ASTROLOGIES

*Plurality and Diversity
in the History of
Astrology*

ASTROLOGIES

Plurality and Diversity in the History of Astrology

Edited by
Nicholas Campion and Liz Greene

SOPHIA CENTRE PRESS

Sophia Centre Press
University of Wales, Trinity Saint David,
Ceredigion, Wales SA48 7ED, United Kingdom.
www.sophiacentrepress.com

Publisher's Cataloging-in-Publication
(Provided by Cassidy Cataloguing Services, Inc.).

Names:　Sophia Centre for the Study of Cosmology in Culture. Annual Conference (8th : 2010 : Bath, England), author. | Campion, Nicholas, editor. | Greene, Liz, editor.

Title:　Astrologies : plurality and diversity in the history of astrology / edited by Nicholas Campion and Liz Greene.

Description:　Ceredigion, Wales, United Kingdom : Sophia Centre Press, 2011. | Series: Studies in cultural astronomy and astrology ; vol. 2 | Includes bibliographical references and index.

Identifiers:　ISBN: 978-1-907767-01-2 (paperback) | 978-1-907767-51-7 (ebook)

Subjects:　LCSH: Astrology--History--Congresses. | Cosmology--History--Congresses.

Classification:　LCC: BF1708.1 .S66 2011 | DDC: 133.5--dc23

Printed globally by Lighting Source.

CONTENTS

Images

ACKNOWLEDGEMENTS

We would like to thank the Sophia Trust for its generous funding of the Sophia Centre and the Urania Trust for its generous support for the Astrologies Conference. Our thanks to Jennifer Zahrt for her exemplary editing skills.

ASTROLOGIES:
PLURALITY AND DIVERSITY

INTRODUCTION

Nicholas Campion and Liz Greene

We have pleasure in presenting in this volume selected papers from the 'Astrologies' conference organised by the Sophia Centre, University of Wales Trinity Saint David, on 24–25 July 2010 in Bath. This conference was a significant event in the subject area, being the first to bring academics together to investigate the theory and practice of astrology in the modern world, from roughly 1700 to the present day. The range of topics cannot pretend to be comprehensive, but it does represent the work being done in the area. The conference title, 'Astrologies', was designed to reflect the growing scholarly realisation that it is impossible to talk about astrology as a monolithic entity, unchanged since ancient times and the same from culture to culture. It is increasingly apparent that under the general rubric of astrology there are competing methodologies, a diversity of techniques, and a variety of underlying philosophies. In this recognition we are following the examples of other disciplines. For example, Paul Walker speaks of 'Platonisms' in Arabic Philosophy, referring to specific concepts that were borrowed from Plato without direct reception of his works.[1] Peter Childs has written about 'Modernisms', recognising that theories about the 'modern world' cannot be understood as a single entity.[2] Robert M. Schuler, discussing the conflicting scholarly perceptions of alchemy as either a proto-chemistry or a path of spiritual transformation, suggests thinking in terms of 'alchemies', since practical alchemy was modified by different philosophical and scientific traditions and the idea of a 'spiritual' alchemy also

---

[1] Paul E. Walker, 'Platonisms in Islamic Philosophy', *Studia Islamica* 79 (1994), pp. 5–25.
[2] Peter Childs, *Modernism* (London: Routledge, 2005), p. 13.

varies from one cultural and religious context to another.[3] In the religious sphere, Jenny Blain, Douglas Ezzy, and Graham Harvey have acknowledged the diverse forms of modern paganism by writing about 'paganisms'.[4] Arthur Green points out that, within the Jewish Kabbalistic tradition, 'we do not have before us a single linear development of a particular type of mysticism, but rather a variety of mysticisms'.[5] And in a critique of the generalising assumptions of astrology and astrologers—which might equally be applied to the generalising assumptions of many sociologists—Ivan W. Kelly emphasises the multiplicity of astrologies, each of which reflects radically differing world-views and conceptions 'regarding the nature of ultimate reality'.[6] Following the increasing scholarly appreciation of the complexity and variety of any human field of endeavour across time, we are reflecting in this volume the paradoxical nature of astrology's relatively stable tradition of symbolic forms expressed through an inherent multivalence, fluidity, and cultural adaptability.

ASTROLOGICAL SYMBOLISM

The papers in this volume are grouped into three basic themes: the symbolism of astrologies, the history of astrologies within different cultural contexts, and the practice of various astrologies from both insider and outsider perspectives. Although each of these themes focuses on a discrete sphere of astrological provenance, there is in fact a good deal of overlap between them, as it is impossible to explore a complex cultural expression such as astrology as though one could entirely separate philosophy and metaphysics from practice, history from historiography, or symbolism from social context. The first theme, which covers the understanding of astrology and of astrological language

---

[3] Robert M. Schuler, 'Some Spiritual Alchemies of Seventeenth-Century England', *Journal of the History of Ideas* 41, no. 2 (1980): pp. 293–318, on p. 294.

[4] Jenny Blain, Douglas Ezzy, and Graham Harvey (eds.), *Researching Paganisms* (Lanham, MD: Rowman and Littlefield, 2004).

[5] Arthur Green, *A Guide to the Zohar* (Stanford, CA: Stanford University Press, 2004), p. 7.

[6] Ivan W. Kelly, 'The Concepts of Modern Astrology: A Critique', at http://www.astrology-and-science.com/a-conc2.htm (2005), first published in *Psychological Reports* 81 (1997), pp. 1035–66.

as a 'symbolic language', is itself fraught with problems. The term 'symbol' has meant different things to astrological practitioners and scholars across the centuries, from the Greek idea of the *symbolon* or 'trace' as an embodiment in material reality of the divine presence, through Jung's psychological understanding of symbols as imaginal representations of archetypal patterns that are 'discovered' rather than 'invented', to the modern perception of symbols as social constructs.[7] In the opening paper, Liz Greene's discussion of the genesis, development, and interpretation of the astrological 'glyphs' or symbols for the planets and zodiacal signs highlights not only their consistency but also their adaptability and fluidity, from the first horoscopes that display them in the fifth century CE to their uniform presentation in printed astrological textbooks from the fifteenth century onward, and the various metaphysical conceptions imposed on these glyphs by esoterically inclined astrologers from the late nineteenth century into the twentieth and twenty-first. This paper discusses both the current sociological understanding of symbols and the older perception of a symbol as an imaginal form which both hints at and embodies what is being symbolised, evident in various astrological currents from late antiquity to the contemporary world, and suggests that the term 'symbol' as it is presented in the Theosophical currents of astrology that have influenced contemporary astrologies throughout the twentieth century may not do justice to the perceptions of those cultures from which astrological symbols and glyphs—and their association with magical invocation and the importance of the imaginal world as a gateway—first emerged.

Bernadette Brady's paper presents an exploration of the horoscope as an *imago mundi* or 'sacred map'. The idea of the 'image of the world' is first encountered in a Babylonian artifact of the sixth century BCE, which presents not only the city of Babylon on the Euphrates as the centre of the world, but also the great cosmic ocean dividing above and below, with seven outer regions beyond the encircling ocean each of which seems to symbolise the domain of a particular astral potency.[8] This idea of map as cosmology rather than

---

[7] See Peter T. Struck, *The Birth of the Symbol* (Princeton, NJ: Princeton University Press, 2004).
[8] First published in 1899, and also formerly dated to an earlier

geography is also found in the *Book of Jubilees* (c. 160–150 BCE),[9] and later in medieval Christian forms of the *mappa mundi*, such as the 'T-O' map of Isidore of Seville, c. 636 CE, and the *mappa mundi* now located at Hereford Cathedral, c. 1300, which presents Jerusalem at the centre of the world and the Garden of Eden in a circle at its edge.[10] An enigmatic modern representation can be found in C. G. Jung's 'Systema Munditotius' (c. 1917), the 'System of All Worlds', which presents a Gnostic cosmology in the form of a horoscope with significators reflecting his own personal birth-chart, and which was described by Barry Jeromson, in a paper discussing this image in Jung's *Liber Novus*, as a 'psycho-cosmological map'.[11] Brady's paper focuses on the non-cartographical elements in these extraordinary maps, so often misunderstood as evidence of the poor geographical knowledge of the pre-modern world, and which reflect the soul's rather than the body's journey in its transition to higher states of spiritual awareness. This idea of a map that conjoins above and below, inner and outer, finds its way into the approaches adopted by many contemporary astrologers who view the horoscope as a spiritual pathway or 'roadmap of the soul', rather than a mere astronomical representation of the heavens.

---

period, c. 900 BCE. See Kurt A. Raaflaub & Richard J. A. Talbert, *Geography and Ethnography: Perceptions of the World in Pre-Modern Societies* (West Sussex: John Wiley & Sons, 2009), p. 147.

[9] See Orval S. Wintermute, 'Jubilees', in James H. Charlesworth (ed.), *Old Testament Pseudepigrapha*, 2 volumes (Garden City, N.Y.: Doubleday, 1985), Vol. 2, pp. 35–142; P. S. Alexander, 'Notes on the "Imago Mundi" of the Book of Jubilees', *Journal of Jewish Studies* 33 (1982), pp. 197–213.

[10] For Isidore's map, see Jonathan T. Lanman, 'The Religious Symbolism of the T in T-O Maps', *Cartographica* 18, no. 4 (1981): pp. 18–22; Michael Livingstone, 'Modern Medieval Map Myths: The Flat World, Ancient Sea-Kings, and Dragons', *Strange Horizons* (2002), at <http://www.strangehorizons.com/2002/20020610/medieval_maps.shtml>. For the Hereford *mappa mundi*, see Gabriel Alington, *The Hereford Mappa Mundi* (Herefordshire: Gracewing, 1996); P. D. A. Harvey, *The Hereford World Map: Medieval World Maps and Their Context* (London: British Library, 2006).

[11] Barry Jeromson, 'Systema Munditotius and Seven Sermons: Symbolic Collaborators in Jung's Confrontation with the Unconscious', *Jung History* 1, no. 2 (2010), available at <https://www.philemonfoundation.org/resources/jung_history/volume_1_issue_2>.

Although the idea of astrological symbolism might not seem to fit within Garry Philipson's discussion of astrology in the light of the philosophy of William James, who evidenced no particular interest in or sympathy toward astrology, nevertheless the relationship between astrologies and philosophies has been an intimate one since Plato, who, in the *Timaeus* and the *Republic*, provided one of the most powerful and influential philosophical frameworks in history to support the value of astrological insight.[12] Although there is little evidence in many modern philosophies that the views they represent might be congenial to astrological thought, this paper provides a gentle antidote to the more rationalistic and materialistic philosophies favoured in current academic paradigms. Philipson emphasises James' 'spiritual monism', with its pantheistic alignment with a universe in which God is the 'indwelling divine', and its assertion that reality is, if not irrational, then at least non-rational in nature. Echoes of this perception of the nature of reality can be found in much older texts, such as those of the Jewish Kabbalah, and in those philosophies which drew on it, such as the *élan vital* of Henri Bergson in the late nineteenth and early twentieth centuries.[13] Within James' philosophical framework, not only astrology itself but also the relevance of astrological symbols can find a home, in the sense that such symbols were once understood as intermediaries or embodiments providing a link between individual consciousness and what James referred to as 'a continuum of cosmic consciousness'. Although James may not have been interested in astrology *per se*, this paper makes clear his allegiance to a world-view which is entirely compatible with much of the thinking of those astrologies embedded in a psycho-religious framework, from antiquity to the more psychologically inclined astrologies of the contemporary world, as well as the astrologically sympathetic psychologies of important figures such as C. G. Jung.[14]

---

[12] Plato, *Timaeus*, trans. R. G. Bury (Cambridge, MA: Harvard University Press, 1931), esp. pp. 24–55; Plato, *Republic*, 2 vols., trans. Paul Shorey (Cambridge, MA: Harvard University Press, 1935), Book X.

[13] Henri Bergson, *Creative Evolution*, trans. Arthur Mitchell (London: Macmillan, 1911).

[14] For James' influence on Jung, see, for example, C. G. Jung, *Symbols of Transformation*, CW5 (London: Routledge, 1952), ¶18–19; C. G. Jung, *Psychological Types*, CW6 (London: Routledge, 1971), ¶506–9;

ASTROLOGICAL HISTORY

It is only in recent decades that scholarly attention has begun to be given to the history of astrology and astrologers as an important dimension of the history of ideas which merits careful examination free from the Frazerian assumption, evident in the work of earlier scholars such as Franz Cumont, of its apparently pre-modern non-rationality.[15] Since no astrology can be studied without its cultural context, such research requires not only an understanding of the particular astrology under examination, but also a sense of the history and development of the philosophical, religious, and social alignments in which the specific work or individual is embedded. A number of works on ancient religions include sections on astrology, although these tend to throw it into the melting-pot of 'divination' without any careful examination of the specific context of astrological texts and practitioners.[16] Astrological historiography is itself a fraught field; some histories are unabashedly 'emic', that is, written by 'insiders' eager to demonstrate astrology's validity without due regard for either context or, on occasion, texts themselves, while others are unabashedly 'etic' and full of the assumptions generated by late nineteenth- to mid-twentieth-century academic paradigms derived from the work of Frazer and Tylor.[17] Among the important monographs devoted to the history of astrology and published in the last two decades, Patrick Curry's two analyses of astrological currents in

---

527–33; 864–66.

[15] Franz Cumont, *Astrology Among the Greeks and Romans* (1912; repr. New York, NY: Dover, 1960).

[16] See, for example, David Potter, *Prophets and Emperors: Human and Divine Authority from Augustus to Theodosius* (Cambridge, MA: Harvard University Press, 1994), p. 17; Tamsyn Barton *Ancient Astrology* (London: Routledge, 1994), p. 11; 'Astrology', *Encyclopaedia Britannica*, <http:www.britannicacom/eb/article-9108511>.

[17] For two excellent papers on this subject, see Patrick Curry, 'The Historiography of Astrology: A Diagnosis and a Prescription', in K. von Stuckrad, G. Oestmann, and D. Rutkin (eds.), *Horoscopes and History* (Berlin: Walter de Gruyter, 2005), pp. 261–74; Patrick Curry, 'Astrology on Trial, and Its Historians: Reflections on the Historiography of "Superstition", *Culture and Cosmos* 4, no. 2 (2000): pp. 47–56.

eighteenth- and nineteenth-century Britain—*Prophecy and Power: Astrology in Early Modern England* and *A Confusion of Prophets: Victorian and Edwardian Astrology*—provide insightful investigations of the astrologies and astrologers of these centuries,[18] and Tamsyn Barton's *Power and Knowledge: Astrology, Physiognomics, and Medicine Under the Roman Empire* provides an important overview of the astrologies of ancient Rome, as does Frederick H. Cramer's much earlier and ground-breaking work, *Astrology in Roman Law and Politics*.[19] Much more recently, Nicholas Campion's *History of Western Astrology*, published in two volumes, provides an important overview of the central role astrologies have played in the various religious, political, scientific, and social contexts from antiquity to the present day. Although a number of texts by astrologers of the late antique, medieval, and early modern periods have been translated, books and papers dedicated to the work of specific astrologers in their cultural contexts are fewer, although some have recently been published: several papers have been produced on the life and work of the twelfth-century Jewish astrologer and polymath Abraham ibn Ezra,[20] and Kim Farnell's *The Astral Tramp* provides a biography of one of the most important late nineteenth-century astrologers, Walter Gorn Old, who called himself Sephariel.[21] More famous, or infamous, figures such as John Dee and Simon Forman have been the subject of numerous biographies,[22] but many major figures in the history of astrology still await an in-depth analysis. The growing body of work addressed to both individual astrologers and the astrologies of specific cultural contexts

---

[18] Patrick Curry, *Prophecy and Power: Astrology in Early Modern England* (Princeton, NJ: Princeton University Press, 1989); Patrick Curry, *A Confusion of Prophets: Victorian and Edwardian Astrology* (London: Collins & Brown, 1999).

[19] Tamsyn Barton, *Power and Knowledge: Astrology, Physiognomics, and Medicine Under the Roman Empire* (Detroit, MI: University of Michigan Press, 1994); Frederick H. Cramer, *Astrology in Roman Law and Politics* (Philadelphia, PA: American Philosophical Society 1954).

[20] See, for example, Shlomo Sela, *Abraham ibn Ezra and the Rise of Hebrew Medieval Science* (Leiden: Brill, 2003).

[21] Kim Farnell, *The Astral Tramp: A Biography of Sephariel* (London: Ascella Publications, 1998).

[22] See, for example, Peter J. French, *John Dee: The World of an Elizabethan Magus* (London: Routledge, 1987); Lauren Kassell, *Medicine and Magic in Elizabethan London: Simon Forman: Astrologer, Alchemist, and Physician* (Oxford: Oxford University Press, 2005).

suggests how important this field of research is to any understanding of the histories of religions, sciences, and societies in which astrology has played a role in providing insight into the meaningful relationships between the heavenly bodies and life on earth.

The four papers included in this section are devoted to specific areas of the history of cultures and ideas where astrology has played a critically important role. Robert Hand's examination of John Partridge—a late seventeenth- and early eighteenth-century English astrologer whose influence on the development of the astrologies of the subsequent three centuries has, as the paper demonstrates, been seriously overlooked—takes into full account the intellectual and social currents of the time and the critical point which astrological studies in Britain had reached in the wake of the rationalism of the Enlightenment. Efforts to reform astrology by making it more consistent with the sciences of the time and purging it of medieval 'super-stitions' are reflected in Partridge's attempt to revolutionise astrological techniques and return them to the 'pure' astrology he believed was expressed by Ptolemy in the second century, and it is this effort at reform that, according to Hand's assessment, contributed to the movement of later astrologies away from older medieval traditions and eventually toward the more person-centred and spiritually focused astrology of Alan Leo and subsequent Theo-sophically inclined astrologers in the twentieth century. This analysis of the work of a little-known astrologer of the early modern period places the various currents of astrology in a specific context, linking them with greater intellectual and social movements and changes and allowing insight into the ways in which astrologers, no less than any other profession, need to be understood in the context not only of their times, but also of the heritage and complex web of religious, philosophical, and scientific perspectives which came before and after them.

Martin Gansten explores two British astrologers of the late eighteenth and early nineteenth centuries, John Worsdale and Thomas Oxley, in the context of the earlier influential work of the seventeenth-century astrologer Placidus de Titis and its adaptation to the cultural milieu of Britain just after the Enlightenment. Like Robert Hand's examination of the work of John Patridge, this paper places Worsdale and Oxley in the context of post-Enlightenment efforts to reform astrology to ensure its survival in an increasingly sceptical age. Both astrologers, along with Partridge, turned to the work of Placidus, himself a reformer who attempted to restore Ptolemaic astrology to its rightful place as a legitimate aspect of Aristotelian natural philosophy. Gansten explores not only the political and religious allegiances which formed the background for their work, but also the specific techniques each man developed from Placidus' understanding of celestial mechanics, and the unique contributions both men made to the development of astrology into the modern era: Oxley, for example, was the chief exponent of the shift from the traditional square nativity utilised in virtually all medieval and early modern astrological texts to the modern circular nativity used by astrologers today. Gansten argues that Worsdale and Oxley, along with their younger contemporaries, made a major contribution to modern astrologies through their espousal of the Placidean system, which provided the standard for many of the astrologies which followed into the present day.

Robert Collis presents a challenging view of the late seventeenth- and early eighteenth-century reform programme of Peter the Great, who, although well-documented in his enthusiasm for importing European culture and science into Russia, has rarely been acknowledged as an enthusiastic promoter of astrology as a means of synthesising Russian and European religious and scientific world-views. Collis argues that Peter actively promoted various forms of German and Eastern European astrologies at his court, and highlights through a series of examples—in particular calendars and almanacs providing information on the qualities of the planets and zodiacal signs—the ways in which astrological motifs and information were used not only for predictive purposes, but also for political and religious propaganda. This paper explores the specific ways in which European astrologies were adapted to the Russian Orthodox calendar and religious framework, revealing a czar who, far from being merely 'not an opponent of astrology', in fact enthusiastically adopted and promulgated many aspects of astrological thought to promote himself and his reform programme.

Nicholas Goodrick-Clarke examines the 'hybrid' or cross-disciplinary sphere of study known as archaeo-astronomy, which, although rooted in speculations by ancient historians such as Diodorus Siculus, began as an independent discipline in the seventeenth century with John Aubrey's interpretation of Stonehenge as an ancient Druidic solar temple, and reached its modern and more apparently scientific flowering with Norman Lockyer's exploration of the astronomical alignments of ancient monuments. This paper, which is concerned with the historiography of the astronomical alignments of ancient structures and the various speculations by particular esoterically inclined British, German, and French archaeologists and historians about their possible religious and cosmological meanings, argues that the work of these archaeo-astronomers is an esoteric discipline which, rather than focusing on ancient astronomy *per se*, deals instead with the perceived meanings of the alignments according to the specific social and religious agendas of the individual researchers. Goodrick-Clarke argues that many of the various arguments of archaeo-astronomers support the idea of a *prisca theologia*: the belief in a body of religious-scientific astronomical knowledge known to the ancient sages but lost over the centuries and absent in the present 'scientistic' age, which nevertheless exists to be discovered in ancient monuments that serve as 'repositories' for these lost secrets.

ASTROLOGICAL PRACTICE

What do astrologers actually do, and how do they experience their work? The answers are as varied as there are astrological practitioners, but certain patterns and modes of thinking are highlighted in the papers that focus on this theme. Most importantly, the papers that explore the issue of astrological practice emphasise the relationships between current astrologies and specific traditions and spheres of human endeavour that are usually thought of as independent of astrology itself. This underlines the ways in which astrologies of various persuasions have integrated themselves into a range of discourses—religious, artistic, political, social, scientific—over the centuries and continue to do so in the twenty-first century. Darrelyn Gunzburg's discussion of the practice of astrology comprises an approach rooted in qualitative research, based on interviews with working astrologers in the contemporary world, and suggests, through descriptions of direct experience, a comparison between the inspirational moment of the artist and the inspirational understanding that arises spontaneously, for many astrologers, during the contemplation and discussion of the astrological chart. Although historically many astrologers in the past defined their work as a 'divine science', the understanding of science has changed over the centuries: as Thomas Kuhn once suggested, science lurches from paradigm to paradigm,[23] and spheres which might now be viewed as exclusive to religion or artistic creativity were once part of what was understood as 'science': the divine work of creation itself may have provided the rationale behind the pursuit of science.[24] Some contemporary astrologers perceive their work as an 'art' rather than a science, and this paper highlights the similarities in experience which might make this understanding a valid interpretation of the process involved in the practice of particular astrologies. Much work remains to be done on the connections between altered states, creative processes, the function of the human imagination, and the overlap between religious or mystical experience and the experience of the artist engaged in the timeless state generated through the formation of a creative work.

Jay Johnston's illuminating investigation into the relationship between astrological practice and healing focuses on a particular current within contemporary astrologies, concerned with the healing of the body/psyche through the sympathetic connections between the individual's 'subtle bodies' and the heavenly bodies. As the paper points out, the concept of a 'subtle body' is very ancient. It can be found in Western traditions not only in the Neoplatonic literature of late antiquity but also in early Jewish esoteric texts, where it is related to the *tselem*, the 'spiritual' body or 'double' which provides the link between the divine and the human.[25] The many currents of medieval and early modern medicine and

---

[23] Thomas Kuhn, *The Structure of Scientific Revolutions* (Chicago, IL: University of Chicago Press, 1962).

[24] See Stanley Jeyeraja Tambiah, *Magic, Science, Religion and the Scope of Rationality* (1984; repr. Cambridge: Cambridge University Press, 1990); Charles Webster, *From Paracelsus to Newton: Magic and the Making of Modern Science* (Cambridge: Cambridge University Press, 1982); Frances Yates, *The Occult Philosophy in the Elizabethan Age* (London: Routledge & Kegan Paul, 1979).

[25] See Gershom Scholem, 'The Concept of the Astral Body', in Gershom Scholem, *On the Mystical Shape of the Godhead: Basic Concepts in the Kabbalah* (New York, NY: Schocken Books, 1991), pp. 251–74.

esoteric thought appropriated by late nineteenth-century Theosophy and its offshoots are highlighted in the paper, reflected in the eclectic nature of those contemporary astrologies which are concerned with healing and well-being through attending to, or manipulating, the imbalances in the 'subtle bodies'. Although the relationship between astrology and healing through the 'subtle bodies' is presented here in its modern context, the tradition is a very old one and highlights the vigour of particular idea complexes that are adapted to particular cultural milieux through language and conceptual frameworks but which retain a structural stability, in this case rooted in the idea of the unity of the cosmos and the consubstantiality between human and cosmic substance.

Nicholas Campion's discussion on 'Astrology's Place in Historical Periodisation' challenges current sociological assumptions about the 'post-modern' nature of astrological practice in the contemporary world. Such discussions about the anachronistic survival of astrology in modern times have proliferated since the 1950s, rooted in the assumption that there is no place for 'belief' in astrology in the rational ambience of the modern world, and hence astrology must represent that diversified and pluralistic escape from modernity currently classified under the rubric of 'postmodern'. This paper highlights the inconsistency of these assumptions about astrology, including the assumption that all astrologies, whatever their context, can be understood as a single monolithic set of beliefs, and that modernity, likewise, can be explained by a single, simple definition and as a single, simple period of historical time. There is no universally accepted meaning of the terms 'modern' and 'post-modern' and, as all the papers in this volume demonstrate, there is no universally accepted single definition of the term 'astrology' devoid of cultural context. Focusing on the historiography of astrology in the present world, Campion's paper questions many current academic paradigms which seek to reduce fluid, shifting human perceptions to rational classifications, highlighting not only the creative and category-resistant pluralism of astrologies and astrologers, but also the protean and uncertain nature of human self-reflection.

All the papers in this volume reflect one of the most profound paradoxes of astrological thought and practice: the existence of a relatively stable tradition of cosmological and astral representations and ideas combined with an immensely creative fluidity and adaptability that has enabled astrologies to meld with virtually every sphere of human endeavour in every culture and in every historical epoch, even when prevailing religious or scientific authorities have attempted to eradicate that tradition. The diversity of astrologies from the ancient world to the modern might suggest that such apparent fragmentation reveals a fundamental flaw in astrological thought, since no two astrologers appear to be able to agree on what it is they believe in, how they define their work, and what metaphysical or religious framework, if any, they espouse to justify what they do. Yet the continuing traditions on which contemporary astrologies draw are highlighted by the historical research presented in these papers, all of which reflect the broad definition of astrology as the perception of meaningful relationships between the heavenly bodies and life on earth. All of the traditions generated by this perception, however variegated and culture-specific, share this persistent idea that occupies such an important role in the human religious imagination and, despite Keith Thomas's belief, articulated in 1971, that 'astrology, witchcraft, magical healing, divination, ancient prophecies, ghosts and fairies, are now all rightly disdained by intelligent persons',[26] shows little sign of rolling over and dying.

BIBLIOGRAPHY

'Astrology'. *Encyclopaedia Britannica*
    <http:www.britannicacom/eb/article-9108511>
Alexander, P. S. 'Notes on the "Imago Mundi" of the Book of Jubilees'. *Journal of Jewish Studies* 33 (1982): pp. 197–213.
Alington, Gabriel. *The Hereford Mappa Mundi*. Herefordshire: Gracewing, 1996.
Barton, Tamsyn. *Ancient Astrology*. London: Routledge, 1994.
———. *Power and Knowledge: Astrology, Physiognomics, and Medicine Under the Roman Empire*. Detroit, MI: University of Michigan Press, 1994.
Bergson, Henri. *Creative Evolution*. Translated by Arthur Mitchell. London: Macmillan, 1911.
Blain, Jenny, Douglas Ezzy, and Graham Harvey, eds. *Researching*

---

[26] Keith Thomas, *Religion and the Decline of Magic* (London: Weidenfeld & Nicolson, 1971), p. ix.

Paganisms. Lanham, MD: Rowman and Littlefield, 2004.

Campion, Nicholas. *A History of Western Astrology*. 2 volumes London: Continuum, 2008–2009.

Childs, Peter. *Modernism*. London: Routledge, 2005.

Cramer, Frederick H. *Astrology in Roman Law and Politics*. Philadelphia, PA: American Philosophical Society 1954.

Cumont, Franz. *Astrology Among the Greeks and Romans*. 1912. Reprinted by New York, NY: Dover, 1960.

Curry, Patrick. *Prophecy and Power: Astrology in Early Modern England*. Princeton, NJ: Princeton University Press, 1989.

———. *A Confusion of Prophets: Victorian and Edwardian Astrology*. London: Collins & Brown, 1999.

———. 'Astrology on Trial, and Its Historians: Reflections on the Historiography of "Superstition"'. *Culture and Cosmos* 4, no. 2 (2000): pp. 47–56.

———. 'The Historiography of Astrology: A Diagnosis and a Prescription'. In K. von Stuckrad, G. Oestmann, and D. Rutkin, eds. *Horoscopes and History*. Berlin: Walter de Gruyter, 2005, pp. 261–74.

Farnell, Kim. *The Astral Tramp: A Biography of Sephariel*. London: Ascella Publications, 1998.

French, Peter J. *John Dee: The World of an Elizabethan Magus*. London: Routledge, 1987.

Green, Arthur. *A Guide to the Zohar*. Stanford, CA: Stanford University Press, 2004.

Harvey, P. D. A. *The Hereford World Map: Medieval World Maps and Their Context*. London: British Library, 2006.

Jeromson, Barry. 'Systema Munditotius and Seven Sermons: Symbolic Collaborators in Jung's Confrontation with the Unconscious'. *Jung History* 1, no. 2 (2010), at <https://www.philemonfoundation.org/resources/jung_histor y/volume_1_issue_2>

Jung, C. G. *Symbols of Transformation*, CW5. London: Routledge, 1952.

———. *Psychological Types*, CW6. London: Routledge, 1971.

Kassell, Lauren. *Medicine and Magic in Elizabethan London: Simon Forman: Astrologer, Alchemist, and Physician*. Oxford: Oxford University Press, 2005.

Kelly, Ivan W. 'The Concepts of Modern Astrology: A Critique', at http://www.astrology-and-science.com/a-conc2.htm   (2005), first published in *Psychological Reports* 81 (1997), pp. 1035–66.

Kuhn, Thomas. *The Structure of Scientific Revolutions*. Chicago, IL: University of Chicago Press, 1962.

Lanman, Jonathan T. 'The Religious Symbolism of the T in T-O Maps'. *Cartographica* 18, no. 4 (1981): pp. 18–22.

Livingstone, Michael. 'Modern Medieval Map Myths: The Flat World, Ancient Sea-Kings, and Dragons'. *Strange Horizons* (2002), at <http://www.strangehorizons.com/2002/20020610/ medieval_maps.shtml>

Plato, *Timaeus*. Translated by R. G. Bury. Cambridge, MA: Harvard University Press, 1931.

———. *Republic*. 2 vols. Translated by Paul Shorey. Cambridge, MA: Harvard University Press, 1935.

Potter, David. *Prophets and Emperors: Human and Divine Authority from Augustus to Theodosius*. Cambridge, MA: Harvard University Press, 1994.

Raaflaub, Kurt A., and Richard J. A. Talbert. *Geography and Ethnography: Perceptions of the World in Pre-Modern Societies*. West Sussex: John Wiley & Sons, 2009.

Scholem, Gershom. *On the Mystical Shape of the Godhead: Basic Concepts in the Kabbalah*. New York, NY: Schocken Books, 1991.

Schuler, Robert M. 'Some Spiritual Alchemies of Seventeenth-Century England'. *Journal of the History of Ideas* 41, no. 2 (1980): pp. 293–318.

Sela, Shlomo. *Abraham ibn Ezra and the Rise of Hebrew Medieval Science*. Leiden: Brill, 2003.

Struck, Peter T. *The Birth of the Symbol*. Princeton, NJ: Princeton University Press, 2004.

Tambiah, Stanley Jeyeraja. *Magic, Science, Religion and the Scope of Rationality*. 1984. Reprinted by Cambridge: Cambridge University Press, 1990.

Thomas, Keith. *Religion and the Decline of Magic*. London: Weidenfeld & Nicolson, 1971.

Walker, Paul E. 'Platonisms in Islamic Philosophy'. *Studia Islamica* 79 (1994): pp. 5–25.

Webster, Charles. *From Paracelsus to Newton: Magic and the Making of Modern Science*. Cambridge: Cambridge University Press, 1982.

Wintermute, Orval S. 'Jubilees'. in James H. Charlesworth, ed., *Old Testament Pseudepigrapha*, 2 vols. Garden City, NY: Doubleday, 1985. Vol. 2, pp. 35–142.

Yates, Frances A. *The Occult Philosophy in the Elizabethan Age*. London: Routledge & Kegan Paul, 1979.

SIGNS, SIGNATURES, AND SYMBOLS: THE LANGUAGES OF HEAVEN

Liz Greene

ABSTRACT: This paper explores the perception and use of astrological symbols—'glyphs' and stylised images for the planets and zodiacal signs—in contemporary astrological currents as well as in different historical contexts. Can there be such a thing as a 'symbolic' astrology, or is all astrology symbolic? And if so, what does this term mean? How does a symbol differ from a sign, a metaphor, a signature, or an allegory? 'Symbol' is assigned a variety of connotations in contemporary academic usage, from a linguistic referent to a means of establishing social identity, and these connotations may differ widely from the way astrological symbols have been understood in the past and are understood now by astrological practitioners of various persuasions. The manner in which symbols, at different historical epochs, have been perceived as magical or talismanic—containing or embodying the thing symbolised—will be examined in relation to both the astrological glyphs and the *charactêres* or 'eye-writing' found in astral magic over the centuries.

THE POWER OF IMAGES

I would like to begin my paper with a brief scenario. Two astrologers—they might be contemporary, or they might belong to an earlier historical epoch—are discussing the natal horoscope of one of their clients. They might have an actual horoscope in front of them, laboriously hand-drawn on parchment, papyrus, or vellum; or they may be viewing a computer-generated horoscope on a PowerPoint presentation at a conference. The design of the 'nativity', as it was once called, might differ according to the cultural context, as the three birth charts shown in figures 1.1 and 1.2 below—from late antiquity, the early modern period, and the twenty-first century—demonstrate.

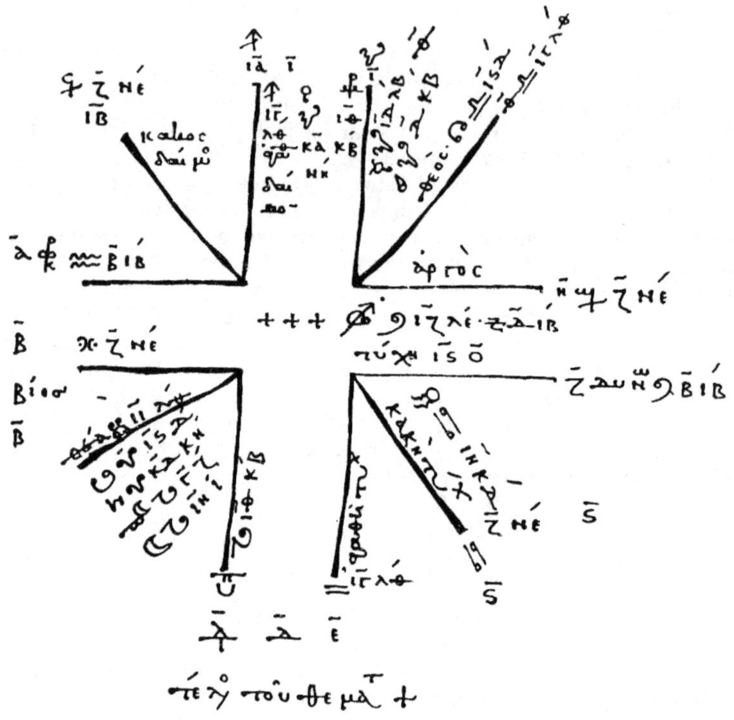

Fig. 1.1: *Greek horoscope set for 28 October, 497* CE.[1]

[1] Otto Neugebauer and H. B. van Hoesen, *Greek Horoscopes* (Philadelphia: American Philosophical Society, 1987), p. 156.

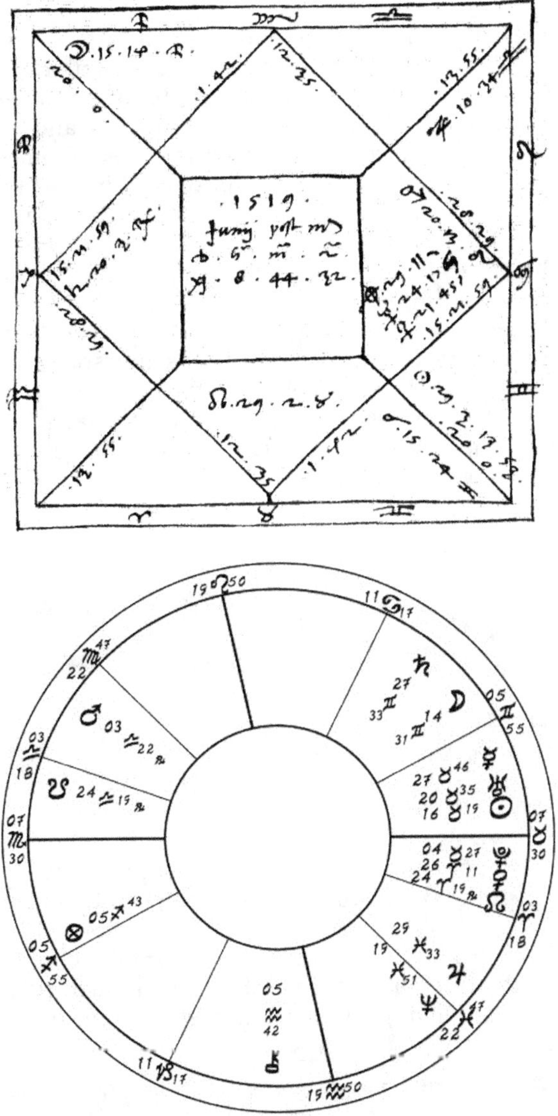

Fig. 1.2: Top, horoscope of Cosimo I de' Medici (1519–1574), produced in 1537. Bottom, horoscope of Sigmund Freud (1856–1939), calculated on an Apple iMac with software produced by Time Cycles Research.[2]

---

[2] Horoscope of Cosimo I, Firenze, Bibl. Medicea Laurenziana, Pluteo

Horoscopes from the Renaissance and early modern period tend to be square, while modern ones are circular. For many centuries only the seven 'planets' visible to the naked eye—Sun, Moon, Mercury, Venus, Mars, Jupiter, and Saturn—were included; in more recent times the celestial objects have proliferated and include planets discovered in the eighteenth and nineteenth centuries such as Uranus and Neptune, as well as asteroids and 'centaurs' from the Kuyper Belt beyond Pluto. But the structure and primary components of the horoscope have remained consistent.

Equally, our two astrologers might not have any actual document before them, but are discussing something they can see in their mind's eye. And they can both see the same thing. One of them gestures toward a particular point in the chart; it is the planet Mars, whose symbol or glyph has remained recognisable for a millennium and a half.

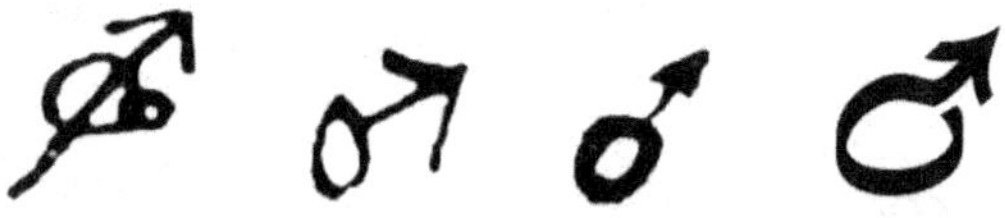

Fig. 1.3: Left to right, Greek Mars, 497 CE; Mars from the horoscope of Cosimo I de' Medici, 1537; Francis Barrett's Mars, from The Magus, 1801; computer-generated Mars, 2010.[3]

This consistency might lead us to imagine that the same principle applies to all the astrological symbols. But other planetary glyphs are not so obliging. Among the extant horoscopes from the Hellenistic period analysed by Neugebauer and van Hoesen, the only planetary symbols that appear, according to these authors, are those of the Sun

89 sup., 34, 'Astrologia, magia e alchimia nel Rinascimento fiorentino ed europeo', in Claudia Beltramo Ceppi and Nicoletta Confuorto, eds., *Firenze e la Toscana dei Medici nell' Europa del Cinquecento* (Florence: Electa Editrice, 1980), p. 380.
[3] Greek Mars: Neugebauer and van Hoesen, *Greek Horoscopes*, p. 156. Mid-sixteenth-century Mars: Ceppi and Confuorto, 'Astrologia, magia e alchimia', p. 378. Early nineteenth-century Mars: Francis Barrett, *The Magus, or Celestial Intelligencer, Being a Complete System of Occult Philosophy* (London: Lackington & Allen, 1801), p. 175.

and Moon; there are no glyphs for the zodiacal signs, and those for the five planets, as well as the signs, only begin to appear during the fifth century CE. The symbol for the Moon in these nativities is, not surprisingly, connoted by the lunar crescent, but the Sun appears in this peculiar form:

Fig. 1.4: *Left, Greek Sun, late fifth century* CE; *right, the Sun in the horoscope of the emperor Hadrian (76–138* CE), *fourth century* CE.[4]

No early astrological text has illuminated the meaning and origin of this symbol, which is so unlike the obvious rayed solar symbols found in much older Bronze Age monuments. This late antique rendition of the Sun also ignores the Apollonian symbol of the point within the circle, evidenced on coins from the Sun-god's shrine at Delphi dated as early as the fifth century BCE.[5] The point in the circle, ubiquitous in contemporary astrological texts, appears for the first time as a specific astrological significator in Renaissance printed books.[6]

Fig. 1.5: *The Sun as it has been portrayed in horoscopes from the Renaissance to the present.*

The solar symbol in these Greek horoscopes from late antiquity might easily be mistaken for Mars, since there is a

---

[4] Greek Sun: Neugebauer and van Hoesen, *Greek Horoscopes*, p. 156. Hadrian's horoscope, cast in the second century CE and drawn in the fourth century by Hephaistion of Thebes, in Frederick H. Cramer, *Astrology in Roman Law and Politics* (Chicago: Ares, 1996), p. 165.
[5] See *British Museum Catalogue of Greek Coins, Central Greece* (1963), Plate 14, no. 4, 24, and 33.
[6] See Neugebauer and van Hoesen, *Greek Horoscopes*, p. 163.

decidedly phallic quality implicit in its shape. It is certainly not intended to reproduce in diagrammatic form the physical disc of the Sun: it is a symbol, rather than a stylised representation. There is, however, one textual source which might possibly illuminate why the Sun was symbolised in these horoscopes as a phallic power: the recently discovered papyrus document known as the Derveni Papyrus, an Orphic text comprising a hymn, probably written in the fifth century BCE or earlier, and interpreted by an Orphic initiate and allegorist of the time of Philip II of Macedon, the father of Alexander the Great, in the early fourth century BCE. The allegorist informs us:

> Since in his [Orpheus'] whole poetry he speaks about facts enigmatically, one has to speak about each word in turn. Seeing that people consider that generation is dependent upon the genitalia, and that without the genitals there is no becoming, he used this word, likening the sun to a phallus. For without the sun the things that are could not have become such...[7]

It is possible that Orphic currents, emerging in Presocratic Greece and exercising a profound influence on the development of Platonic and Neoplatonic philosophies, might also, in their preoccupation with astral and eschatological matters, have contributed to the development of a system of astral symbols to connote not any physical heavenly body, but the specific qualities and attributes of those celestial divinities for whom the actual planets were themselves understood to be symbols.[8]

---

[7] Gábor Betegh, *The Derveni Papyrus: Cosmology, Theology and Interpretation* (Cambridge: Cambridge University Press, 2004), Col. 13.

[8] For Orphic cosmologies and theogonies, see Betegh, *Derveni Papyrus*; W. K. C. Guthrie, *Orpheus and Greek Religion* (Princeton, NJ: Princeton University Press, 1952); M. L. West, *The Orphic Poems* (Oxford: Oxford University Press, 1983); Walter Burkert, *Babylon, Memphis, Persepolis: Eastern Contexts of Greek Culture* (Cambridge, MA: Harvard University Press, 2004), pp. 71–98; M. L. West, 'Ab ovo: Orpheus, Sanchuniathon and the Origins of the Ionian World Model', *The Classical Quarterly* 44, no. 2 (1994): pp. 289–307; Robert Eisler, *Orpheus the Fisher: Comparative Studies in Orphic and Early Christian Cult Symbolism* (London: Watkins, 1921); Vittorio D. Macchioro, *From Orpheus to Paul: A History of Orphism* (London: Constable, 1930); Peter Kingsley, *Ancient Philosophy, Mystery, and*

Our two astrologers are therefore not looking at any literal representation of a concrete object. The consistency of the symbols of the signs and planets which comprise what today's astrologers understand as a birth chart has been firmly established since the arrival of the printed book, but the origins of these figures are obscure and they seem to have followed a complex and circuitous route over the centuries which has been anything but consistent—not only in their visual presentation, but in the ways in which they have been understood. Contemporary astrologers tend to describe these figures as symbols, as we will see later; but the word 'symbol' has itself gone through considerable shifts in meaning depending on which culture, and which academic paradigm, it is being viewed through. I would like now to explore some of these views on the nature of symbolism, and a few of the ways in which astrological symbols, now thoroughly codified and recognised by any astrologer anywhere in the world familiar with Western astrological practices, have been and are perceived.

Symbols and Pictorial Representations

Pictorial images of the constellations can be dated back to the Babylonians. Figure 1.6 shows a *kudurru* or boundary-stone, ca. 1100 BCE, portraying various celestial objects including the constellation of the Scorpion. Iconographic representations of the circle of the zodiac can likewise be dated back to antiquity; the so-called 'altar' of Gabii, ringed by the twelve Olympian gods associated with the zodiacal signs as described in Manilius' poem, the *Astronomica*, is, like the poem, from the first century CE. The artifact shown below (fig. 1.7) is unusual because its specific iconography is clarified by Manilius' text.[9] There are innumerable examples of such pictorial representations of the circle of the zodiac throughout history, expressed in many cultures and embedded in settings ranging from calendars to churches to iPhone apps. It might seem simple to work out how the symbols for the zodiacal signs could have been derived from

---

Magic: Empedocles and Pythagorean Tradition (Oxford: Clarendon Press, 1995); Alberto Bernabé and Ana Isabel Jiménez San Cristóbal, *Instructions for the Netherworld: The Orphic Gold Tablets* (Leiden: Brill, 2008).

[9] For the twelve gods as rulers of the signs of the zodiac, see Manilius, *Astronomica*, 2.433.

such pictorial forms—the horns of the ram are replicated in
the glyph for Aries, the head of the bull in Taurus, the twins
in the two pillars of Gemini, the claws of the crab in Cancer,
and so on. But here, as with the symbols for the planets, there
are considerable variations, and some bear no resemblance to
the zodiacal creatures they are meant to designate (fig. 1.8)

Fig. 1.6: Babylonian kudurru ca. 1100 BCE *portraying the constellation of
the Scorpion.*[10]

---

[10] British Museum 102485. See Leonard King, *Babylonian Boundary-
Stones and Memorial-Tablets in the British Museum* (London: British
Museum, 1912), pp. 76–79, Plates I–IV.

Fig. 1.7: Top, the altar of Gabii, first century CE, *Louvre MA 666. Bottom, the altar from the side, showing the zodiacal signs around the rim*

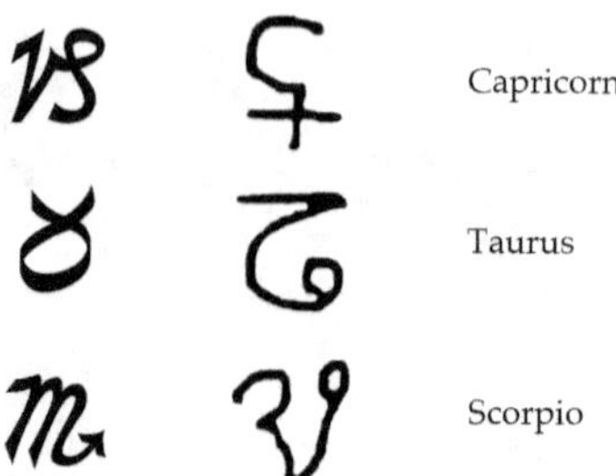

Fig. 1.8: Left column, modern glyphs for Capricorn, Taurus and Scorpio; right column, glyphs from the horoscope given in Fig. 1.1, dated 497 BCE.[11]

And there is also the question of why these particular images—ram, bull, twins, crab—have themselves became meaningful symbols. It seems somewhat specious to assume that they are imaginative projections by gullible, unscientific pre-moderns onto groups of stars which might or might not bear a resemblance to the image; why project twins rather than the columns flanking the door to a temple, or even two trees?

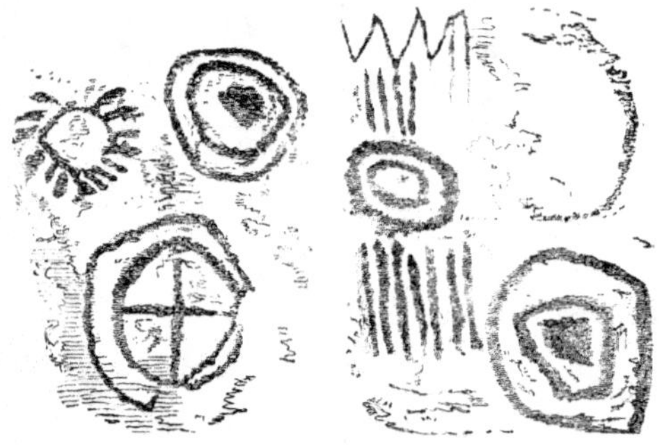

Fig. 1.9 Carvings from the Dowth passage tomb at Meath, Ireland.[12]

---

[11] For other variations, see Wilhelm Spiegelberg, 'Die ägyptischen Namen und Zeichen der Tierkreisbilder in demotischer Schrift', *Zeitschrift für ägyptische Sprache und Altertumskunde* 48 (Leipzig: Hinrich, 1864–84): pp. 146–52; Alexandra von Lieven, 'Divination in Ägypten', *Altorientalische Forschungen* 26 (1999): pp. 77–126.
[12] Drawing from William Frederick Wakeman, *Wakeman's Handbook*

The planetary symbols are even more baffling in terms of their derivation, although the symbol for the Moon is understandable enough and reflects the perception of a visible heavenly phenomenon, the lunar crescent. Symbols for the Sun are also found in very ancient cultures, but they do not resemble the phallic symbol used in the horoscopes of late antiquity; they are more obviously representational, as demonstrated by the images found in the Dowth passage tomb at Meath, Ireland, dated ca. 11,000–8500 BCE (fig. 1.9). More elusive planetary symbols, such as those of Mercury and Saturn, could be related to the objects or instruments that designate the planetary god's attributes in myth and iconography: Mercury's winged helmet might be seen in his planetary symbol, and Saturn's sickle—the instrument he used to castrate his father Ouranos in Hesiod's theogony— might be glimpsed in the shape of *his* planetary symbol. But if this is so, we must consider the possibility that these objects are themselves symbols of qualities, powers, and mythic narratives associated with the planetary god, and have a much more complex web of associations.

So, are the planetary and zodiacal symbols really a species of shorthand—condensed images of larger but nevertheless literal pictorial representations? Were they always under- stood as a culturally agreed celestial alphabet to designate specific concepts? Or might they be related to the Greek perception of Egyptian hieroglyphics—a word which literally means 'divine inscription'—and the understanding of these characters as a mode of symbolically representing aspects of the divine? In this context the symbol becomes a kind of magic key, seal, or password which transcends ordinary rules of communication, and can reveal divine secrets through images which hint at and embody that which has no image, for those who have the facility to understand them. The late-second-century Christian theologian Clement of Alexandria wrote about the Egyptians:

> When they want to indicate the sun, for example, they make
> a circle, and the moon a crescent shape, according to the
> literal form...Other things they engrave figuratively...and
> they transpose and alter their character; they change some
> things, others they recast entirely.[13]

---

of Irish Antiquities, ed. John Cooke (Dublin: Hodges, Figgis, 1903), 95.

[13] Clement, *Stromateis* 5.4.20–21, in Peter Struck, *The Birth of the*

In other words, some symbols appear to be diagrammatic or stylised representations of physical reality, like the lunar crescent, although they also intimate knowledge beyond the object; while others, like the planetary glyphs, appear to bear no relation to any physical object, and are meant to refer to patterns, potencies, and narratives that cannot be communicated in any conceptual form. To use Peter Struck's words, the symbol 'can tell us more than we can possibly know'.[14]

Mary LeCron Foster, expressing the perspective of many cultural anthropologists, asserts that a symbol 'is any entity that has socially participative meaning'.[15] The meaning perceived in symbols thus exists only in the concordant minds of the participants in a given culture; symbols do not contain any ontically intrinsic meaning, but are constructions which form the binding glue of cultures and their customs. LeCron goes on to say:

> Symbolism arose and evolved into human culture because of a growing appreciation and social utilization of abstract likenesses between objects and events separated in time and space.[16]

This functional understanding of the symbol as a cultural construct based on observed resemblances is certainly relevant to the development and use of the astrological symbols: there must obviously be some agreement between astrologers as to the meaning of the symbols in order for them to be useful in texts read by other astrologers. The symbol must be 'institutionalised' or 'routinised' for the purposes of communication. But this approach does not answer the question of why a particular symbol should develop in relation to a particular planetary or zodiacal potency, particularly when there is no observed resemblance to a physical object. It would seem that Foster is referring not to symbols, but to signs or significators. The degree of resonance of a symbol, in her view, is determined by its 'use-

---

Symbol: Ancient Readers at the Limits of Their Texts (Princeton, NJ: Princeton University Press, 2004), p. 199.

[14] Struck, *Birth of the Symbol*, p. 201.

[15] Mary LeCron Foster, 'Symbolism: The Foundation of Culture', in Tim Ingold, ed., *The Companion Encyclopedia of Anthropology* (London: Routledge, 1994), p. 366.

[16] Ibid., p. 370.

potential', like the logo for a company or a household product: the wider and more useful the application, the more potent the symbol. If this is so, then human beings, apparently oblivious to such theoretical interpretations, have found astrological symbols useful in a vast variety of different contexts for an extremely long time, and continue to do so even when prevailing cultural dominants oppose any suggestion of their relevance. This implies that the formation and continuity of symbols are more dependent on the degree of meaning and resonance experienced through them than on common cultural usage, and another approach to the astrological glyphs may need to be considered which is far older than LeCron's perspective and which seems to be more deeply interiorised and related more specifically to the religious imagination—which might or might not be a culturally generated form of human expression, depending on which academic paradigm one wishes to adopt.

SYMBOLS AS EMBODIMENTS

Some scholars credit the writers of the German Romantic movement of the nineteenth century, such as Johann Gottfried Herder (1744–1803) and Friedrich Wilhelm Joseph von Schelling (1775–1854), with the idea that symbols, and the mythic narratives that accompany them, express an ontic reality independent of the humans who articulate the symbols.[17] This understanding of the symbol is also found in Jung's analytical psychology, which stresses the intimate connection between myth and symbol, both of which express archetypal patterns that are both psychological and ontically objective.[18] Planetary myths encrust planetary symbols, and the glyph representing the planet communicates not only a characteristic astrological concept such as 'Mars equals aggression', but also a dense and intricate web of mythic associations which can best be expressed through narrative and ritual. In the view of the promulgators of this current in nineteenth- and twentieth-century Western thought,

---

[17] See Adolf Allwohn, *Der Mythos bei Schelling* (Charlottenburg: Verlag Rolf Heise, 1927), pp. 32–33; Alexander Altmann, 'Myth and Symbol', *Philosophy* 20, no. 76 (1945): pp. 162–71.
[18] See, for example, C. G. Jung, *Psychological Types*, CW6 (London: Routledge & Kegan Paul, 1970), ¶202, 401; C. G. Jung, *The Archetypes and the Collective Unconscious*, CW9i (London: Routledge & Kegan Paul, 1968), ¶7.

symbolic images arise from the unconscious; they are not invented or constructed, but are discovered or encountered. This understanding in fact long predates the German Romantics: the term 'symbol', in ancient Greek divinatory practice, carries the notion of a meeting, an encounter, or a 'bumping into' something.[19] Seen from this perspective, symbols are not made, but happen; cultures do not generate symbols, but instead, symbols generate cultural patterns through an encounter with the potency of the ideas associated with them. They are simultaneously omens, the events portended by the omen, and that which stands behind both omen and event.

This perception of symbols approaches them as both representations and embodiments of an objective reality that exists both within and outside the human being; they are generated by the human psyche through the organ of the imagination rather than being constructed by the intellect as a cultural and social edifice, and they are capable of inaugurating the transformation of psychic energy while at the same time describing that transformation. This approach to the symbol can be found throughout the Greek world, from Orphic funerary plaques to early medieval Byzantine astral magic, and seems to have inhabited those currents of astrology that did not succumb, as Ptolemy did, to the influence of Aristotle's profoundly antagonistic approach to the poetics of symbolic expression.[20] Iamblichus, a Neoplatonist writing in the late third to early fourth century CE, asserts that the power of symbols to transform the devotee lies in the symbols themselves; they do not awaken something within the human soul, but derive their power from their identity with the divine potency embodied in the symbol:

> It is the power of ineffable symbols comprehended by the gods alone that establishes theurgical union. Thus, we don't perform these acts intellectually...In fact, these very symbols, by themselves, perform their own work, and the ineffable power of the Gods with which these symbols are charged, itself, recognizes, by itself, its own images. It is not awakened to this by our thinking.[21]

---

[19] See Struck, *Birth of the Symbol*, pp. 90–94.
[20] See Struck, *Birth of the Symbol*, pp. 59–68, for Aristotle's antagonism toward the symbol in poetry.
[21] Iamblichus, *De mysteriis*, 96:13–97.9, in Gregory Shaw, *Theurgy and*

Although symbols may, and usually do, encompass biology—such as the Sun as a phallus, or the Moon as a womb—they represent, from this perspective, the meaningful end of a spectrum which encompasses instinct at one pole and psyche at the other. They are, in other words, both spirit and flesh, and provide a bridge between the two.

Peter Struck, discussing the understanding of a symbol in the Hellenistic world, suggests that the symbol is:

> ... a form of representation that has an intimate, ontological connection with its referent and is no mere mechanical replication of the world, that is transformative and opens up a realm beyond rational experience, that exists simultaneously as a concrete thing and as an abstract and perhaps transcendent truth, and that conveys a unique density of meaning.[22]

This understanding of an ontological link between symbol and symbolised reflects an idea of sympathies or correspondences that was clearly formulated in Stoic circles in the last two centuries BCE, but appears in poetic forms three or four centuries earlier in Orphic texts such as the Derveni papyrus, which portrays a cosmos in which everything has a share of every other thing in it, and is part of an underlying unity.[23]

> Orpheus named this [divine] breath Moira...For before Zeus received his name, Moira was the wisdom of the god always and through everything.[24]

The idea of an organic, interconnected universe filled with a single, primal divine substance is an idea with great agency and continuity, running from Presocratic to Platonic, Neoplatonic, Stoic, Hermetic, and early Jewish cosmologies, and continuing through medieval and early modern alchemy and Kabbalah to modern Theosophy and the astrologies

---

the Soul: The Neoplatonism of Iamblichus (University Park, PA: Pennsylvania State University Press, 1995), p. 84.

[22] Struck, *Birth of the Symbol*, p. 5.

[23] For Stoic cosmology and physics, see F. H. Sandbach, *The Stoics* (London: Duckworth, 1989); A. A. Long and D. N. Sedley, *The Hellenistic Philosophers, Vol. 1* (Cambridge: Cambridge University Press, 1987), pp. 158–437.

[24] Betegh, *Derveni Papyrus*, Col. XIX.

influenced by it. It is also one of the basic building-blocks of Jung's psychological models, although the 'world soul' or *anima mundi* in Jung's work receives the more neutral terminology of 'collective unconscious' or 'objective psyche'.[25] In this world of sympathies, a planetary symbol enjoys a secret identity with the planet it symbolises, and the planet, in turn, is itself a symbol for potencies both interior and exterior, in the human being and in the world, which can only be articulated through the symbol. This idea also stands as the foundation-stone of magic: if everything reflects and contains everything else, then deliberately invoked transformation on one level will result in transformations on other levels.

The astrological symbols in this context are thus not merely representations or signifiers, but embody the thing portrayed; symbols in pictorial or linguistic form may be stylised or condensed forms of larger, more complex pictorial representations, but the latter too embody the essence of the thing portrayed and are thus themselves symbols. An example of this approach to the astrological symbols is the use to which they were put in magical rituals from the early medieval period onward. In magical grimoires such as the fourteenth-century *Liber iuratus* (figs. 1.10 and 1.11), planetary symbols are combined with what are known as *charactêres*: arrangements of lines and dots that form visual/linguistic entities understood to both embody and represent celestial potencies or angelic entities associated with particular planets and groups of stars.[26]

---

[25] For Jung's explication of the 'collective unconscious', see Jung, CW9i.

[26] For the *charactêres*, see Gideon Bohak, *Ancient Jewish Magic: A History* (Cambridge: Cambridge University Press, 2008), p. 272, for possible derivations of the term *charactêre* (*kalaqtiraia* in Aramaic), used by Jewish magicians in late antiquity. For a Greco-Egyptian example of the *charactêres*, see *PGM* X.24–35, in Hans Dieter Betz, ed. and trans., *The Greek Magical Papyri in Translation, Including the Demotic Spells* (Chicago: University of Chicago Press, 1992), p. 149, and the various examples in John G. Gager, *Curse Tablets and Binding Spells from the Ancient World* (Oxford: Oxford University Press, 1992). For early modern examples, see the pseudo-Paracelsian *Archidoxis Magica*, written ca. 1560, translated into English by Robert Turner in *Archidoxes of Magic: Of the Supreme Mysteries of Nature: Of the Spirits of the Planets: Of the Secrets of Alchemy: Of Occult Philosophy: The Mysteries of the Twelve Signs of the Zodiack: The Magical Cure of Diseases: Of Celestial Medicines* (London: N. Brook

Fig. 1.10: Charactêres *for the Martial angel Samael from the* Liber iuratus, *with the planetary glyph on the right*[27]

Fig. 1.11: Charactêres *for the Martial angel Samael from the late medieval Hebrew grimoire,* Sefer Maphtea Shelomo[28]

Texts such as the *Liber iuratus* combine *charactêres* with planetary glyphs in the understanding that both contain magical potency, and the drawing of the glyph is itself a ritual act which can invoke the chosen entity. These glyphs and *charactêres* have been used on magical seals and talismans from late antiquity to the present day for the purpose of invoking the heavenly powers.

Fig. 1.12: Left, sigil for the Martial angel Samael from the Heptameron *(1496), attributed to Pietro d'Abano. Right, Francis Barrett's sigil for Samael (Camael), from* The Magus *(1801). Barrett probably copied it from the seventeenth-century English translation of the* Heptameron. *The* charactêres *are the same as those from the* Liber iuratus.[29]

---

and J. Harison, 1656; repr. London: Askin Publishers, 1975); Juris G. Lidaka, '*The Book of Angels, Rings, Characters and Images of the Planets*: Attributed to Osbern Bokenham', in Claire Fanger, ed., *Conjuring Spirits: Texts and Traditions of Medieval Ritual Magic* (University Park, PA: Pennsylvania State University Press, 1998), pp. 32–75. See also Campbell Bonner, *Studies in Magical Amulets, Chiefly Greco-Egyptian* (Ann Arbor, MI: University of Michigan Press, 1950), pp. 12–13.

[27] *Liber iuratus*, Royal MS 17 A XLII, ff. 68v–69, British Library.

[28] Hermann Gollancz, ed. and trans., *Sefer Maphteah Shelomo (Book of the Key of Solomon): An Exact Facsimile of an Original Book of Magic in Hebrew* (Oxford: Oxford University Press, 1914), ms 35a, p. 89.

[29] *Heptameron*, trans. Robert Turner, in *Henry Cornelius Agrippa, His*

This idea has continued into some contemporary astrological currents, and may lie—albeit unconsciously—behind the insistence on the part of some astrologers that it is important to draw the birth horoscope by hand, even if it is initially calculated by a computer programme, because 'something' happens when these figures are inscribed by the astrologer. Whether understood as a mode of meditation allowing a deeper understanding of the birth chart, or as a form of preparatory ritual, or simply as a way of facilitating an attentive and relaxed state in which to greet the client, this emphasis on the drawing of the glyphs belongs to the complex realm of ritual magic, because it concerns the establishment of a relationship with that which the symbol both represents and embodies.

ASTROLOGICAL SYMBOLS IN MODERNITY

We might, with considerable justification, assume that so-called 'modern' astrology begins with Alan Leo at the turn of the twentieth century.[30] In *Esoteric Astrology*, a work first published in 1913, Leo opens with a chapter entitled 'Astrological Symbology', and proceeds to explain in detail the meaning of the glyphs.

> So far as the planets are concerned, these symbols are built up of the circle, the semi-circle, and the cross... The half-circle is 'employed as the symbol of the Soul, regarded as intermediate between Spirit above and Body below. The cross 'implies complete manifestation and incessant

---

Fourth Book of Occult Philosophy. Of Geomancy. Magical Elements of Peter de Abano. Astronomical Geomancy. The Nature of Spirits. Arbatel of Magick (London: John Harrison 1655), p. 139; Barrett, *The Magus*, Book II, Part III frontispiece.

[30] For Leo's contribution to 'modern' astrology, see Kim Farnell, *The Astral Tramp* (London: Ascella, 1998); Patrick Curry, *A Confusion of Prophets: Victorian and Edwardian Astrology* (London: Collins & Brown, 1992), pp. 122–59; Nicholas Campion, *A History of Western Astrology, Vol. 2: The Medieval and Modern Worlds* (London: Hambledon Continuum, 2009), pp. 231–34; Bessie Leo, *The Life and Work of Alan Leo, Theosophist-Astrologer-Mason* (London: Fowler, 1919). For Leo's own publications, see, among others Alan Leo, *How to Judge a Nativity* (London: Modern Astrology, 1903); Alan Leo, *Astrology for All* (London: Modern Astrology, 1904); Alan Leo, *The Key to Your Own Nativity* (London: Modern Astrology, 1910); Alan Leo, *Esoteric Astrology* (London: Modern Astrology, 1913).

> activity...This cross stands for Body, as distinguished from
> the circle, Spirit, and the semi-circle, Soul.[31]

Leo's understanding of the planets which these glyphs represent is that 'it is not the physical planets themselves that affect mankind, but the supreme Intelligences who use the planetary bodies as their physical vehicles'.[32] This is a very different and far more literal view than that of the planet as itself a symbol.

Margaret Hone, writing forty years later in her *Modern Textbook of Astrology*, also refers to the planetary and zodiacal glyphs as 'symbols'. She then goes on to describe these 'symbols', offering an interpretation directly derived from Alan Leo's understanding of them:

> [The symbols of the planets]...may be seen to be composed
> of different combinations of three parts, the circle, the half
> circle, the cross. This will have more meaning to the modern
> student if he understands that they date from the earliest
> days of mankind before reading was known, when an idea
> had to be taught to the people in pictorial form. The circle is
> said to symbolise eternity, the never-ending: hence spirit or
> primal power. The half-circle signifies soul. The cross
> signifies the material world.[33]

Hone uses the term 'signifies', suggesting that these figures, although she calls them symbols, were deliberately and consciously constructed to designate a specific concept such as 'material world' or 'soul'. Hone presents this idea without any critical discussion of what is meant by 'soul', by 'symbol', or, for that matter, by the extraordinary idea that such figures date to a period 'before reading was known'—extraordinary because the first textual appearance of recognisable zodiacal and planetary glyphs occurs in the fifth century CE, and earlier astrological works tend to spell out the name of the planet or zodiacal sign. Generations of astrologers have nevertheless accepted Hone's interpretation, as they have Leo's; her book was the standard textbook for astrological students in Britain for several decades following its publication in 1951.

The idea that the glyphs were consciously constructed

---

[31] Leo, *Esoteric Astrology*, pp. 1–4.

[32] Ibid., p. 7.

[33] Margaret Hone, *The Modern Textbook of Astrology* (London: Fowler, 1951), p. 21.

does have an important precedent: in the sixteenth century, the Elizabethan magus John Dee (1527–1608) designed a figure which he used as the basis for a cosmo-logical/alchemical exegesis entitled *Monas hieroglyphica*.[34]

Fig. 1.13: Emblem from John Dee's Monas hieroglyphica. *The emblem contains the lunar crescent, the solar point within a circle, and the planetary glyphs for Mercury and Venus, as well as the glyph for the zodiacal sign of Aries as the symbol of the element of fire.*

Dee comments throughout his short work that the circle, crescent, and cross are the only symbols used to construct the glyphs of the planets, and this is probably the source for the later interpretations of the Theosophists. But Dee's 'Monad' is itself not an astrological glyph or symbol; it is an emblem, a kind of condensed signature constructed to convey pictorially the major themes in Dee's philosophy. Dee uses his explication of the emblem to articulate his cosmology and philosophy, and the *Monas* is thus a form of shorthand deliberately utilising a particular arrangement of already extant astrological symbols to convey specific ideas.

The influence of Theosophy, and of Alan Leo's Theosophical astrology, on twentieth-century astrological

---

[34] John Dee, *Monas hieroglyphica* (Antwerp: G. Sylvius, 1564). Dee explains the construction of the emblem in a series of twenty-four 'Theorems'. For English translations of the *Monas hieroglyphica*, see C. H. Josten, trans., 'A Translation of John Dee's *Monas Hieroglyphica*', *Ambix* 12, no.2/3 (1964): pp. 84–221; John Dee, *The Hieroglyphic Monad* (York Beach, ME: WeiserBooks, 2000). See also Peter J. Forshaw, 'The Early Alchemical Reception of John Dee's Monas Hieroglyphica', *Ambix* 52, no. 3 (2005): pp. 247–69; Frances A. Yates, *The Occult Philosophy in the Elizabethan Age* (London: Routledge & Kegan Paul, 1979), pp. 83–89; Federico Cavallaro, 'The Alchemical Significance of John Dee's *Monas Hieroglyphica*', in Stephen Clucas, ed., *John Dee: Interdisciplinary Studies in English Renaissance Thought* (Dordrecht: Kluwer Academic Publishers, 2006), pp. 159–76.

currents has been pervasive. This understanding of the deliberate derivation of the glyphs from the circle, semi-circle, and cross has proved to be a tenacious concept. So, for example, the Theosophically inclined astrologer Isabel Hickey, in a work published in 1970 called *Astrology: A Cosmic Science*, presents a section called 'Planetary Symbols and Their Meanings', in which the circle 'represents the eternal self' while the point in the middle (the glyph for the Sun) 'represents the divine spark at the centre of every living cell'; the half-circle is 'the symbol of the personality' [note the difference between 'personality' and the idea of 'soul']; the cross is the 'symbol of earth-manifestation'.[35] Composite glyphs such as that of Mercury, according to Hickey, combine the three symbols, and their position—for example, whether the circle is at the top, in the middle, or at the bottom—determines how the glyph is to be read, rather like an algebraic formula.

The Theosophical understanding of these symbols, although purportedly based on a very ancient symbolic code, is virtually mechanistic, implying that someone—perhaps an enlightened individual or a secret group of initiates—sat down and constructed them specifically to designate the various relationships of spirit, soul, and matter according to where the emphasis lies in the interpretation of the planet. In fact the planetary glyphs from late antique horoscopes do not contain any crosses at all, and it is possible that, as the pagan world gradually succumbed to the spread of Christianity, the glyphs were also 'Christianised' and the planetary gods rendered subservient to Christ through the imposition of the cross. The Theosophical understanding of the glyphs presents them not as symbols, but as signs or significators: a kind of shorthand like the periodic table in chemistry, where specific letters and numbers are assigned in a codified manner to indicate particular qualities. This approach, perhaps in part derived from John Dee (with whose work Blavatsky was familiar), is entirely contradictory to the manner in which the glyphs emerged and developed slowly over many centuries, altering according to cultural context and understood from diverse perspectives, including both pedagogical and magical.[36]

---

[35] Isabel Hickey, *Astrology: A Cosmic Science* (Bridgeport, CT: Altieri Press, 1970), p. 30.

[36] For Blavatsky's familiarity with Dee's work, see H. P. Blavatsky,

A particularly interesting perception of the zodiacal symbols was presented in the early 1940s in a work called *Astrological Physiognomy* by an American astrologer called Gloria Barrett.[37] Barrett did not offer an explanation of the origin of the symbols as did earlier Theosophical astrologers such as Leo, but understood each zodiacal symbol to represent not only psychological characteristics but also a myriad of associations ranging from the macrocosmic (such as correspondences in religions and philosophies) to microcosmic (correspondences in individual occupations, character, and health) as well as representatives of the animal, plant, and mineral kingdoms. This listing of correspondences in relation to an astrological symbol is neither unique nor modern, and may be found in many astrological texts from late antiquity, although the emphasis on signs rather than planets is characteristic of the astrologies emerging from Alan Leo's work. But Barrett offers her unique contribution by illustrating pictorially the 'energy' of each symbol as reflected in human physiognomy.

The idea that the human body is a symbolic representation of the human soul even in the smallest details is not new; physiognomy was pursued as a window into character and fate from the medieval period onward, and various derivations, such as cheiromancy (palmistry), metaposcopy (analysis of the lines on the forehead), and phrenology (analysis of the features of the skull) have remained popular in esoteric circles from the late eighteenth century to the present day.[38] But Barrett's perspective is focused specifically on the physical embodiment of the astrological glyphs. Glyph, energy, and physical body are seen as a unity, each expressing a different level of a central archetypal pattern for which the symbol is the optimum description. Barrett illustrates her concept with some

---

The Letters of H. P. Blavatsky, Vol. 1, 1861–1879 (Wheaton, IL: Theosophical Publishing House, 2003), p. 242.

[37] Gloria Barrett, *Astrological Physiognomy* (Chicago: Aries Press, 1941).

[38] For academic works on these subjects, see, among others, John van Wyhe, *Phrenology and the Origins of Victorian Scientific Naturalism* (Farnham: Ashgate, 2004); Lawrence Fine, 'The Art of Metoposcopy: A Study in Isaac Luria's Charismatic Knowledge', *AJS Review* 11, no. 1 (1986): pp. 79–101; P. G. Maxwell-Stuart, ed. and trans., *The Occult in Early Modern Europe: A Documentary History* (London: Palgrave Macmillan, 1999).

extraordinary images (fig. 1.13). What she calls the 'symbolic picture' for Aries is meant to represent an abstract image of a particular kind of energy in motion. Next to it is the 'form principle', portraying the energy as it determines the form of various natural objects; finally we see the 'form of forehead'—an image of the structure of the upper portion of the human skull, correlated with a list of physical attributes including stature, skin, nose, chin, jaw, hands, movements, gait, voice, and speech.

Fig. 1.14: Left, the Aries 'energy'; centre, the Aries 'form principle'; right, the Aries forehead.[39]

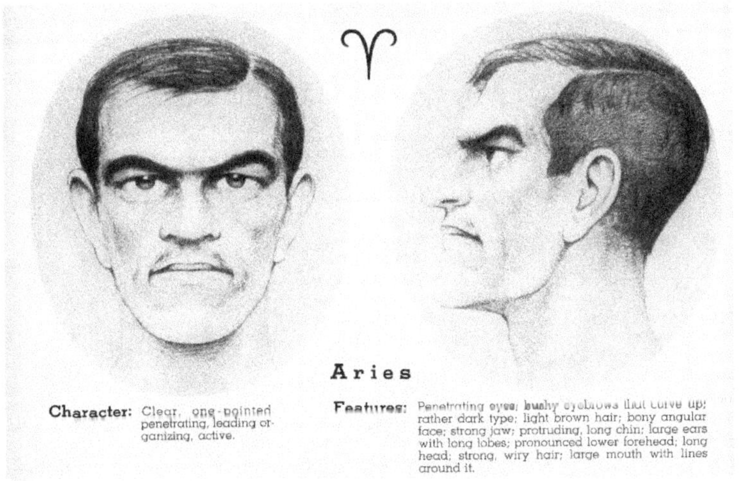

Fig. 1.15: The Aries face.[40]

---

[39] Barrett, *Astrological Physiognomy*, pp. 46–47.
[40] Ibid., Plate 10.

Among the plates accompanying Barrett's book is a complete 'Aries face' (fig. 1.14), which might be terrifying if one met the gentleman in a dark alley—he looks rather like Sean Connery on a bad day—but which is meant to represent the archetypal qualities of Aries, personified by its zodiacal symbol embodied in the human face. Another example, this time of the zodiacal symbol for Capricorn, indicates the extent to which this particular mid-twentieth–century astrologer understands the symbols as a limitless chain of correspondences, including the distillation of energy into human form through the specific features of the human face.

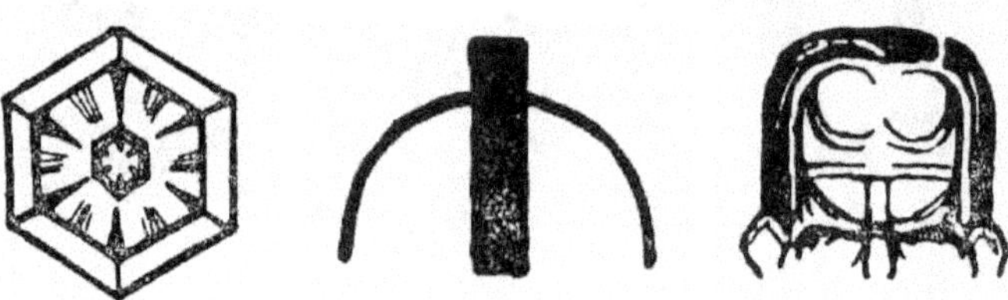

Fig. 1.16: Left, the Capricorn 'energy'; centre, the Capricorn 'form principle'; right, the Capricorn forehead.[41]

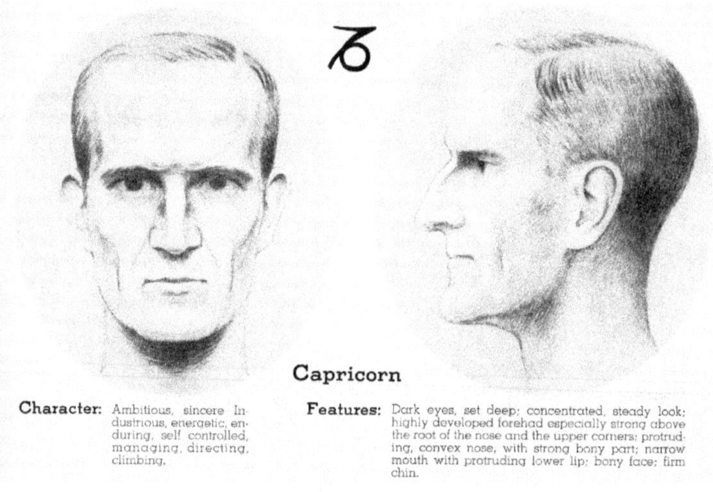

Character: Ambitious, sincere In-
dustrious, energetic, en-
during, self controlled,
managing, directing,
climbing.

Features: Dark eyes, set deep; concentrated, steady look;
highly developed forehad especially strong above
the root of the nose and the upper corners; protruding, convex nose, with strong bony part; narrow
mouth with protruding lower lip; bony face; firm
chin.

Fig. 1.17: The Capricorn face.[42]

---

[41] Ibid., pp. 91–92.
[42] Ibid., Plate 19.

This is the symbol solidified and concretised: in other words, the symbol 'made flesh'. It echoes the ancient idea of the cosmic *anthropos* or 'primordial man' upon whom the human body is modelled: symbol as flesh and flesh as symbol. Jung, irritated with Freud's insistence on the reducibility of so many symbols to the concrete reality of the male sexual organ, remarked laconically in a footnote that even the penis should be understood as a phallic symbol.[43] Barrett appears to understand the glyphs not as something designed to convey a specific set of concepts, but as images of ontically autonomous energies that participate in every level of existence, including the human body. The symbols are thus everywhere because everything encapsulates everything else. It is not that the symbol represents the zodiac sign, but rather, that symbol and zodiac sign are both reflections of an archetypal principle which cannot be grasped by the rational mind alone, but which can be apprehended best through the complex web of the symbol.

The cultural functionalism of the astrological symbols is a valid perspective on their role in various historical contexts. The development of symbolic systems—visual, linguistic, or both—cannot be separated from the cultural context within which they are formed. But at the same time, it might also be appropriate to suggest that these symbols, rather than being 'invented' or 'designed', emerged through a long process that incorporated cosmological, philosophical, and experiential perspectives from a wide variety of cultures; and that they had, and continue to have, an agency independent of their cultural 'use-potential'. This raises a final and perhaps unanswerable question: If the astrological symbols themselves have agency, does it make any difference whether or not the astrologer who utilises them is aware of it? I would like to conclude with a quote from William Butler Yeats, whose particular understanding of symbols was rooted in his training and experience in both astrology and magic in the occult orders of the late nineteenth and early twentieth centuries:

Symbols and formulae are powers, which act in their own

---

[43] See C. G. Jung, *Civilization in Transition*, CW10 (London: Routledge & Kegan Paul, 1964), ¶637, n. 3: 'The phallus is not just a sign that indicates the penis; it is a "symbol" because it has so many other meanings'.

right and with little consideration for our intentions...They are, indeed, personifying spirits that we had best call Gates and Gate-Keepers, because through their dramatic power they bring our soul to crisis.[44]

BIBLIOGRAPHY

Allwohn, Adolf. *Der Mythos bei Schelling*. Charlottenburg: Verlag Rolf Heise, 1927.

Altmann, Alexander. 'Myth and Symbol'. *Philosophy* 20, no. 76 (1945): pp. 162–71.

Barrett, Francis. *The Magus, or Celestial Intelligencer, Being a Complete System of Occult Philosophy*. London: Lackington & Allen, 1801.

Barrett, Gloria. *Astrological Physiognomy*. Chicago: Aries Press, 1941.

Bernabé, Alberto and Ana Isabel Jiménez San Cristóbal. *Instructions for the Netherworld: The Orphic Gold Tablets*. Leiden: Brill, 2008.

Betegh, Gábor. *The Derveni Papyrus: Cosmology, Theology and Interpretation*. Cambridge: Cambridge University Press, 2004.

Betz, Hans Dieter, ed. and trans. *The Greek Magical Papyri in Translation, Including the Demotic Spells*. Chicago: University of Chicago Press, 1992.

Blavatsky, Helena P. *The Letters of H. P. Blavatsky, Vol. 1, 1861–1879*. Wheaton, IL: Theosophical Publishing House, 2003.

Bohak, Gideon. *Ancient Jewish Magic: A History*. Cambridge: Cambridge University Press, 2008.

Bonner, Campbell. *Studies in Magical Amulets, Chiefly Greco-Egyptian*. Ann Arbor, MI: University of Michigan Press, 1950.

Brennan, Martin. *The Boyne Valley Vision*. Dublin: Dolmen Press, 1980.

British Museum Catalogue of Greek Coins, Central Greece (1963).

Burkert, Walter. *Babylon, Memphis, Persepolis: Eastern Contexts of Greek Culture*. Cambridge, MA: Harvard University Press, 2004.

Campion, Nicholas. *A History of Western Astrology, Vol. 2: The Medieval and Modern Worlds*. London: Hambledon Continuum, 2009.

Cavallaro, Federico. 'The Alchemical Significance of John Dee's *Monas Hieroglyphica*'. In *John Dee: Interdisciplinary Studies in English Renaissance Thought*, edited by Stephen Clucas, pp. 159–76. Dordrecht: Kluwer Academic Publishers, 2006.

Ceppi, Claudia Beltramo and Nicoletta Confuorto, eds. *Firenze e la Toscana dei Medici nell' Europa del Cinquecento*. Florence: Electa

---

[44] William Butler Yeats, letter to Florence Farr, cited in Kathleen Raine, *Yeats, the Tarot, and the Golden Dawn* (Dublin: Dolmen Press, 1972), p. 44, and William Butler Yeats, *The Autobiography of William Butler Yeats* (New York: Macmillan, 1953), p. 272, cited in Raine, *Yeats, the Tarot, and the Golden Dawn*, p. 45.

Editrice, 1980.

Clucas, Stephen, ed., *John Dee: Interdisciplinary Studies in English Renaissance Thought*. Dordrecht: Kluwer Academic Publishers, 2006.

Cramer, Frederick H. *Astrology in Roman Law and Politics*. Chicago: Ares, 1996.

Curry, Patrick. *A Confusion of Prophets: Victorian and Edwardian Astrology*. London: Collins & Brown, 1992.

Dee, John. *Monas hieroglyphica*. Antwerp: G. Sylvius, 1564.

———. *The Hieroglyphic Monad*. York Beach, ME: WeiserBooks, 2000.

Eisler, Robert. *Orpheus the Fisher: Comparative Studies in Orphic and Early Christian Cult Symbolism*. London: Watkins, 1921.

Fanger, Claire, ed. *Conjuring Spirits: Texts and Traditions of Medieval Ritual Magic*. University Park, PA: Pennsylvania State University Press, 1998.

Farnell, Kim. *The Astral Tramp*. London: Ascella, 1998.

Fine, Lawrence. 'The Art of Metoposcopy: A Study in Isaac Luria's Charismatic Knowledge'. *AJS Review* 11, no. 1 (1986): pp. 79–101.

Forshaw, Peter J. 'The Early Alchemical Reception of John Dee's Monas Hieroglyphica'. *Ambix* 52, no. 3 (2005): pp. 247–69.

Foster, Mary LeCron. 'Symbolism: The Foundation of Culture'. In *The Companion Encyclopedia of Anthropology*, edited by Tim Ingold, pp. 366–95. London: Routledge, 1994.

Gager, John G. *Curse Tablets and Binding Spells from the Ancient World*. Oxford: Oxford University Press, 1992.

Gollancz, Hermann, ed. And trans. *Sefer Maphteah Shelomo (Book of the Key of Solomon): An Exact Facsimile of an Original Book of Magic in Hebrew*. Oxford: Oxford University Press, 1914. MS 35a.

Guthrie, W. K. C. *Orpheus and Greek Religion*. Princeton, NJ: Princeton University Press, 1952.

Hickey, Isabel. *Astrology: A Cosmic Scioence*. Bridgeport, CT: Altieri Press, 1970.

Hone, Margaret. *The Modern Textbook of Astrology*. London: Fowler, 1951.

Josten, C. H., trans. 'A Translation of John Dee's *Monas Hieroglyphica*'. *Ambix* 12, no. 2/3 (1964): pp. 84–221.

Jung, C. G. *Civilization in Transition*, CW10. Translated by R. F. C. Hull. London: Routledge & Kegan Paul, 1964.

———. *The Archetypes and the Collective Unconscious*, CW9i. Translated by R. F. C. Hull. London: Routledge & Kegan Paul, 1968.

———. *Psychological Types*, CW6. Translated by R. F. C. Hull. London: Routledge & Kegan Paul, 1970.

King, Leonard. *Babylonian Boundary-Stones and Memorial-Tablets in the British Museum*. London: British Museum, 1912.

Kingsley, Peter. *Ancient Philosophy, Mystery, and Magic: Empedocles and Pythagorean Tradition*. Oxford: Clarendon Press, 1995.

Leo, Alan. *How to Judge a Nativity*. London: Modern Astrology, 1903.

———. *Astrology for All*. London: Modern Astrology, 1904.

————. *The Key to Your Own Nativity*. London: Modern Astrology, 1910.

————. *Esoteric Astrology*. London: Modern Astrology, 1913.

Leo, Bessie. *The Life and Work of Alan Leo, Theosophist-Astrologer-Mason*. London: Fowler, 1919.

Liber iuratus, Royal MS 17 A XLII. British Library.

Lidaka, Juris G. 'The Book of Angels, Rings, Characters and Images of the Planets: Attributed to Osbern Bokenham'. In *Conjuring Spirits: Texts and Traditions of Medieval Ritual Magic*, edited by Claire Fanger, pp. 32–75. University Park, PA: Pennsylvania State University Press, 1998.

Long, A. A. and D. N. Sedley. *The Hellenistic Philosophers, Vol. 1*. Cambridge: Cambridge University Press, 1987.

Macchioro, Vittorio D. *From Orpheus to Paul: A History of Orphism*. London: Constable, 1930.

Manilius, Marcus. *Astronomica*. Translated by G. P. Goold. Cambridge, MA: Harvard University Press, 1977.

Maxwell-Stuart, P. G., ed. and trans. *The Occult in Early Modern Europe: A Documentary History*. London: Palgrave Macmillan, 1999.

Neugebauer, Otto and H. B. van Hoesen. *Greek Horoscopes*. Philadelphia: American Philosophical Society, 1987.

Page, Sophie. *Magic in Medieval Manuscripts*. London: British Library, 2004.

Raine, Kathleen. *Yeats, the Tarot, and the Golden Dawn*. Dublin: Dolmen Press, 1972.

Sandbach, F. H. *The Stoics*. London: Duckworth, 1989.

Shaw, Gregory. *Theurgy and the Soul: The Neoplatonism of Iamblichus*. University Park, PA: Pennsylvania State University Press, 1995.

Sibly, Ebenezer and Frederick Hockley, ed. and trans. *The Clavis or Key to the Magic of Solomon*. Lake Worth, FLA: Ibis Press, 2009.

Spiegelberg, Wilhelm. 'Die ägyptischen Namen und Zeichen der Tierkreisbilder in demotischer Schrift'. *Zeitschrift für ägyptische Sprache und Altertumskunde* 48 (1864–84): pp. 146–52.

Struck, Peter T. *The Birth of the Symbol: Ancient Readers at the Limits of Their Texts*. Princeton: Princeton University Press, 2004.

Turner, Robert, in Paracelsus. *Archidoxes of Magic: Of the Supreme Mysteries of Nature: Of the Spirits of the Planets: Of the Secrets of Alchemy: Of Occult Philosophy: The Mysteries of the Twelve Signs of the Zodiack: The Magical Cure of Diseases: Of Celestial Medicines*. London: N. Brook and J. Harison, 1656. Repr. London: Askin Publishers, 1975.

————, trans. *Heptameron, in Henry Cornelius Agrippa, His Fourth Book of Occult Philosophy. Of Geomancy. Magical Elements of Peter de Abano. Astronomical Geomancy. The Nature of Spirits. Arbatel of Magick*. London: John Harrison, 1655.

Van Wyhe, John. *Phrenology and the Origins of Victorian Scientific Naturalism*. Farnham: Ashgate, 2004.

Von Lieven, Alexandra. 'Divination in Ägypten'. *Altorientalische*

Forschungen 26 (1999): pp. 77–126.
Wakeman, William Frederick. *Wakeman's Handbook of Irish Antiquities*. Edited by John Cooke. Dublin: Hodges, Figgis, 1903.
West, M. L. *The Orphic Poems*. Oxford: Oxford University Press, 1983.
———. 'Ab ovo: Orpheus, Sanchuniathon and the Origins of the Ionian World Model'. *The Classical Quarterly* 44, no. 2 (1994): pp. 289–307.
Yates, Frances A. *The Occult Philosophy in the Elizabethan Age*. London: Routledge & Kegan Paul, 1979.
Yeats, William Butler. *The Autobiography of William Butler Yeats*. New York: Macmillan, 1953.

THE HOROSCOPE AS AN IMAGO MUNDI: RETHINKING THE NATURE OF THE ASTROLOGER'S MAP

Bernadette Brady

ABSTRACT: Field work into belief in determinism within contemporary western astrology has revealed a wide diversity of opinion and philosophy amongst astrologers. This diversity encompasses beliefs that range from a fatalistic expectation or acceptance of God's Providence to a humanistic position of the self as the sole creator of one's life. Despite this diversity there is, however, a common unifying theme—that of the role of the horoscope, the astrologer's map. This is viewed, not as a mill-stone of determinism, as suggested by critics of astrology, but rather as a symbolic or sacred map suggestive of what Mircea Eliade defined as an *imago mundi*. That is to say a map of sacred space, where time is non-linear—*illud tempus*, used to locate an individual in a unique position within their world while at the same time providing a personal link to the cosmos.[1] In this light the horoscope can be reappraised: instead of a profane object, a simple tool or map of the solar system open to criticism for its lack of rational representation of the sky, it for the astrologer, is a sacred map belonging within the tradition of other cosmological maps from the medieval period. Such a reappraisal of the nature of the horoscope as a personal, unique cosmological map can contribute to the debates on the role that astrology plays in contemporary culture.

Astrology's existence in popular culture is considered an enigma in that it persists despite its ongoing dismissal by the scientific community. Patrick Curry writes that 'it has attracted as many as it has repelled, springing up afresh after every apparent defeat whether by science, religion, or simply "reason"'.[2] A less sympathetic view is expressed by Martin Ince who, after defining astrology as a form of superstition, commented: 'Astrology is apparently immune to extinction

---

[1] Mircea Eliade, *The Sacred and the Profane: The Nature of Religion,* trans. and ed. Willard R. Trask (1957; repr. London: Harcourt, Inc., 1987), pp. 42, 70.

[2] Patrick Curry, *Prophecy and Power: Astrology in Early Modern England* (Princeton, NJ: Princeton University Press, 1989), p. 1.

despite scientific advances and spread of education'.[3] This persistence in popular culture over millennia has led scholars to attempt definitions. One such definition, put forward by David Pingree, was 'the study of the impact of the celestial bodies—Moon, Sun, Mercury, Venus, Mars, Jupiter, Saturn, the fixed stars and sometimes the lunar nodes—upon the sublunar world'.[4] But such clarity is not so easily found when one is looking for definitions amongst its practitioners. The English astrologer Margaret Hone (1892–1969) prefaced her definition of celestial influence on life by saying 'there are as many angles of approach to astrology as to religion or art'.[5] Prior to this, another English astrologer, Alan Leo (1860–1917), wrote that astrology was 'the soul of astronomy, and by it the inequalities of humanity are explained'.[6] Nicholas Campion addresses this diversity by pointing out that astrology 'will always be plagued by problems of definition' and states that astrology 'may be speculative, but it can also be operative; it involves not only myth and ritual, but also action…'[7]

This diversity was apparent in my own investigation into the belief in determinism amongst practitioners of twentieth and early twenty-first century western astrology. The result of my doctoral field work, in which I surveyed over 1300 astrologers and interviewed 21 professional astrologers within the English speaking world from the period of 2007–2010, revealed that the practice of astrology contains a highly personalized and diverse set of expectations, applications and techniques. Indeed, as Campion had found earlier, with personal nuances added by each individual's spiritual beliefs or life philosophy, the idea of a single definition of astrology, or a single idea of what astrologers believed, proved difficult to sustain.[8] However, even in the face of this diversity, the

---

[3] Martin Ince, *Dictionary of Astronomy* (Teddington, Middlesex: Peter Collins Publishing, 1997), p. 12.

[4] David Pingree, 'Astrology', in *Dictionary of the History of Ideas* (1968; repr. New York: Scribner, 1973), p. 118.

[5] Margaret E. Hone, *The Modern Text-Book of Astrology*, 5th ed. (1951; repr. London: L. N. Fowler & Co. Ltd, 1973), p. 16.

[6] Alan Leo, *The Complete Dictionary of Astrology (C 1900)*, ed. Vivian Robson (Rochester, VT: Destiny Books, 1989), p. 8.

[7] Nicholas Campion, *The Dawn of Astrology. A Cultural History of Western Astrology, the Ancient and the Classical Worlds* (London: Continuum Books, 2008), p. xi.

[8] Nicholas Campion, 'Prophecy, Cosmology and the New Age Movement. The Extent and Nature of Contemporary Belief in

field work revealed two recurring themes. One of these themes is the prime subject of my research, that of the perceived link between the order of nature, in this case celestial determinism, and the perceived determinism of life. The second common theme was the construction and use of a map—a horoscope—to provide a unique view of the individual in time and space. All astrologers who took part in my field work constructed and worked with maps. Furthermore, while personal philosophies varied considerably, the actual diagram used to make the map was universal amongst these western astrologers. In the periphery, along the margins of my research notes, astrologers reported how they would construct diagrammatical horoscopes, carry them as mental images, discuss them with other astrologers and pursue a lifelong journey of understanding their own personal and unique map. The importance of the astrologer's map was unspoken and so accepted that it could easily have been overlooked in the research. It became apparent that, far from being an artifact of astrology, the map seemed to provide the base on which all other astrological philosophy and techniques stood.

The diagrammatical horoscope itself appeared to be the *prima materia* of the astrologer's world. In discussing how astrologers read horoscopes, Curry commented that 'surely a horoscope is a symbolic map of someone's psyche ..... a soul-map...'[9] A symbol according to C. G. Jung (1875–1961) can be 'a picture that may be familiar in daily life, yet that possesses specific connotations in addition to its conventional and obvious meaning....Thus an image is symbolic when it implies something more than its obvious and immediate meaning'.[10] Additionally Jung considered that, 'the symbol is alive only so long as it is pregnant with meaning'.[11] With Jung's definitions therefore the map of the sky which to the astrologer's eye was embodied with the meaning of their life

---

Astrology' (PhD, Bath Spa University College, 2004), p. 257; Nicholas Campion, *What Do Astrologers Believe?* (London: Granta Books, 2006), pp. 1–11.

[9] Roy Willis and Patrick Curry, *Astrology, Science and Culture: Pulling Down the Moon* (New York: Berg, 2004), p. 62.

[10] C. G. Jung, 'Approaching the Unconscious', in *Man and His Symbols*, ed. C. G. Jung, et al. (London: Aldus Books, Jupiter Books, 1964), p. 20.

[11] C. G. Jung, *Psychological Types*, trans. and ed. R. F. C. Hull (1923; repr., Princeton, NJ: Princeton University Press, 1971), p. 815.

became a symbol, a map that moved beyond the mundane into the sacred.

Francesca Rochberg notes that the first horoscopes came from Mesopotamia and they were list maps, a text based description of the sky, with the earliest known being dated from 410 BCE.[12] Johannes Thomann points out that the tradition of the horoscope as a written list perpetuated into the Hellenistic period, arguing that there are only eleven known diagrams existing in more than one hundred Greek astrological documents.[13] He suggests that the horoscope, as a diagram rather than a list map, remained scarce in the West until Arabic influences reached the west in the twelfth century. His argument is that the diagram of the square horoscope was of Chinese origin and moved into the Islamic world and hence to the West via the trade of the Silk Road.[14] However, once the horoscope as a diagram was established within the western astrological tradition, whether it was represented as a square diagram (see fig. 2.1) or in its later nineteenth-century version of a circular form (see fig. 2.2), it maintained its dominant position in Western astrology.[15]

---

[12] Francesca Rochberg, *Babylonian Horoscopes* (Philadelphia: American Philosophical Society, 1998), p. 3.

[13] Johannes Thomann, 'Square Horoscope Diagrams in Middle Eastern Astrology and Chinese Cosmological Diagrams: Were These Designs Transmitted Through the Silk Road?' in *The Journey of Maps and Images on the Silk Road*, ed. Andreas Kaplony and Philippe Forêt (Leiden: Brill, 2008), p. 98.

[14] Ibid., pp. 107–13.

[15] Robert Hand argued that the circular form of the horoscope was drifting into western astrology by the time of William Lilley in the seventeenth century but was firmly established in the nineteenth century by the English astrologer Zadkiel, the pseudonym of Richard James Morrison (1795–1874). 'Astrologies' conference, Bath, UK, 24–25 July 2010. See Robert Hand, 'John Partridge—One of the Founders of Modern Astrology?', in this volume.

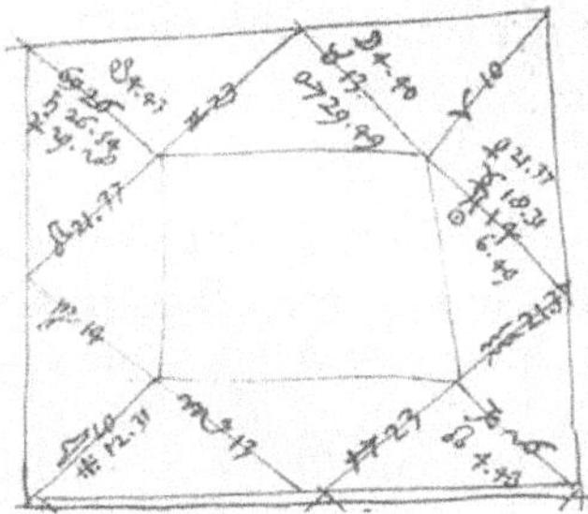

Fig. 2.1: A square chart. Galileo's self-drawn natal horoscope (dated 26 February, 1564, Pisa Italy).[16]

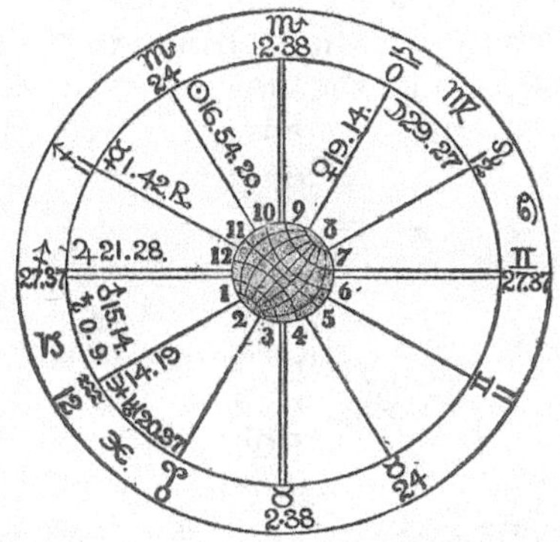

Fig. 2.2: A circular horoscope — the horoscope of King Edward VII published by Alan Leo in 1908 Data: 9 November 1841, 10:48 am, Buckingham Palace, London.[17]

Whether the map is drawn as a square or a circle, it locates the zodiac, tropical or sidereal, around the perimeter of the diagram. The planets are then placed onto the zodiac band representing their celestial position at the time of birth or a moment of time. Additionally the planets and zodiac signs are aligned to represent their orientation to the individual at this moment. Unlike the earlier list maps, this style of representation places the individual in the centre.

---

[16] Image from the *Astrologica nonulla,* a collection of some fifty pages in Galileo's own hand and is the first volume of the sixth part of Galileo's Manuscripts at the Biblioteca Nazionale in Florence.

[17] Alan Leo, *How to Judge a Nativity* (London: Modern Astrology, 1908), p. 282.

The horoscope as a diagram thus embraces the individual, inviting one into the map itself. The astrolabe and the horoscope are both orientated in a similar manner with the observer in the centre of the instrument, facing south with east on the left. In the northern hemisphere the ecliptic is located south of the observer so this orientation allowed for the planets to culminate overhead. The heavens are thus seen to move from left to right in the movement that we now define as clockwise motion. This matching orientation between a horoscope and the astrolabe may well have been due to their close association, with the astrolabe, a time finder, being used to construct horoscopes, a time marker.[18] Additionally, the astrolabe and the square diagram of the horoscope were introduced into Europe at the same time.[19] The similarity between the astrolabe and the horoscope potentially implied that the horoscope was meant to be a simplified map of the heavens. However this assumption was seriously challenged when European astrologers moved into the southern hemisphere.

When European astrologers, in the late eighteenth and early nineteenth century, began to cast their maps for southern hemisphere locations, the northern hemisphere astrolabe had already been put to one side as the major instrument of time, and astrologers used sets of printed tables to orientate the zodiac around an individual. However, to create a horoscope for a birth in the southern hemisphere, a different methodology was needed with these tables.[20] However, even though astrologers made these adjustments to compensate for their southern latitudes, they ignored the fact that the sun actually moved in an anti-clockwise direction during the course of the day. They continued to place east on the left of their horoscopes and the

<hr>

[18] Silke Ackermann, 'The Astrological Scales on the National Maritime Museum Astrolabes', in Lippincott, *Astrolabes at Greenwich*, p. 73.

[19] Koenraad van Cleempoel, 'Representations of Astrolabes in Western Art', in Lippincott, *Astrolabes at Greenwich*, p. 99.

[20] Astrologers used what was known as Tables of Houses. They would, firstly, using a particular algorithm, calculate the local sidereal time, then use this, linked with the latitude, to consult a set of tables to find the rising and culminating degrees of the ecliptic. For the southern hemisphere the algorithm needed to be adjusted by 12 hours and all the zodiac signs read from the Table of Houses needed to be reversed. See Alan Leo, *Casting the Horoscope* (London: Modern Astrology, 1908), p. 41.

point of culmination of the planets (which was now north) above the head of the individual. In doing this the astrological community revealed that they were comfortable with, or ignorant of, the contradiction that the southern hemisphere sky presented. Such disregard for the actual sky challenges the very idea that the horoscope is intended to be a simplified piece of celestial cartography and suggests instead a drive, almost in a Platonist manner, for an object's ideal form; the astrologer was seeking to create or reveal a symbolic ideal form of the individual relationship to the sky.

Indeed the map as a purely factual representation of a landscape or topography is an eighteenth-century construct. As Matthew Edney states, 'The later eighteenth and early nineteenth centuries constitute a period of profound significance for modern Western cartography. ...From this period dates the widespread acceptance that cartography is an empirical, objective and unproblematic science concerned only with the presentation of geographic information'.[21] Edney argues that to the eighteenth-century cartographer the world was 'deemed to be ultimately knowable through active investigation by humans...Each new investigation would add to the existing body of knowledge; that corpus would not need revision and would never become outmoded because the world was fixed'.[22] This classification process of the eighteenth century sought total knowledge of the world with both natural historians and encyclopaedists pursuing full understanding, a pursuit based on the assumption of the absolute perceptibility of the world.[23] From this the concept of a map became synonymous with the idea of knowledge. For example, the eighteenth-century naturalist Carl von Linnaeus (1707–1778) eventually created a *mappa naturae* to show the outline of his taxonomic system in an attempt to bring order to the biological and geological world. As Gunnar Broberg states, Linnaeus sought to map from 'God to gravel as he aimed for a complete inventory or encyclopaedia of the world'.[24] The pursuit of an entire inventory of the

---

[21] Matthew Edney, 'Mathematical Cosmography and the Social Ideology of British Cartography, 1780–1820', *Imago Mundi* 46 (1994): p. 101.

[22] Ibid., p. 104.

[23] Gunnar Broberg, 'The Broken Circle' in *The Quantifying Spirit in the Eighteenth Century*, ed. J. L. Heilbron, Tore Frängsmyr, Robin E. Rider (Berkeley, CA: University of California Press, 1990), p. 45.

[24] Ibid., p. 55.

world was also the desire to understand God's Creation, and in this way the spiritual nature of a map, once represented symbolically in medieval maps, now embraced the pursuit of factuality. These factual maps of an idea (evolution, for example) or place would produce gaps which then became the quest of explorers to fill, usually with species or places or ideas linked with the explorer's name. In this way the map became the bedrock of science, a symbol of unchangeable and fixed truth, a rock on which to stand, that which was fixed and known about the world.

However, a map in the medieval period could be as much concerned with philosophy and theology as with geography, and represent all of these positions within a single diagram. David Woodward argues that the *mappaemundi* of the medieval period were 'primarily to provide a visual narrative of Christian history cast in a geographical framework'.[25] In discussing the philosophy of map-making from the medieval period. Evelyn Edson states '... world maps were philosophical rather than practical, providing a cosmic overview rather than information for some mundane journey'.[26] She points out that these maps were a mixture of metaphor, history, spiritual realms and physical places arranged in a manner to help the individual undertake a lifelong spiritual pilgrimage physically or mentally.[27] Eliade also described such maps; for him they were traditional sacred maps. He called these maps *imago mundi* and defined their features as maps divided into quadrants by the cardinal points, which placed the sacred or known world in the centre and enabled the individual to communicate with the transcendental world by a ritual iteration of the moment of birth or origin of the world.[28] This constant activity of returning to the moment of origin placed the map, in Eliade's opinion, in circular time, which he defined as sacred time, 'indefinitely recoverable, indefinitely repeatable'.[29]

---

[25] David Woodward, 'Reality, Symbolism, Time and Space in Medieval World Maps', *Annals of the Association of American Geographers* 75, no. 4 (1985): p. 519.

[26] Evelyn Edson and Emilie Savage-Smith, 'An Astrologer's Map: A Relic of Late Antiquity', *Imago Mundi* 52 (2000): p. 21.

[27] Evelyn Edson, *The World Map 1300–1492: The Persistence of Tradition and Transformation* (Baltimore: Johns Hopkins University Press, 2007), pp. 14–15.

[28] Eliade, *The Sacred and the Profane*, pp. 42–45, 52.

[29] Ibid., p. 69.

In the nineteenth century when scholars turned their attention to medieval maps, as Woodward points out, they completely misunderstood the *mappaemundi*. From their cultural perspective they considered that all maps attempted to show factual knowledge. This anachronistic approach led to the assumption that the medieval knowledge of the world was simplistic as it appeared ill-informed—believing in a flat world and assuming that Jerusalem was located in the centre.[30] Today it is recognised that such maps offer information at a symbolic level, yet such an anachronistic approach is still encountered when it comes to assumptions concerning the nature of horoscopes. Contemporary western astrologers are accused of being simplistic or ignorant because their maps are geocentric, placing the earth or more precisely the individual in the centre of the map, as well as inaccurate since they locate the planets in a way that does not represent the actual placement of the constellations. This style of judgment was displayed by Richard Dawkins when he wrote in the *Independent on Sunday* on 31 December 1995:

> My birthday (26 March) is listed in the papers as Aries but this is the sun sign which somebody with my birthday would have had when Ptolemy codified all that stuff. Because of the processional shift....my sun sign is in fact (if you can call it that) Pisces. If astrologers were doing something that had any connection with reality, this presumably ought to make a difference. Since they aren't, it doesn't...[31]

Dawkins has assumed that astrologers are seeking perfection in celestial cartography. If this was the case then he would be justified in his assumption of ignorance. However, the nature of the construction of southern hemisphere horoscopes implies that the horoscope is indeed not a modern map fitting into Dawkins' idea of knowledge. Since historically the western astrologer's map has remained largely unchanged in its layout and concept since the twelfth century, it may share more with the encyclopaedic and symbolic medieval *mappaemundi* and/or Eliade's concept of an *imago mundi* than with modern cartography.

In an interview conducted in August 2009, Melanie

---

[30] Woodward, 'Reality, Symbolism, Time and Space in Medieval World Maps', p. 510.
[31] Richard Dawkins, 'The Real Romance in the Stars', *The Independent on Sunday*, 31 December 1995, p. 2.

Reinhart, a professional consulting astrologer and author who lives in England, mirrored Eliade's concept of a sacred map with which one personally engaged as well as used to transcend the mundane world. She commented on the horoscope by saying it '... describes our unique portion of participation in this constantly unfolding universe. And in this sense we neither own our charts nor are we our charts but the chart describes a process that we fully participate in'. This view of the chart as something that provides access to a cosmic whole was a repeated theme in other interviews. Stephanie Johnson, an Australian astrologer and director of Esoteric Technologies, one of the world's leading providers of astrological software, when interviewed in 2010, replied to the question of what she gained from astrology by saying 'I think we belong in the same sense that all nature belongs so I do like the idea of belonging to this earth and sense of uniqueness and cooperation and community on this earth'. For Johnson, as for many astrologers, the horoscope provided simultaneous uniqueness and citizenship in the cosmos. Other astrologers I surveyed talked of 'Being able to see the intelligence of poetic mapping playing out', or 'It connects my little life with a bigger picture and provides understanding combined with awe'. In the manner of Eliade's concept of circular time an English astrologer wrote that what she liked about astrology was 'The feeling of being in touch with the cosmos; the feeling of being in touch with something ancient; the feeling of picking up on a cycle which helps to explain the whys and wherefores of life'.

If the horoscope operated within the tradition of the medieval *mappaemundi*, a spiritual or sacred map, it would also be used as guidance throughout one's life journey. In an interview in 2010, Barbara Dunn, an English horary astrologer[32] who has been practicing, writing and teaching for the last 25 years, answered the question of what astrology gave to her life by saying, ' Well I suppose ... I suppose... well by doing any type of chart or by looking at your own nativity it gives you ... well I suppose it gives you an idea of how your life is going to be and what your areas of strengths are'. Similarly Dutch astrologer Karen Hamaker-Zondag, author and teacher and Jungian specialist who has been practicing astrology since 1975, when interviewed in 2008 about what astrology gave to any individual, replied, 'The

---

[32] A Horary astrologer is one who seeks to answer questions by casting horoscopes for the moment of the asking of the question.

chart is a road map, it tells you about your dynamics and what you need to become you, and so the more you fulfil your chart the happier you will be. This does not mean that you will have less difficulties but you can handle them better and so for me living the chart is actually the key'. Both astrologers are using the map as guidance, one for finding one's strength; the other for finding a form of happiness. An anonymous English astrologer with over 22 years of study in astrology also talked of this when she wrote in her survey form:

> The natal blue print [the horoscope] will often bring us back to our evolutionary path through transits or progressions— when we have strayed from it by exploring another side road or seemingly taken a wrong turning but what we have learnt through our experiences of making such 'mistakes' will enhance our understanding of ourselves and others and enable us to choose more wisely the route we take in the future to reach our evolutionary goals in this life.

Adding to this picture were comments within interviews and on survey forms concerning the use of circular time. In this respect, Mircea Eliade talked of non-linear time, *illud tempus*, which was used to locate an individual both in the mundane as well as sacred world.[33] In an interview Robert Hand, who has been studying astrology since 1960 and works as a consultant, translator, author and lecturer, replied to a question about his use of cycles in his own horoscope, by saying, 'Yes, but they are, nevertheless, only a pre-figuration, they are not going to be repeated. Nothing is ever repeated. For example both Saturn returns, interestingly enough, coincided with the same style of personal problems but the second one worked out fine'.[34] Here Hand is expressing a common theme amongst the astrologers I surveyed and interviewed. Cycles and the events which occurred at an earlier time were used to give insight into the likely expression of future events when that cycle returned. For astrologers involved in the investigation, time past and future was cyclic in nature and its theme, which was predefined by astrological symbolism, was placed firmly into the chronological perimeters defined by the individual's

---

[33] Eliade, *The Sacred and the Profane*, pp. 42, 70.
[34] The Saturn return for astrologers is the time that Saturn returns to its location at the time of the person's birth, a cycle that takes 29 and a half years.

horoscope. Some astrologers saw the resulting events in a more fateful light while others tended to agree with Hand's opinion that the timing was certain but the expression of the event was not.

The ability of the horoscope to provide a private chronology which could then be used to give feedback on one's life journey was referred to in a comment by an American astrologer who had been working with astrology for 34 years. She wrote that she liked astrology because of 'The cyclical quality that it presents to us. If you live long enough, you see those cycles coming back. If you've learned anything at all, then when the tough ones come back, you handle them better and when the great ones come back, you appreciate them more'. This theme of watching cycles and using them as a way of gaining greater alignment to perfection (however defined by the astrologer) was referred to in an interview with Roy Gillett, current President of the Astrological Association of Great Britain and involved with astrology since the 1970s. He commented on free will and fate by saying '… I think you do have a certain amount of control over your destiny. If you are conscious of the cycles [to your chart] as they are and you approach them with a selfless but mindful compassion, … you are free up to a point within the range of possibilities. But if you approach them with, "Oh God how can I get as much as I can out of them", then you are just going to be tossed and blown'.

Unlike a mundane map the sacred map also embodied emotions. For most of the astrologers involved in the project this emotion was hope. One Norwegian astrologer who had worked in astrology for 12 years replied that what she liked about astrology was 'When life is difficult, astrology gives it meaning and hope, even in the darkest hours. You know that soon this too will pass'. This astrologer was referring to timed events in her horoscope, the coming and going of life events as indicated by her private chronology. Another comment from an English astrologer of 20 years, when talking about what she liked about astrology, referred to this same idea when she wrote, 'It shows me that the bad times won't last forever and the ability to make "lemonade out of lemons" and to make the most of the good times when they are here'.

As well as hope, however, it can also inspire fear. Some astrologers talked of the fear of the knowing. One US astrologer wrote, 'For some people it would be better they do not use it at all, for it scares them…' One male American astrologer expressed concern with the actions of some astrologers when they worked with their own horoscope by commenting, '…you can feel the fear rolling off them as they work to arrange every detail of their lives so that nothing untoward will ever occur'. The astrologer was referring to the philosophy that one can mitigate foreseen negative events by undertaking evasive action. Talking more personally, an Australian astrologer wrote of both her fear and her approach to that fear: 'At times I am fearful of the future transits [to my chart], but I can prepare for crisis points, and know that there is purpose for going through difficult times. Usually things don't turn out as badly as I fear they will, and I try to use the energies in a positive way, rather than to let them work negatively'.

This small sample of voices of astrologers is reflective of the majority of comments, notes and conversations of the whole project. The field work revealed that contemporary western astrologers use the horoscope as a symbolic map which, for them, contains information about their times of joy and their times of sadness. This personal map establishes their uniqueness in the world, providing them with a personal chronology based on a version of circular time. However, at the same time as it gives uniqueness to each individual, this uniqueness was viewed within the larger set of planetary cycles which enables membership of the cosmos in the past, present and future. It also became apparent that most of the astrologers viewed their own map as a reflection of their perfect self and used it as a guide to help achieve this perfection. Moreover, in the same way as Eliade described the need to return to the point of origin by revisiting the birth of the world, each astrologer constantly revisited their personal moment of creation, returning to their birth horoscope for guidance, timing and understanding. At least for the astrologers who took part in this field work, the horoscope had moved beyond its simplistic representation of the sky and become instead an encyclopaedia of the self, written at birth but never finished being read.

This paper has argued for a reconsideration of the nature of the diagrammatical horoscope, seeing it as it is seen by contemporary western astrologers, as a sacred map having more in common with the medieval *mappaemundi* than with twentieth-century celestial cartography. In this regard the horoscope, rather than the sky itself, may have a greater claim to being the *prima materia* of astrology. In addition, by recognising the role of the horoscope in astrology, insights can be gained into its resilient nature for, having been offered an independent, unique personal guide for life which reflects back to its owner a perfect form of the self, never judging but always guiding, it is possible that few astrologers put it back down again. As summed up by an anonymous astrologer in 2008: 'I like having a map, a place where I can turn to understand and manage my life'.

BIBLIOGRAPHY

Ackermann, Silke. 'The Astrological Scales on the National Maritime Museum Astrolabes'. In Lippincott, *Astrolabes at Greenwich*, pp. 73–89.

Broberg, Gunnar. 'The Broken Circle'. In *The Quantifying Spirit in the 18th Century*. Edited by J. L. Heilbron, Tore Frängsmyr, Robin E. Rider, pp. 45–72. Berkeley, CA: University of California Press, 1990.

Campion, Nicholas. *The Dawn of Astrology: A Cultural History of Western Astrology, the Ancient and Classical Worlds*. London: Continuum Books, 2008.

———. 'Prophecy, Cosmology and the New Age Movement. The Extent and Nature of Contemporary Belief in Astrology'. PhD, Bath Spa University College, 2004.

———. *What Do Astrologers Believe?* London: Granta Books, 2006.

Curry, Patrick. *Prophecy and Power: Astrology in Early Modern England*. Princeton, NJ: Princeton University Press, 1989.

Dawkins, Richard. 'The Real Romance in the Stars'. *The Independent on Sunday*, 31 December 1995.

Edney, Matthew. 'Mathematical Cosmography and the Social Ideology of British Cartography, 1780–1820'. *Imago Mundi* 46 (1994): pp. 101–16.

Edson, Evelyn. *The World Map 1300–1492: The Persistance of Tradition and Transformation*. Baltimore: Johns Hopkins University Press, 2007.

———, and Emilie Savage-Smith. 'An Astrologer's Map: A Relic of Late Antiquity'. *Imago Mundi* 52 (2000): pp. 7–29.

Eliade, Mircea. *The Sacred and the Profane: The Nature of Religion*. 1957. Translated by Willard R. Trask. London: Harcourt, Inc., 1987.

Hone, Margaret E. *The Modern Text-Book of Astrology*. 1951. 5th ed. London: L. N. Fowler & Co. Ltd, 1973.

Ince, Martin. *Dictionary of Astronomy*. Teddington, Middlesex: Peter Collins Publishing, 1997.

Jung, C. G. ' Approaching the Unconscious'. In *Man and His Symbols*, edited by C. G. Jung, M-L von Franz, Joseph L. Henderson, Jolande Jacobi, and Aniela Jaffé, pp. 18–104. London: Aldus Books, Jupiter Books, 1964.

———. *Psychological Types*. 1923. Translated and edited by R. F. C. Hull. Princeton, NJ: Princeton University Press, 1971.

Leo, Alan. *Casting the Horoscope*. London: Modern Astrology, 1908.

———. *The Complete Dictionary of Astrology (C 1900)*. Edited by Vivian Robson. Rochester, VT: Destiny Books, 1989.

———. *How to Judge a Nativity*. London: Modern Astrology, 1908.

Lippincott, Kristin, ed. *Astrolabes at Greenwich*. Oxford: Oxford University Press, 2005.

Pingree, David. 'Astrology'. In *Dictionary of the History of Ideas*. 1968. Reprinted by New York: Scribner, 1973.

Rochberg, Francesca. *Babylonian Horoscopes*. Philadelphia: American Philosophical Society, 1998.

Thomann, Johannes. 'Square Horoscope Diagrams in Middle Eastern Astrology and Chinese Cosmological Diagrams: Were These Designs Transmitted Through the Silk Road?' In *The Journey of Maps and Images on the Silk Road*, edited by Andreas Kaplony and Philippe Forêt, pp. 97–117. Leiden: Brill, 2008.

van Cleempoel, Koenraad. 'Representations of Astrolabes in Western Art'. In Lippincott, *Astrolabes at Greenwich*, pp. 99–111.

Willis, Roy, and Patrick Curry. *Astrology, Science, and Culture: Pulling Down the Moon*. New York: Berg, 2004.

Woodward, David. 'Reality, Symbolism, Time and Space in Medieval World Maps'. *Annals of the Association of American Geographers* 75, no. 4 (1985): pp. 510–21.

THE PHILOSOPHY OF WILLIAM JAMES AS A CONTEXT FOR ASTROLOGY

Garry Phillipson

ABSTRACT: According to William James reality is "if not irrational, then at least non-rational in its constitution".[1] What he meant can be illustrated by a marginal note he added to a lecture: "All 'classic', 'clean', cut and dried, 'noble', 'fixed', 'eternal' *Weltanschauungen* [worldviews] seem to me to violate the character with which life concretely comes and the expression which it bears, of being, or at least involving a muddle and a struggle, with an 'ever not quite' to all our formulas, and novelty and possibility forever leaking in".[2] This paper will consider reason, reality, and the disjunction alleged by James to exist between them. Some key elements of James's thought—such as pluralism, radical empiricism and pragmatism—will be touched on, together with parallels from other thinkers. After noting that astrology is often dismissed as lacking rationality,[3] consideration will be given to James's non-rational reality as a context for the understanding and practice of astrology.

Astrology is commonly characterised as having been invalidated for all time—as when, for instance, the *Oxford English Dictionary*, in defining the noun, notes: 'By 1700 astrology had lost intellectual credibility in the West, but continued to have popular appeal'.[4] This paper is informed

---

[1] William James, 'Lecture V: The Compounding of Consciousness' in *A Pluralistic Universe* in William James, *William James: Writings 1902–10: The Varieties of Religious Experience; Pragmatism; A Pluralistic Universe; The Meaning of Truth; Some Problems of Philosophy; Essays*, ed. Bruce Kuklick (New York: Library of America, 1988), p. 726.

[2] William James, *Manuscript Lectures* (Cambridge, MA: Harvard University Press, 1988), p. 326.

[3] For example in Edward W. James' essay 'On Dismissing Astrology and Other Irrationalities' in Patrick Grim, ed., *Philosophy of Science and the Occult*, 2nd ed. (Albany, NY: State University of New York Press, 1990), pp. 28–36.

[4] 'Astrology (noun)', *The Oxford English Dictionary*, rev. ed., ed. Catherine Soanes and Angus Stevenson (Oxford: Oxford University Press, 2005).

by the idea that reports of astrology's invalidation rest upon a set of questionable philosophical assumptions. This is a theme that has recently been developed by Willis and Curry, amongst others.[5] Since the theme is too large develop fully here, this paper will confine itself to surveying some elements of William James's philosophy which—I will suggest—throw into relief the assumptions generally made by critics of astrology, and sketch an approach that could be more congenial to an understanding of the subject. My hope is that locating the discussion in the work of one philosopher will make it relatively straightforward for subsequent commentators to critique the position developed here. It may be worth emphasising at the start that no attempt is made, in what follows, to resolve or prove anything once and for all. The aim is simply to question what are often taken to be certainties, and to discuss a precedent in the Western philosophical tradition for doing so.

RATIONALITY V. ASTROLOGY

As an expedient to introduce the theme that will be developed here, it can be noted that the invalidation of astrology is frequently defined in terms of it lacking rationality, or—which amounts to much the same—being built upon reasoning errors. For example:

> It is only when we encounter one piece of bogus reasoning after another, as we do with astrology, that we have a clear case of irrationality.[6]

> [Belief in astrology is a] massive rejection of rationality stemming from ignorance of the facts...[7]

> [C]ould astrology deliver the necessary goods? For twenty-five years we have tried to find out... we have found nothing that could not be explained by reasoning errors and other artifacts.'[8]

---

[5] Roy Willis and Patrick Curry, *Astrology, Science and Culture: Pulling Down the Moon* (Oxford: Berg, 2004).
[6] James, 'On Dismissing Astrology', p. 35.
[7] Roger B. Culver and Philip A. Ianna, *Astrology: True or False? A Scientific Evaluation* (Buffalo NY: Prometheus Books, 1988), p. 207.
[8] Geoffrey Dean et al., quoted in Garry Phillipson, *Astrology in the Year Zero* (London: Flare, 2000), p. 153.

> Astrology, for instance, is but the largest component of larger phenomenon—the growing receptivity to irrational spiritual doctrines and practices...[9]

William James suggested that reality is 'if not irrational, then at least non-rational in its constitution', and it is the vista opened up by this statement which is the focus of this paper, in particular for the perspective it lends to evaluations of astrology.[10] What James meant can be illustrated by a marginal note he added to a lecture:

> All 'classic', 'clean', cut and dried, 'noble', 'fixed', 'eternal' *Weltanschauungen* [worldviews] seem to me to violate the character with which life concretely comes and the expression which it bears, of being, or at least involving a muddle and a struggle, with an 'ever not quite' to all our formulas, and novelty and possibility forever leaking in.[11]

James does not discuss astrology, nor show any sympathy towards it—to the best of my knowledge he directly mentions the subject only once, and then dismissively.[12] Nonetheless, the case to be developed here is that certain elements of James's thought provide an environment congenial to an understanding of astrology as a subject which, whilst it cannot be contained and explained within the framework of 'scientific rationality', is not invalidated thereby.[13]

A thorough examination of James's views on rationality and non-rationality will not be undertaken here. In the first place there is not sufficient time—particularly if we were to

---

[9] Robert P. Crease, 'Top Scientists Must Fight Astrology or All of Us Will Face the Consequences', *The Scientist* 3, no. 5 (1989): p. 9. http://www.the-scientist.com/article/display/9209/ (accessed 24 October 2010).

[10] James, 'Lecture V', p. 726.

[11] James, *Manuscript Lectures*, p. 326.

[12] '...alchemy, magic, astrology, imposed on every one's belief...' William James, 'Philosophy and its Critics', ch.1 in *Some Problems of Philosophy* (1911), in James, *William James: Writings 1902–10*, p. 993.

[13] For an example of the phrase 'scientific rationality', the argument that it distinguishes science from pseudosciences such as astrology, together with reflection on the difficulty of reaching a complete and satisfactory definition of it, see: Alan Sokal, *Beyond the Hoax: Science, Philosophy and Culture* (Oxford: Oxford University Press, 2008), particularly p. 180.

consider James's assertion that 'rationality has at least four dimensions, intellectual, aesthetical, moral and practical'.[14] In the second place, it is possible to get a good general idea of what is understood by 'rationality' here from James's statements that 'the subconscious and non-rational... hold primacy in the religious realm'; and that '[i]ntellectually, the world of mechanical materialism is the most rational, for we subject its events to mathematical calculation'.[15] In the third place, a detailed account of James's views on rationality and non-rationality can already be found in an essay by Michel Weber.[16]

The aim of the present paper is, then, relatively modest: to note some of the major elements of James's thought—particularly concerning matters ontological and epistemological—that can be applied to the consideration of astrology. This is undertaken, not with any aspiration to establish or prove any particular view within the compass of the paper, but rather with the hope of introducing a philosophical context which may facilitate future discussion about, and evaluation of, astrology.

MATERIALISTIC AND SPIRITUALISTIC PHILOSOPHIES

In identifying the overarching worldviews that can be held, James distinguishes between *materialistic* and *spiritualistic* philosophies.[17] The former, he writes, defines the world 'so as to leave man's soul upon it as a sort of outside passenger or alien, while the latter insists that the intimate and human must surround and underlie the brutal.'[18] As James uses the term here, 'spiritualism' is used 'merely as the opposite of materialism'. In other words there is, despite modern usage, no reference to clairvoyance. James then proceeds to

---

[14] William James, 'Lecture III: Hegel and His Method', in *Pluralistic Universe*, p. 680.
[15] William James, *The Varieties of Religious Experience* (1902; repr. London: Penguin, 1985), p. 74; James, *Pluralistic Universe*, p. 680.
[16] Michel Weber, 'James's non-rationality and its religious extremum in the light of the concept of pure experience', in *William James and the Varieties of Religious Experience—A Centenary Celebration*, ed. Jeremy Carrette (London: Routledge, 2005), pp. 203–20.
[17] For example James, *Pluralistic Universe*, p. 640.
[18] Ibid.

distinguish 'two very distinct types or stages in spiritualistic philosophy':[19]

> *Dualistic theism, which* depicts 'God and his creation as entities distinct from each other, [and so] still leaves the human subject outside the deepest reality in the universe".[20] Under this view, '[God's] action can affect us, but he can never be affected by our reaction.'[21]

> *Monistic pantheism,* by contrast, is 'the vision of God as the indwelling divine rather than the external creator, and of human life as part and parcel of that deep reality.'[22] This is the position that James favours.

An additional pair of terms that James coined, and which overlap to a considerable extent with dualistic theism/monistic pantheism, are:

- Universalistic (or Refined) Supernaturalism
- Piecemeal (or Crass) Supernaturalism

As James describes it, for the universalistic supernaturalist, 'the world of the ideal has no efficient causality, and never bursts into the world of phenomena at particular points.'[23] Whereas the piecemeal supernaturalist

> admits miracles and providential leadings, and finds no intellectual difficulty in mixing the ideal and the real worlds together by interpolating influences from the ideal region among the forces that causally determine the real world's details.[24]

James numbers himself amongst the ranks of the piecemeal supernaturalists.

---

[19] Ibid.

[20] Ibid., p. 641.

[21] Ibid., p. 642.

[22] Ibid., p. 644.

[23] James, *Varieties of Religious Experience*, p. 521.

[24] Ibid., pp. 520–21. For an extended discussion, see: T. L. S. Sprigge, 'Refined and Crass Supernaturalism', in *Philosophy, Religion and the Spiritual Life*, ed. Michael McGhee (Cambridge: Cambridge University Press: 1992), pp. 105–25.

DIVINATION AND SCIENCE

At this point it may appear that James's 'piecemeal supernaturalism' would naturally map onto a view of astrology as divination; and that his 'universalistic supernaturalism' would ally itself with a view of astrology as science. This is based on the discussion of these matters found in works such as those of Geoffrey Cornelius, who writes that 'the main body of astrology's practice…is properly to be understood as a form of divination. It is divination despite all appearances of objectivity and natural law.'[25]

To say of astrology that it is divination, or any particular type of thing *sub specie aeternitatis* is, however, just what Liz Greene has recently argued against:

> Astrology cannot be explained by any single theoretical framework, but must be viewed within a specific religious, philosophical, social and political background and, equally importantly, from the perspective of individual practitioners working within a particular milieu.[26]

It will be argued in what follows that elements of James's philosophy provide a way of thinking within which the epistemological and ontological dilemmas posed by astrology can be accommodated and—up to a point—made sense of, and that part of this process involves an explication of how it is that the subject can take a plurality of forms.

PRAGMATISM

For James, experience rather than concepts should be the arbiter of truth. This is the essence of his pragmatic approach:

> There can *be* no difference anywhere that doesn't *make* a difference elsewhere—no difference in abstract truth that doesn't express itself in a difference in concrete fact and in

---

[25] Geoffrey Cornelius, *The Moment of Astrology*, 2nd ed. (Bournemouth: Wessex Astrologer, 2003), p. xxii.
[26] Liz Greene, 'Is Astrology a Divinatory System?', *Culture and Cosmos* 12, no.1 (Spring/Summer 2008): p. 3.

conduct consequent upon that fact, imposed on somebody, somehow, somewhere and somewhen.[27]

The need for the pragmatic approach follows, for James, from the relativism he illustrated on more than one occasion with analogies concerning household pets. James wrote:

> I firmly disbelieve, myself, that our human experience is the highest form of experience extant in the universe. I believe rather that we stand in much the same relation to the whole of the universe as our canine and feline pets do to the whole of human life. They inhabit our drawing-rooms and libraries. They take part in scenes of whose significance they have no inkling. They are merely tangent to curves of history the beginnings and ends and forms of which pass wholly beyond their ken. So we are tangent to the wider life of things.[28]

In another work he put it this way:

> That the world of physics is probably not absolute, all the converging multitude of arguments that make in favour of idealism tend to prove; and that our whole physical life may lie soaking in a spiritual atmosphere, a dimension of being that we at present have no organ of apprehending, is vividly suggested to us by the analogy of the life of our domestic animals. Our dogs, for example, are in our human life but not of it. They witness hourly the outward body of events whose inner meanings cannot, by any possible operation, be revealed to their intelligence,—events in which they themselves often play the cardinal part.[29]

The suggestion in these passages is that it may not in fact be rational to believe the human mind central, privy to everything there is to know about the world. As to what *is* rational, James argued that rationality is to some extent *a feeling*, and therefore intrinsically perspectival.[30] In consequence, therefore, 'the ultimate philosophy… must not be too strait-laced in form, must not in all its parts divide heresy from orthodoxy by too sharp a line'.[31]

---

[27] William James, *Pragmatism and Other Writings*, ed. Giles Gunn, (London: Penguin, 2000), p. 27. Emphasis in the original.

[28] James, *Pragmatism*, p. 131.

[29] William James, *The Will to Believe* (in James, *Pragmatism*), p. 237.

[30] See, in particular, 'The Sentiment of Rationality' in ibid.

[31] Ibid., p. 539.

This reintroduces a theme referred to, with a quotation from James, at the beginning of this paper. In a fuller version of that quotation, James states that:

> For my own part, I have finally found myself compelled to give up the logic, fairly, squarely, and irrevocably. [...] Reality, life, experience, concreteness, immediacy, use what word you will, exceeds our logic, overflows and surrounds it... I prefer bluntly to call reality if not irrational then at least non-rational in its constitution,—and by reality here I mean reality where things *happen*, all temporal reality without exception.[32]

As part of his critique of the rational, conceptual, mind, James denied the ultimate reality of familiar mind-created dualities such as 'thoughts and things', 'spirit and matter', 'soul and body' and advocated an understanding in terms of what he called 'pure experience'. He wrote that:

> My thesis is that if we start with the supposition that there is only one primal stuff or material in the world, a stuff of which everything is composed, and if we call that stuff 'pure experience', then knowing can easily be explained as a particular sort of relation towards one another into which portions of pure experience may enter.[33]

Perhaps the most cogent way to encapsulate the significance of James's 'pure experience' is to say that it is opposed to Cartesian dualism. This is significant for astrology because an absolute split between mind and matter poses the problem of how there could be any sort of meaningful relationship between the inner life of an individual and the planets. Under a dualistic view, some sort of 'influence' would be needed—as when the philosopher Kanitscheider suggested that astrology could only be credible if there was evidence of 'F-Rays' to mediate astrological influence:

> For the sake of brevity, let us introduce the term 'F-ray' for a supposed type of stellar influence (F for fate determinant) of unknown ontological status, whether physical or spiritual. [...]

---

[32] James, *Pluralistic Universe*, p. 725–26.
[33] William James, 'Does 'Consciousness' Exist?', in James, *William James: Writings 1902–10*, pp. 1141–42.

If F-rays are somehow phenomena that exist in space-time, then distance must somehow be pertinent in the judging the influence of individual stellar bodies. Every known macroscopic force varies with the inverse square of distance, and in the case of F-rays the emitter and receiver are spatiotemporal objects; it is therefore all the more plausible that such interactions should obey the laws of space-time.[34]

Despite some attempts to identify a causal mechanism for astrology—found, for instance, in some works of the astronomer Percy Seymour—astrology has generally failed to produce convincing candidates for the role of 'F-rays'.[35] Rather than attempting to find a viable explanation within Newtonian physics, it seems natural to see James's 'pure experience' as having more affinity with views found in quantum physics. This is not the place for a long discussion of the relevance of developments in modern physics to astrology.[36] For the purpose presently in hand, it will suffice to note the response of the physicist Max Planck (1858–1947) who, on being asked if he thought consciousness could be explained in terms of matter and its laws, replied, 'Consciousness I regard as fundamental. I regard matter as derivative from consciousness. We cannot get behind consciousness. Everything that we talk about, everything that we regard as existing postulates consciousness.'[37] This view—which is, or at least is close to, panpsychism—would have sat well with James, whose panpsychist leanings can be seen in his warm and sympathetic appraisal of the

---

[34] Bernulf Kanitscheider, 'A Philosopher Looks at Astrology', *Interdisciplinary Science Reviews* 16, no. 3 (1991): pp. 261–62. For an argument from an astrologer to the effect that astrology works 'within the accepted laws of space/time physics' (and not through synchronicity), see Mike Harding, *Hymns to the Ancient Gods* (London: Arkana, 1992), p. 35.

[35] In particular, Percy Seymour, *The Scientific Basis of Astrology* (London: Quantum, 1997).

[36] More on the subject can be found in: Garry Phillipson, 'Modern Science, Epistemology and Astrology', *Correlation (Astrological Association Journal of Research in Astrology)* 23, no. 2 (2006): pp. 4–23.

[37] J. W. N. Sullivan, 'Interview with Max Planck', *Observer*, 25 January 1931. Cited in C. E. M. Joad, *Philosophical Aspects of Modern Science* (London: Allen and Unwin, 1932), p. 16.

works of the psychologist and animist mystic Gustav
Fechner (1801–1887):[38]

> The vaster orders of mind go with the vaster orders of body.
> The entire earth on which we live must have, according to
> Fechner, its own collective consciousness. So must each sun,
> moon, and planet; so must the whole solar system have its
> own wider consciousness, in which the consciousness of our
> earth plays one part. So has the entire starry system as such
> its consciousness; and if that starry system be not the sum of
> all that is, materially considered, then that whole system,
> along with whatever else may be, is the body of that
> absolutely totalized consciousness of the universe to which
> men give the name of God.[39]

These remarks will have reached many twentieth century
students of the occult via the lengthy citation of them in the
international best-seller *Tertium Organum* by P. D.
Ouspensky (1878–1947).[40]

If it is true, however, that consciousness informs
everything—and particularly if this consciousness is
somehow synonymous with what is often thought of as
'God'—this raises as many questions as it answers. For
astrology, an obvious question is: If there is already a
connection between the astrologer's mind and the entire
world, why would they need to refer to astrological charts at
all? In fact the question of how astrology could allow anyone
to know anything may seem to have been exchanged for the
question of why the astrologer (or anyone whatsoever) does
not know everything in the normal course of things, without
recourse to the technical apparatus of horoscopic charts and
so forth. This issue may be illumined somewhat by reference
to James's studies of clairvoyant phenomena.

---

[38] For a discussion of James's panpsychism, see: David Skrbina,
Panpsychism in the West (Cambridge, MA: MIT Press, 2005), pp. 145–
49, and David C. Lamberth, *William James and the Metaphysics of Experience* (Cambridge: Cambridge University Press, 1999), pp. 185–96.
[39] James, *Pluralistic Universe*, p. 699.
[40] P. D. Ouspensky, *Tertium Organum* (1922; London: Routledge &
Kegan Paul, 1970), pp. 188–91. In describing the book as an
'international best-seller' I follow: Jacob Needleman, 'Ouspensky' in
Dictionary of Gnosis & Western Esotericism, ed. Wouter J. Hanegraaff
(Leiden: Brill, 2006), p. 912.

A 'PSYCHICAL RESEARCHER'

William James was interested in clairvoyant phenomena and psychical research for much of his life. This interest can be dated back at least as far as 1869, when he reviewed a book on the subject—albeit without great enthusiasm.[41] In 1885 he began visiting a clairvoyant by the name of Mrs Piper, who he at length concluded had 'supernormal powers'.[42] And he was involved from the start in the *American Society for Psychical Research*, founded in 1885.[43] The measured interest that James brought to the subject is illustrated by an episode that occurred in 1906, when his wife conveyed a clairvoyantly received message to Henry James (the novelist and William's brother, 1843–1916). The message purported to be from their mother, who at that point had been dead for 24 years. Henry wrote that it contained

> an allusion to a matter known (so personal is it to myself) to no other individual in the world but *me*—not *possibly* either to the medium or to my sister-in-law, and an allusion so pertinent and *initiated* and tender and helpful, and yet so unhelped by any actual earthly knowledge on any one's part, that it quite astounds as well as deeply touches me.[44]

William's thoughts on the matter can be found in his response to Henry:

> The episode of the message so exactly hitting your mental condition is very queer. There is something back there that shows that minds communicate, even those of the dead with those of the living, but the costume, so to speak, and accessories of fact, are all symbolic and due to the medium's stock of automatisms—what it all means I don't know but it means at any rate that the world that our 'normal' consciousness makes use of is only a fraction of the whole world in which we have our being.[45]

---

⁴¹ See: Robert D. Richardson, *William James in the Maelstrom of American Modernism* (New York: Mariner, 2007), pp. 99–100.

⁴² William James, *Essays in Psychical Research* (Cambridge, MA: Harvard University Press, 1986), pp. 80–81.

⁴³ See Richardson, *William James in the Maelstrom*, p. 259.

⁴⁴ *Henry James Letters Vol. 4 1895–1916*, ed. Leon Edel (Cambridge, MA: Harvard University Press, 1984), pp. 396–97.

⁴⁵ *The Correspondence of William James Vol. 3*, ed. Elizabeth Berkeley, John J. McDermott, and Ignas K. Skrupskelis (Charlottesville, VA:

Three years later—in 1909, the year before his death—James characterised himself as 'neither a convinced believer in parasitic demons, nor a spiritist, nor a scientist, but still… a psychical researcher waiting for more facts before concluding'.[46] He noted that, 'at times I have been tempted to believe that the Creator has eternally intended this department of nature to remain *baffling*, to prompt our curiosities and hopes and suspicions all in equal measure'.[47] It may be as well, at this point, to be clear that it is not my intention to conflate astrology and 'psychical' phenomena, but only to suggest that James's thought about the latter may shed light on the former as regards two particulars:

-       That the interaction typically involves a mediating figure who plays midwife to the communication whilst inevitably colouring and shaping it thereby

-       The suggestion that the phenomena may be seen as elusive, or chimerical, and that this may in some sense be a 'design feature'.

Perhaps the issue here was pointed toward by Max Planck, when he remarked that '[s]cience cannot solve the ultimate mystery in nature. And it is because in the last analysis we ourselves are part of the mystery we try to solve.'[48] This certainly seems to be a good fit with James's views, as when for instance he wrote:

Out of my experience, such as it is (and it is limited enough) one fixed conclusion dogmatically emerges, and that is this, that we with our lives are like islands in the sea, or like trees in the forest. The maple and the pine may whisper to each other with their leaves, and Conanicut and Newport hear each other's fog-horns. But the trees also commingle their roots in the darkness underground, and the islands also hang together through the ocean's bottom. Just so there is a continuum of cosmic consciousness, against which our

---

University of Virginia Press, 1994), p. 310. For discussion of this episode, see Richardson, *William James in the Maelstrom*, pp. 475–76.
[46] William James, 'The Confidences of a "Psychical Researcher"', in *William James: Writings 1902–10*, p. 1263.
[47] James, 'Psychical Researcher', p. 1250.
[48] Max Planck, *Where is Science Going?*, trans. James Murphy (New York: W. W. Norton, 1932), p. 217.

individuality builds but accidental fences, and into which our several minds plunge as into a mother-sea or reservoir. Our 'normal' consciousness is circumscribed for adaptation to our external earthly environment, but the fence is weak in spots, and fitful influences from beyond leak in, showing the otherwise unverifiable common connection.[49]

This passage is quoted approvingly by the PSI researcher Dean Radin, who remarks that 'James's cosmic consciousness metaphor has reverberated throughout the ages, ranging from ancient concepts like the Akashic record of Hindu mysticism, to psychiatrist Carl Jung's collective unconscious, to biologist Rupert Sheldrake's morphogenetic fields.'[50] Such views—wherein the detail of individual lives forms part of a bigger picture—have often been invoked as a context for astrology, as when Howard Sasportas cited a statement attributed to Einstein:

> A human being is part of the whole, called by us 'Universe', a part limited in time and space. He experiences himself, his thoughts and feelings as something separated from the rest— a kind of optical delusion of his consciousness. This delusion is a kind of prison for us...[51]

As Sasportas went on to say, the significant thing here is that 'we... have to put the ego in its proper relation to the Higher Self'.[52]

The search and struggle to put his ego into a proper relation to a 'Higher Self' is, it is probably fair to say, *the*

---

[49] James, 'Psychical Researcher', pp. 1263–64.

[50] Dean Radin, *Entangled Minds: Extrasensory Experiences in a Quantum Reality* (New York: Pocket/Simon & Schuster, 2006), p. 234.

[51] Albert Einstein quoted in: Howard Sasportas, 'The Quest for the Sublime', in Liz Greene and Howard Sasportas, *Dynamics of the Unconscious—Seminars in Psychological Astrology* (London: Arkana, 1988), p. 171. As his source, Sasportas cites: Peter Russell, *The Awakening Earth* (London: Routledge & Kegan Paul, 1982), p. 129. The exact provenance of the quotation is disputed. It was quoted as presented here in the *New York Times* of 29 March 1972, where it was attributed to a letter sent by Einstein on 4 March 1950; however *The New Quotable Einstein* by Alice Calaprice (Princeton, NJ: Princeton University Press, 2005), p. 206 reproduces a different version of the letter, dated to 12 February 1950. The substance of the quotation as it appears here remains, however, unaltered.

[52] Sasportas, 'The Quest for the Sublime', p. 175.

central theme of James's life. He spoke of the difference that could be made by what he called a 'religious' attitude, writing that '[t]he universe is no longer a mere *It* to us, but a *Thou*... and any relation that may be possible from person to person might be possible here.'[53]

GOD, SIGNS AND GAMES

It may seem somewhat incongruous, given James's avowed pantheism and the apophatic orientation of much of his work, to find him writing of a finite God, a *thou*.[54] I believe the point for James, here, is not however to attempt to define God—his own philosophy bars him from the attempt—but to submit what he sees as the most pragmatically useful way of thinking about God. And the payload of the finite God is that

> my powers, such as they are, are not irrelevant to [the universal essence], but pertinent, that it speaks to them and will in some way recognise their reply, that I can be a match for it if I will, and not a footless waif...'[55]

This can be seen as one implication of James's analogy of islands that meet under the sea, and indeed as 'pure experience'. Although the 'universal essence' is beyond our conception, the apparent individual is not ultimately separate from it, and therefore interaction is possible. There are a number of parallels that could be pursued here. For instance, the idea is found in the Upanishads that Brahman has two aspects: saguna Brahman (Brahman with qualities), and nirguna Brahman (Brahman without qualities). Hence, the *Ramatapinya Upanishad* states: 'Brahman is pure consciousness, without parts, without form. In order to help the seeker in his efforts to surrender, symbols and qualities are added to Brahman.'[56] This is a view which can be seen

---

[53] James, *Pragmatism*, p. 216.

[54] For more on James's thought concerning a finite God, see: Lamberth, *James and the Metaphysics of Experience*, pp. 196–202.

[55] William James, *The Psychology of Belief* in William James, *William James: Writings 1878–1899* (New York: Library of America, 1992), pp. 1053.

[56] *Ramatapaniya Upanishad*, quoted in 'Saguna Brahman', in Ingrid Fischer-Schreiber, Franz-Karl Ehrhard, Kurt Friedrichs & Michael S. Diener, *Rider Encyclopedia of Eastern Philosophy and Religion*, trans.

when, for instance, the Indian sage Ramana Maharshi (1879–1950), said, 'God assumes any form imagined by the devotee through repeated thinking in prolonged meditation.'[57]

This need to play an active part in characterising the transcendental can also be found in Plato, when Socrates remarks that:

> The first and finest line of investigation, which as intelligent people we must acknowledge, is this, that we admit that we know nothing about the gods themselves or about the names they call themselves... [and] we hope the gods are pleased by the names we give them, since we know no others.[58]

In somewhat similar vein, James approvingly quotes his friend Myers's view of prayer:

> If we then ask to *whom* we pray, the answer (strangely enough) must be that *that* does not much matter. The prayer is not indeed a purely subjective thing... but we do not know enough of what takes place in the spiritual world to know how the prayer operates;—who is cognizant of it, or through what channel the grace is given.[59]

It would surely not be helpful, in this paper, to conflate astrology with prayer, any more than with psychic phenomena. What I suggest here is that there may be *something* in common between prayer (as it appears in Myers's account) and astrological work. The commonality seems to exist in the need for an element of creative engagement—as, for instance, when Nicholas Campion wrote that:

> Astrology is like a game of chess with an invisible partner. We set out the board and the rules, make a move, and then

---

Michael H Kohn, Karen Ready, and Werner Wünsche (London: Rider, 1989), p. 294.

[57] David Godman, *Be As you Are: The Teachings of Sri Ramana Maharshi* (London: Arkana, 1985), p. 205.

[58] Plato, *Cratylus* 400d: this translation by C. D. C. Reeve in *Plato: Complete Works*, ed. John M. Cooper (Indianapolis, IN: Hackett, 1997), p. 119.

[59] James, *Varieties of Religious Experience*, p. 467. And see the discussion of this passage at: G. William Barnard, *Exploring Unseen Worlds: William James and the Philosophy of Mysticism* (Albany, NY: State University of New York Press: 1997), p. 326f.

find that the pieces are moving themselves, as if by an invisible hand.[60]

It can be noted that, in order to locate Campion's analogy entirely with the present discussion, it would be necessary to further specify that the rules of the game are themselves devised, to some extent at least, as part of the game. From this perspective, the involvement of the individual in characterising the gods, or forces, of astrology makes it inevitable that astrology should take a broad plurality of forms.

THE RIGHT TO BELIEVE

It was a major concern of James's to exhort his readers, and indeed himself, to engage with life. He argued that we have—as he put it—a 'right to believe' and insisted that 'evidence might be forever withheld from us unless we [meet] the hypothesis half-way.'[61] He encapsulated his argument by saying, '[i]f I refuse to bale out a boat because I am in doubt whether my efforts will keep her afloat, I am really helping to sink her.'[62]

If this is applied to engagement with astrology, I think it will be clear that it tends in the opposite direction to that advocated by critics of astrology such as Dean *et al.* when they say that we should '[b]e careful because pitfalls are everywhere' and that the possibility of seeing corre-spondences where none exist explains 'why researchers have to be so careful. They cannot afford to be misled.'[63] Or, indeed, Richard Dawkins when he writes that belief in 'astrology, paranormalism and alien visitations' stems from 'a normal and, from many points of view, desirable credulity in children which, unless we are careful, can spill over into adulthood, with unfortunate results.'[64]

In words which could have been written specifically about the popular work of Dawkins, James says that he is

---

[60] Nicholas Campion, 'Mythical Moments in the Rectification of History', in *Astrology Looks at History* , ed. Noel Tyl (St. Paul, MN: Llewellyn Publications, 1995), p. 47.

[61] James, *Pragmatism*, p. 216.

[62] James, *The Will to Believe*, p. 538.

[63] Dean et al., quoted in Phillipson, *Astrology in the Year Zero*, p. 135.

[64] Richard Dawkins, *Unweaving the Rainbow* (London: Penguin, 2006), p. 138.

worried for the 'thousands of innocent magazine readers [who] lie paralyzed and terrified in the network of shallow negations which the leaders of opinion have thrown over their souls.'[65]

James's conclusion on the matter is this:

> I...cannot see my way to accepting the agnostic rules for truth-seeking, or wilfully agree to keep my willing nature out of the game. I cannot do so for this plain reason, that *a rule of thinking which would absolutely prevent me from acknowledging certain kinds of truth if those kinds of truth were really there, would be an irrational rule.*[66]

In conclusion, it has been argued that James challenges many of the assumptions most inimical to astrology, and that he articulates a worldview which can help make sense of astrologers' work and experience, as situated on a shoreline where distinctions between individual and universe blur. As already stated, none of the discussion here *proves* astrology, nor has it aimed to. What such reflections may eventually serve to establish, however, is the viability of a different worldview to the rational-scientific one that is generally assumed by astrology's critics. In this view, the uncertainty, doubts and lack of overwhelming proof of astrology within a scientific framework need not point to the subject's invalidity. Rather, these qualities may be entirely fitting for a subject that aspires to hold a mirror up to life. For, as James put it:

> If this life be not a real fight, in which something is eternally gained for the universe by success, it is no better than a game of private theatricals from which one may withdraw at will. But it *feels* like a real fight—as if there were something really wild in the universe which we, with all our idealities and faithfulnesses, are needed to redeem; and first of all to redeem our own hearts from atheisms and fears. For such a wild, half-saved universe our nature is adapted.[67]

---

[65] James, *The Will to Believe*, p. 538.
[66] James, *Pragmatism*, p. 216. Original emphasis.
[67] James, *The Will to Believe*, p. 502.

BIBLIOGRAPHY

Barnard, G. William. *Exploring Unseen Worlds: William James and the Philosophy of Mysticism*. Albany, NY: State University of New York Press: 1997.

Calaprice. Alice. *The New Quotable Einstein*. Princeton, NJ: Princeton University Press, 2005.

Campion, Nicholas. 'Mythical Moments in the Rectification of History'. In *Astrology Looks at History*, edited by Noel Tyl. St. Paul, MN: Llewellyn Publications, 1995.

Cornelius, Geoffrey. *The Moment of Astrology*. 2nd ed. Bournemouth: Wessex Astrologer, 2003.

Crease, Robert P. 'Top Scientists Must Fight Astrology or All of Us Will Face the Consequences', *The Scientist* 3, no. 5 (1989): p. 9. http://www.the-scientist.com/article/display/9209/

Culver, Roger B., and Philip A. Ianna. *Astrology: True or False? A Scientific Evaluation*. Buffalo NY: Prometheus Books, 1988.

Dawkins, Richard. *Unweaving the Rainbow*. London: Penguin, 2006.

Godman, David. *Be As you Are: The Teachings of Sri Ramana Maharshi*. London: Arkana, 1985.

Greene, Liz. 'Is Astrology a Divinatory System?'. *Culture and Cosmos* 12, no.1 (Spring/Summer 2008): pp. 3–29.

Harding, Mike. *Hymns to the Ancient Gods*. London: Arkana, 1992.

James, Edward W. 'On Dismissing Astrology and Other Irrationalities'. In Patrick Grim, ed., *Philosophy of Science and the Occult*, 2nd ed., 28–36. Albany, NY: State University of New York Press, 1990.

James, Henry. *Henry James Letters Vol. 4 1895–1916*. Edited by Leon Edel. Cambridge, MA: Harvard University Press, 1984.

James, William. *The Varieties of Religious Experience*. 1902. Reprint, London: Penguin, 1985.

———. *Essays in Psychical Research*. Cambridge, MA: Harvard University Press, 1986.

———. *Manuscript Lectures*. Cambridge, MA: Harvard University Press, 1988.

———. *William James: Writings 1902–10: The Varieties of Religious Experience; Pragmatism; A Pluralistic Universe; The Meaning of Truth; Some Problems of Philosophy; Essays*. Edited by Bruce Kuklick. New York: Library of America, 1988.

———. 'The Confidences of a "Psychical Researcher"'. in James, *William James: Writings 1902–10*.

———. 'Does 'Consciousness' Exist?', in James, *William James: Writings 1902–10*.

———. 'Lecture III: Hegel and His Method', in James, *William James: Writings 1902–10*.

———. 'Lecture V: The Compounding of Consciousness'. In *A Pluralistic Universe*, in James, *William James: Writings 1902–10*.

———. 'Philosophy and its Critics'. In *Some Problems of Philosophy* (1911), in James, *William James: Writings 1902–10*.

———. *William James: Writings 1878–1899*. New York: Library of America, 1992.

———. *The Correspondence of William James Vol. 3*. Edited by Elizabeth Berkeley, John J. McDermott, and Ignas K. Skrupskelis. Charlottesville, VA: University of Virginia Press, 1994.

———. *Pragmatism and Other Writings*. Edited by Giles Gunn. London: Penguin, 2000.

———. *The Will to Believe* in James, *Pragmatism and Other Writings*.

———. 'The Sentiment of Rationality' in James, *Pragmatism and Other Writings*.

Kanitscheider, Bernulf. 'A Philosopher Looks at Astrology'. *Interdisciplinary Science Reviews* 16, no. 3 (1991): pp. 261–62.

Lamberth, David C. *William James and the Metaphysics of Experience*. Cambridge: Cambridge University Press, 1999.

Needleman, Jacob. 'Ouspensky'. In *Dictionary of Gnosis & Western Esotericism*, edited by Wouter J. Hanegraaff. Leiden: Brill, 2006.

Ouspensky, P. D. *Tertium Organum*. 1922. Reprint, London: Routledge & Kegan Paul, 1970.

Phillipson, Garry. *Astrology in the Year Zero*. London: Flare, 2000.

———. 'Modern Science, Epistemology and Astrology'. *Correlation (Astrological Association Journal of Research in Astrology)* 23, no. 2 (2006): pp. 4–23.

Planck, Max. *Where is Science Going?* Translated by James Murphy. New York: W. W. Norton, 1932.

Plato, *Cratylus* 400d. In *Plato: Complete Works*. Edited by John M. Cooper. Translated by C. D. C. Reeve.Indianapolis, IN: Hackett, 1997.

Radin, Dean. *Entangled Minds: Extrasensory Experiences in a Quantum Reality*. New York: Pocket/Simon & Schuster, 2006.

Ramatapaniya Upanishad. Quoted in 'Saguna Brahman'. In Ingrid Fischer-Schreiber, Franz-Karl Ehrhard, Kurt Friedrichs, and Michael S. Diener, *Rider Encyclopedia of Eastern Philosophy and Religion*. Translated by Michael H Kohn, Karen Ready, and Werner Wünsche. London: Rider, 1989.

Richardson, Robert D. *William James in the Maelstrom of American Modernism*. New York: Mariner, 2007.

Russell, Peter. *The Awakening Earth*. London: Routledge & Kegan Paul, 1982.

Sasportas, Howard. 'The Quest for the Sublime', in Liz Greene and Howard Sasportas. *Dynamics of the Unconscious — Seminars in Psychological Astrology*. London: Arkana, 1988.

Seymour, Percy. *The Scientific Basis of Astrology*. London: Quantum, 1997.

Skrbina, David. *Panpsychism in the West*. Cambridge, MA: MIT Press, 2005.

Sokal, Alan. *Beyond the Hoax: Science, Philosophy and Culture*. Oxford: Oxford University Press, 2008.

Sprigge, T. L. S. 'Refined and Crass Supernaturalism', in *Philosophy, Religion and the Spiritual Life,* edited by Michael McGhee, pp. 105–25. Cambridge: Cambridge University Press: 1992.
Sullivan, J. W. N. 'Interview with Max Planck', *Observer,* 25 January 1931. Cited in C. E. M. Joad, *Philosophical Aspects of Modern Science.* London: Allen and Unwin, 1932.
Weber, Michel. 'James's non-rationality and its religious extremum in the light of the concept of pure experience'. In *William James and the Varieties of Religious Experience—A Centenary Celebration,* edited by Jeremy Carrette, pp. 203–20. London: Routledge, 2005.
Willis, Roy and Patrick Curry. *Astrology, Science and Culture: Pulling Down the Moon.* Oxford: Berg, 2004.

JOHN PARTRIDGE—ONE OF THE FOUNDERS OF MODERN ASTROLOGY?

Robert Hand

ABSTRACT. John Partridge was located in a pivotal point in the history of European astrology. He was the last major seventeenth century astrologer. Consequently his influence on subsequent astrology was enormous especially on a technical level. The techniques he chose to respect continued in use after his time. The methods he rejected fell into disuse largely up until the traditionalist revival of the late twentieth century. Among the methods he favored were those of Placidus de Titis which became standard until the early twentieth century. Among those he rejected were all surviving systems of time lords, profections and the extensive use of lots. When interest in astrology began to increase in the late eighteenth and early nineteenth centuries, Partridge was one of the chief astrologers that the new generation of astrologers, especially Raphael, turned to as a guide. In this way his influence on the development of nineteenth century as early twentieth century astrology may have been out of all proportion to his real talents as an astrologer.

In the historiography of the decline and fall of astrology in the early modern period there has been a shift from the traditional, triumphalist view. In that view the decline of astrology was seen as the inevitable result of the rise of modern science, philosophy, rationalism, and the retreat from all forms of 'medieval superstition'. The bibliography of this historiography is far too large to go into here. Suffice to say that this view can still be found in most encyclopedia articles and popular treatises on this history of science. However, a rather different view has surfaced among historians who attribute the decline of astrology in the early modern period more to social, religious and political forces, and less to a simple triumph of 'Reason' over 'Superstition'.

Among these historians three stand out presenting this newer, more complex view, and much of what I have to present in this paper will only make sense to those who are familiar with this new historiography. These historians are as follows: Patrick Curry in *Prophecy and Power: Astrology in*

Early Modern England, Nicholas Campion in *History of Western Astrology, Volume II, the Medieval and Modern Worlds* and Stuart Clark in *Thinking with Demons: The Idea of Witchcraft in Early Modern Europe.* In Curry the entire work is devoted to expounding this point of view especially in the context of England. In Campion all of the work relating to early modern and modern astrology is relevant, and for Clark see especially the passage below. These three works are most useful in establishing the context of the material discussed in this paper. Enough of this contextual material will be presented in this paper so that most readers should have no difficulty in following along.

This paper will present evidence that, although John Partridge (1644–1715) was probably not one of the most brilliant or accomplished astrologers of his day, his influence in shaping the course of eighteenth-, nineteenth-, and early twentieth-century astrology was out of all proportion to his talents and abilities as an astrologer. This is due to his placement at a critical point in the history of astrology in which astrology had entered its period of decline. By the end of the seventeenth and the beginning of the eighteenth century astrology had been for the most part excluded from the universities, and had ceased to be a subject appropriate for discussion among intellectuals, except for purposes of derision. This is well exemplified by the almanac battle between Partridge and Jonathon Swift (posing as the astrologer Isaac Bickerstaff) in 1707–8.[1]

The following passage from Clark sets the stage for the intellectual currents that came to afflict astrology in this period. I quote at length.

> In the aftermath of the Civil Wars and Interregnum and in the culturally eclectic conditions of the 1660s, 1670s, and 1680s, intellectuals like Glanvill, More, and Boyle sought to develop a natural philosophy that would protect traditional Anglican theology, and the orthodoxies that went with it. The two threats they feared, above all, were from what they saw as atheism and subversive sectarian enthusiasm . . . Specifically, they wanted knowledge that would demonstrate the real power of God not only as the original creator of the

---

[1] See Patrick Curry, *Prophecy and Power: Astrology in Early Modern England* (Cambridge: Polity Press, 1989), pp. 89–91 for a good and concise account of what happened.

natural order but as the providential supplier of some of nature's most crucial effects in the present. This would prevent God being dispensed with altogether, as in the case of Hobbes's radically materialistic philosophy, or dispersed throughout the world, as in the pantheism and immanentalism of the radical sects. At the same time, this natural theology had to be empirical. It had to be accessible to the senses and capable of being experimentally verified.[2]

The passage speaks directly to the situation in England but a little consideration makes it clear that what it describes can be applied to the continent as well. In the sixteenth and seventeenth centuries Europe had been the scene of major religious conflict resulting from the destruction of the religious unity of the middle ages which gave way to the fragmentation of the reformation and Counter-Reformation. The final culmination of this on the Continent was the Thirty Years War (1618–1648). What began as a religious war ended having become an almost completely secular war as houses of Bourbon and Habsburg struggled with each other throughout Europe. At the end Catholics and Protestants were on both sides. However, in England the most severe religious conflict was delayed until the mid-seventeenth century with the English Civil War and Interregnum (1642–1660). On both the Continent and in England it is readily apparent that from the chaos of religious conflict there might arise a desire for order and certainty. Also, as Curry makes clear in the case of England, while there were astrologers on both sides of the conflicts, more of them were on the side of 'subversive sectarian enthusiasm'. On the continent this pattern is perhaps a bit less clear, but in both cases, aside from the context of orthodox and established religion, any idea of a mystical, occult, or spiritual nature was suspect and regarded as subversive to the social order. This is the situation in which Partridge lived and wrote.[3]

A basic outline of Partridge's life is in order. He was born near London and according to most sources became a cobbler. He began to study astrology at 18 and taught

---

[2] Stuart Clark, *Thinking with Demons: The Idea of Witchcraft in Early Modern Europe* (Oxford; New York: Oxford University Press, 1997), p. 299.
[3] Thomas Seccombe, *Dictionary of National Biography*, vol. 15, ed. Sydney Lee (New York: MacMillan, 1909), pp. 428–30.

himself Latin and later Greek and Hebrew. He was a student of John Gadbury but in his later years turned against Gadbury as much for religious as astrological reasons. Gadbury was a Catholic; Partridge (as we will see below) was a nonconformist protestant, therefore not a member of the Church of England. Partridge became a full-time astrologer about 1678. He published his first major astrological work, the *Mikropanastron*, in 1679. His astrological lineage therefore is directly traceable from William Lilly, the most important astrologer of the Civil War period by way of Gadbury. Because Lilly, like Partridge, was a vigorous protestant, he and Gadbury also fell out over the religious issue.

During the reign of James II, Partridge deemed it expedient to get out of England and went, like many other radical nonconformists had in the past, to the Netherlands. It is a subject of debate as to whether Partridge did or did not obtain an M.D. at the University of Leyden in 1689. The evidence is unclear but suggests that he did not. In any case he returned to England shortly thereafter.

Partridge's conflict with Gadbury broke out into the open in the 1690's but then by the early 1700's he was England's most important astrologer. Indeed he was the only one with a national reputation. Near the end of his life his career and reputation were badly damaged by the previously mentioned activities of Jonathon Swift in the Isaac Bickerstaff hoax. Those in brief are the main circumstances of his life. However, for the purposes of this paper it will be much more useful to examine Partridge's astrology and the historical environment in which it took place than to look further at his biographical details. The remainder of the paper will deal primarily with these two subjects.

There are three important aspects of his life that we must consider with regard to the two main foci mentioned in the previous paragraph. First of all there is the issue of where he was located in history, specifically English history. He was born during the English Civil War, a period of maximum unrest as well as social and intellectual instability. However, he lived well into the time of what is usually referred to as the Enlightenment. In the period after the Civil War under the Restoration of Charles II those who were interested in what they called the 'Mechanical Philosophy' organized themselves into the Royal Society and, having made peace with the crown, removed from themselves whatever lingering opprobrium that might have remained because of the involvement of some of them with the previous regime. From the study of the mechanical philosophy both in England and abroad there arose the foundations of modern science both in content and institutionally. It is precisely the period mentioned in the passage from Clark.

Second, we have Partridge's own intellectual and historical antecedents. He was an extreme nonconformist protestant and this in a time when the Church of England was once again in the ascendant. Also, because most of the important English astrologers of the seventeenth century died in the decades after the Civil War, Partridge became the last of the major seventeenth-century English astrologers. Thus, when Jonathon Swift launched his attack by means of the bogus almanac of Isaac Bickerstaff, there were no other astrologers of major standing to come to his defense. Also very important, there were no astrologers of national repute to contradict Partridge and who might have lived to preserve other schools of astrological method. As a result, from the standpoint of the astrological revival of the early nineteenth century it would have been easy to see Partridge *by accident* not merely as the last of the great seventeenth-century astrologers (which he was) but also somehow as a *culmination* of their work (which he arguably was not).

This brings us to the third major point about Partridge's astrology: his desire to reform it. In *Prophecy and Power*, Curry describes the effort in England to reform astrology.[4] It was widely recognized even among astrologers that intellectual currents of the time made it mandatory (or so it was generally perceived) to purge astrology of superstitious elements and bring it more into line with said currents. What none of the reformers realized was that no amount of reform could have saved astrology, at least not from the point of view of the established elites of the time. As Curry points out the reform took two major tacks. One was to bring astrology more or less into accord with the Baconian methods of the new mechanical philosophy. The other was to purge astrology of its medieval additions and to restore it to the ideal Ptolemaic form which astrology was supposed to have had among the Greeks. This latter movement was also doomed, because, first of all, outside of Ptolemy, there was no such 'pure' Greek astrology because the ancient Greek

---

[4] Curry, *Prophecy and Power*, pp. 34–88.

methods were not that dissimilar from the medieval ones, and, second, Ptolemy's description of his methods was so terse and incomplete that there never could have been a practically applicable astrology based on them alone. Partridge became the leading exponent of this 'back to Ptolemy' movement in seventeenth century English astrology. What Curry does not point out is that these two trends in reform were also to be found in continental astrology, with similar results. This will be taken up below.

While Partridge's reform consisted of this purge from astrology of its medieval methods, and a return to pure Ptolemaic astrology, it was to be conducted particularly along the lines proposed by the Italian astrologer Placidus de Titis (1603–1668). This became very important for the development of astrology in the nineteenth century. I will also return to this below.

The period of early modern astrology, roughly 1500 to 1700, was a period of major crisis which culminated in astrology's near demise at the end. At the beginning of this period astrology was at or near the peak of its prestige. While astrology was never an uncontroversial subject, it was in fact widely practiced in both papal and royal courts.[5] At the end of the period (quite close to Partridge's death date in 1715) astrology had lost all prestige and had entered its period of near but not total extinction.

It has been conventional to date the beginning of astrology's decline in status with the massive attack upon it launched by Pico della Mirandola's *Disputationes adversus astrologiam divinatricem* or *Disputations Against Divinatory Astrology* published in 1496 after Pico's death.[6] The nature of this work is such that if one actually peruses it, as opposed to reading about it, it becomes clear that the thrust of the work is religious and philosophical, not scientific in any modern

---

[5] See Lynn Thorndike, *History of Magic and Experimental Science* [*H.O.M.E.S*], vol. 5, (1941), pp. 252–74 for an account of the court of Paul III and his interest in astrology. For an account of the court of the emperor Rudolf II, see Peter Marshall, *The Magic Circle of Rudolf II: Alchemy and Astrology in Renaissance Prague* (New York: Walker and Company, 2006).

[6] Pico della Mirandola, *Disputationes adversus astrologiam divinitricem*. 2 vols. Eduzione Nazionale Dei Classici Del Pensiero Italiano, ed. Eugenio Garin (Florence: Vallecchi Editore, 1946). This edition contains the original Latin text with an Italian translation by Garin.

sense.[7] Yet Pico's work did become the central focus and a principal source of arguments for those who attacked astrology in the subsequent century. Pico's arguments were hashed out on both sides generating a bibliography of attacks and counterattacks too extensive to summarize here.

Two trends in astrological thought emerged which can be regarded as attempts to deal with the increasing criticism of astrology. The first, which began earlier, was very much in the spirit of early modern humanistic thought. It was to purge astrology of what were regarded as accretions of medievalisms that obscured the purity of ancient classical Greek thought. The main source of these accretions was believed to be Arabic. The second trend, which came later, consisted of attempts to reach an accommodation with the critics by making astrology more consistent with 'science'. In some cases, as we shall see, there were attempts to make astrology more rigorously scientific in terms of Aristotelian science. In others the efforts were to make astrology more scientific in terms of the emerging new science. I have already mentioned that both of these trends can be seen in seventeenth century English astrology. I will add to this below.

As with Partridge, those who desired to purge astrology of its medievalisms did so in the name of restoring 'pure' Ptolemaic astrology. Among the leaders of this movement can be numbered the following. One of the most important was Girolamo Cardano known in English as Jerome Cardan (1501–1576).[8] Cardano wrote the first major commentary on Ptolemy since Ali ibn Ridwan. Cardano's work contained not only his own commentary but the complete text of the *Tetrabiblos* in a new Latin translation done from the original Greek of Ptolemy (as opposed to the Greek of the Proclus Paraphrase).[9] Another *Tetrabiblos* commentary was the one written by Francesco Giuntini (1523–1590), also known as Franciscus Junctinus, as part of his massive *Speculum*

---

[7] Thorndike, *H.O.M.E.S*, vol. 4, (1934), p. 529. This and subsequent sections of *H.O.M.E.S.* contains an excellent account of the impact of Pico's *Disputationes*.

[8] For Cardano's attitude toward medieval astrology see Anthony Grafton, *Cardano's Cosmos: The Worlds and Works of a Renaissance Astrologer* (Cambridge, MA: Harvard University Press, 1999), especially p. 141.

[9] The translation was that of Gogava about whom otherwise I have little information.

astronomiae of 1573.[10]

The most noted of the purgers and the most influential in the subsequent development of astrology was Placidus de Titis (1603–1668). To give astrology a firmer basis, Placidus advocated a new natural philosophy of astrology based on Aristotle and Ptolemy which featured a 'new' type of house system and a reformed system of semi-arc primary directions.[11] The house system was not new. Various authors, such as Fred Gettings, have claimed that it is to be found in Arabic sources.[12] It was also advocated by Ioannes Antonius Maginus (d. 1617). The semi-arc system of directions was derived from Ptolemy and is also found in its pure form in Alcabitius and in Latin authors such as Antonio de Montulmo. However, Placidus extended the system enormously and so it does deserve to be called a 'Placidian' system.[13]

The effort to accommodate astrology with science, be it Aristotelian or early modern, includes several important figures in the history of early modern science as well as astrologers. Among the earliest such efforts is that of John Dee (1527–1608) in his *Propaedumata Aphoristica*.[14] This is an

---

[10] Francesco Giuntini, *Speculum astrologiae quod attinet ad iudiciariam rationem nativitatum atque annuarum revolutionum* (Lyons: Sumptibus Philippi Tinghi Florentini, 1573).

[11] Primary directions consist of a complex technique of rotating the chart by diurnal motion in the hours after birth. The actual methods are far too complex to go into here. The interested reader is referred to the following excellent work: Martin Gansten, *Primary Directions: Astrology's Old Master Technique* (Bournemouth, UK: Wessex Astrologer, 2009).

[12] *Dictionary of Astrology* (London, Boston and Henley: Routledge and Kegan Paul, 1985), 240. 'The system is often said to be named after its (supposed) inventor, the astrologer Placidus di Tito, who lived in the seventeenth century, but the fact is that this particular trisection method was derived from one (correctly) ascribed to the eighth century Arabian astrologer ben Djabir . . .'

[13] An English translation of one of his major works is to be found in the Cooper translation of Placidus, *Primum Mobile* (London: Davis and Dickson, 1814). A reprint of this work with additional commentary by Michael Baigent was printed in 1983 by The Institute for the Study of Cycles in World Affairs, London. The latter is a photo-offset reproduction of the former except for the new introduction by Baigent.

[14] An edition of the original Latin with an English translation is to be found in *John Dee on Astronomy = Propaedeumata Aphoristica (1558 and 1568)*, ed. and trans. Wayne Shumaker (Berkeley, CA:

extremely radical work with little similarity to the astrology of the usual kind of the period, even that practiced by Dee. It is derived instead from the tradition known as 'Light Metaphysics', i.e., metaphysics of light, stemming from late classical neoplatonism, through Al-Kindi's *Stellar Rays*, to Roger Bacon, and thence to Dee.

The most important of all of these authors is undoubtedly Johannes Kepler (1571–1630). He seems to have believed that astrology was basically sound but that its effects could be seen most clearly in the aspects of the planets. He appears to have not accepted any form of house division, sign rulership or any of the other parts of apparatus of natal astrology. That said, Kepler does seem to have been much more traditional in his *practice* than in his *theory*. Another one of those who attempted to base astrology on a reformed natural philosophy was Jean Baptiste Morin (1583–1656). His proposed natural philosophy is clearly derived from Aristotle but introduces a number of changes, which are described in books I to X of his *Astrologia Gallica*.[15]

An Englishman strongly associated with the attempt to accommodate astrology to the new science was John Goad (1616–1689) in his *Astro-meteorologica* of 1686.[16] His was an effort to bring astrology in accordance with Baconian principles of induction by reporting thirty years of observations of the correlation of weather phenomena in London with astrological aspects. His work shows little or none of the conventional methods of natal astrology or even of the astrology of revolutions and great conjunctions normally used to make predictions about the weather, as summarised by Bos and Burnett.[17]

At this point it is appropriate to begin to document the changes in Astrology between the late medieval and early

---

University of California Press, 1978).

[15] Jean Baptiste Morin, *Astrologia Gallica* (Hagae Comitis: Adrianus Vlacq, 1661).

[16] See Curry, *Prophecy and Power*, pp. 67–72 for an extended discussion of Goad. In this section Curry also mentions other authors who could be counted among this type of reformer. For Goad's original work see bibliography.

[17] For a description of more traditional methods of astro-meteorology see Gerrit Bos and Charles Burnett, *Scientific Weather Forecasting in the Middle Ages: The Writings of Al-Kindi* (London: Kegan Paul International, 2000).

modern periods, on one hand, and the revival of astrology in the nineteenth century, on the other. These changes had more to do with changes in technique and method in dealing with astrological charts than with changes in the style and purpose of analyzing such charts. Also, two dominant branches of medieval astrology do nearly die out in this period. These were the method of Elections, or picking the most favorable times for taking actions and the astrology of Interrogations, which attempts to answer questions put to an astrologer by means of charts erected for the moment and place of the asking. Both of these branches of medieval astrology were widely and erroneously believed to have been creations of Arabic astrology. The reason for this error seems to have been that neither were covered by Ptolemy, the only Greek astrologer with whom those in the the Middle Ages were familiar. While other Greek authors became somewhat available in the early modern period, these do not seem to have been widely read. However, both of these topics were covered in Dorotheus of Sidon's *Carmen Astrologicum*.[18] The Arabs did, however, build enormously on whatever they received from the Greeks and these two branches, especially interrogations, became the most widely used branches of medieval astrology.

However, the decline of electional and interrogational astrology was not the only change that occurred in early modern astrology. There were a number of techniques in natal astrology that died out or became extremely simplified. As we shall see, Partridge had a large role to play in this process. Here is a brief tally of these changes.[19] First of all let

---

[18] Dorotheus of Sidon. *Carmen Astrologicum,* ed. David Pingree (Leipzig: Teubner, 1976), book 5. The issue of interrogations in Dorotheus is in dispute. Based on the text that we have of Dorotheus there is abundant evidence of an ancient use of astrology for interrogations. This is reinforced by passages from Hephaestio of Thebes which quotes these passages from the original Greek. David Pingree disputes that there is evidence for Greek interrogational astrology but given that his scholarship has provided most of the text that gives evidence for it, it is difficult to see why he took this position. For his arguments see David Pingree, *From Astral Omens to Astrology: From Babylon to BīKāNer* (Rome: Istituto italiano per l'Africa et l'Oriente, 1997), p. 21.

[19] I do not have the space in this paper to describe the meanings of all of the astrological technical terms that I am about to employ from here on. For readers unfamiliar with these I refer to John Christopher Eade, *The Forgotten Sky: A Guide to Astrology in English*

us look at natal astrology as opposed to predictive astrology.

1) *Essential Dignities, Rulership and Disposition by Essential Dignity which employed the five dignity system.*

      Domicile – This was retained although it came to be called 'sign rulership' as if there were only this one kind.

      Exaltation – This was retained but used mostly as a dignity not as a basis for rulership and disposition.

      Triplicity (with either two or three rulers) – This was rarely used in later astrology until the traditional revival of the late twentieth century.

      Bound or Term – This became rarely used in later astrology until the traditional revival of the late twentieth century.

      Face or Decan (using the Chaldean order rulership.) – This became rarely used in later astrology until the traditional revival of the late twentieth century. The Hindu system or *drekana* for a time replaced it.

      Reception – Only a simplified version of mutual reception was retained.

      Almutens – The use of Almutens either of individual degrees (*victor*) or Almutens with specific domains of rulership derived from several points was not retained.

2) *Accidental Dignities.*

      Angular, succedent and cadent house positions – retained.

      Sect – not retained.

      Dignity by Solar Phase including oriental, occidental, combust, beams, increasing in light etc. – retained but in a confused manner.

      Planetary joys by sign (thrones) – not retained.

      Planetary joys by house – not retained.

      Planetary Dignity according to motion (direct, retrograde etc.) – retained but simplified.

      Specific degree qualities, lucid, smokey, pitted, masculine, feminine, etc. – not retained.

3) *Antiscia and Contra-antiscia* – replaced by the use of Parallels and Contra-parallels of declination.

Literature (New York: Oxford University Press, 1984). Also useful is John David North, *Chaucer's Universe* (New York: Oxford University Press, 1988).

4) *'Arabic' Parts, or Lots* – Mostly not retained except for the Lot of Fortune.

5) *The Use of 'Alcabitius' houses as the dominant domification system* – not retained. This system was replaced by the system advocated by Regiomontanus everywhere at first (with a few exceptions), then in England and other English-speaking nations by the Placidian System.

Then there were major changes in the predictive techniques associated with natal astrology.

1) *Predictive Techniques involving Planetary Periods and Time-Lords or Chronocrators.* None of the following were retained in modern astrology until recently.
> The direction of significators in primary directions to indicate a change of time-lord. – Not retained. Primary directions become used to indicate more or less exact times of events.
> The Seven Ages of Man – not retained.
> *Algebutar* – not retained for either use as above.
> Profections – at first changed as with primaries regarding event timing, then later mostly dropped.
> Alfridaries – not retained.
> Decennials – not retained.
> Lord of the Orb – not retained.

2) *Primary Directions for the Timing of Events* – retained but at first converted from the semi-arc methods of Ptolemy/Alcabitius to the 'circle of position' methods of Regiomontanus. Then, in England the Regiomontanus methods were replaced by the methods of Placidus largely, I suggest, due to the influence of Partridge.

3) *Solar Revolutions* – retained, but the full medieval technique was integrated with Time-Lord systems and therefore weakened by their loss. The technique lost its centrality in later authors and was either neglected completely or used only somewhat.

4) *Transits* – retained but at first de-emphasized. Partridge, as we shall see, particularly downplayed the use of transits. But in one of the major changes in modern astrology, transits have become a widely used predictive technique in the twentieth century.

> 5) *Secondary Directions* – Placidus made extensive use of these and was one of the earliest to use them. He may or may not have been the first. They became very popular in the early twentieth century and came to be called progressions, a word originally used for profections.

So now the following questions arise. 1) How long and by whom were the techniques which were later dropped (at least until the traditional revival) used? 2) How did their survival in England compare with that on the Continent?

We find the complete medieval apparatus of techniques among the following authors on the Continent. This list is not intended to be exhaustive. The apparatus is completely present in the writings of Guido Bonatti (ca. 1210–ca. 1290).[20] They are also found in Johannes Schoener (1477–1547).[21] The complete apparatus tends not to be found in the major astrologers of the Ptolemaic revival mentioned previously.

In England the medieval apparatus is found in varying degrees among the following. First of all we have William Lilly (1602–1681) in Book III of *Christian Astrology*, 1647. We have them in John Gadbury (1628–1704) in his *Genethlialogia*, 1658. We have them in Henry Coley (1633–1707) in his *Clavis Astrologiae Elimata*, 1676, which is a very conservative work. And most interestingly we have them in Partridge in his earliest work, the *Mikropanastron*, 1679.[22] None of the above English writers, except Partridge in his later years, challenged any of the techniques of the medieval apparatus which were later dropped from astrology. They may not have used them in their day-to-day work, we cannot tell for certain, but they did not recommend their disuse.

In the end we have these about-to-be forgotten techniques advocated by authors on the continent until at least the mid-sixteenth century, and some of them into the seventeenth. In England we have them at least mentioned all the way through to early Partridge. Clearly someone like Partridge, the last surviving astrologer with a national reputation in England in the late seventeenth century, was in a position to have an enormous influence on astrological posterity as an

---

[20] See bibliography for an edition of the original Latin and a modern English translation.

[21] Johannes Schoener, *De iudiciis nativitatum libri tres* (Nuremberg: Iannes Montanus, 1545).

[22] See bibliography for complete citations of all of these works.

astrological reformer. I assert that this is exactly what happened.

Let me return at this point to Partridge. There are several major points to be made about his mind set and his astrology. First of all, to some extent the desire to 'purge' and to 'accommodate' were united in Partridge. The 'purge' tendency is the more obvious of the two. His attempt to 'accommodate' astrology to the new emerging science was frustrated because he did not seem to understand what that entailed. Even though ultimately Goad was no more successful than Partridge, Goad at least understood the Baconian model.

Second, Partridge's protestantism was apparently of the more extreme Calvinist/Puritan type, as evidenced in his *Advice to the Protestants of England*, 1678.[23] As was the case with the more extreme protestants of that era, he was a fundamentalist. Therefore, he tended to seek authentic texts as the foundation of his intellectual systems. This meant the Bible for his religion and Ptolemy for his astrology. His error from the point of view of 'accommodation' is that he seems to have believed that basing himself on correct texts would

---

[23] Here is a sample passage:

I.

Touch't with a teeming strain of *English* growth,
My burning Muse into a flame breaks forth
In sacred Passions, scorns to be afraid
Of those vast Murders pious *Rome* hath made.
A gracious Mother, merciful and good,
Her Thoughts are murder, and her Bosom's blood.
II.
The *Priests of Rome* are like their Mother true,
Lazy and Letcherous, yet Obedient too;
Furnish'd with all the Vice that Nature gives:
They are the only *Epicures* that lives.[*sic*]
Yet they converse with God, disperse their Powers,
Confess your Wives, and also get you Heirs.
III.
Of all the Arts the Devil yet made choice,
This think of *Popery* was his Master-piece.
For in revenge with Heaven, being at ods,
He taught the *Papists* how to *Eat* their Gods.
Then t'would not be amiss, since thus they do,
To make clear works, and *Eat* the Devil too.

serve to accommodate. He was completely out of touch with the systematically empirical aspect of the new science. Of course, as we shall, see he did attempt to show by case studies that his astrology was sound, but this sort of anecdotal evidence had been commonly presented by astrologers in the preceding centuries before him with little persuasive effect except for other astrologers. Besides, his extreme protestantism removed him from the effort 'to develop a natural philosophy that would protect traditional Anglican theology', and placed him solidly in the camp of 'subversive sectarian enthusiasm' as Clark has put it.[24]

Partridge's program of reform is largely contained in two works: the *Opus Reformatum*, 1693 and the *Defectio Geniturarum*, 1697.[25] The most comprehensive general description is contained in the *Opus Reformatum* while the specifics are contained in both works but especially the beginning of the *Defectio Geniturarum*. In these two works Partridge describes his program of reform just as we have described, a combination of a purge of medieval techniques with the institution of the Placidian house system and a semi-arc direction system. But there is an interesting question. Exactly what was Partridge's relationship to Placidus?

We know that Partridge read Placidus. In the introduction to the *Opus Reformatum* he wrote 'It [the chart of Cardano's son] was first printed by Placidus de Titis, in his *Primum Mobile*, . . .'[26] However he seems to have regarded Ptolemy as the real source.[27]

> In the whole thing there is much Variety, both in the Matter and Method, and these founded on very good Principles, which I shall deliver more methodically hereafter, according as I shall find this is received in the World. I do not pretend, that either the Matter or Method, is either of them new, but only the old ones revived; and, to say the truth, it is so old,

---

[24] Clark, *Thinking with Demons*, p. 299.

[25] John Partridge, *Opus Reformatum: Or Treatise of Astrology in Which the Common Errors of That Art Are Modestly Exposed and Rejected* (London, 1693), and John Partridge, *Defectio Geniturarum: Being an Essay Towards the Reviving and Proving the True Old Principles of Astrology* (London, 1697).

[26] Partridge, *Opus Reformatum*, p. iv.

[27] In this and all subsequent passages quoting from English sources the punctuation, spelling, capitalization, and italics are as in the original.

that I can safely say, it is forgot, and the whole of it will seem strange to this Age. Which I humbly offer to the consideration of the Ingenious Students, and intreat everyone to examine it seriously and deliberately before he gives a determinate Judgment, either in Approbation or Exprobation of what I have here done'. [28]

There are several possible reasons for this. First of all he may have wanted to give his own work more credibility by attributing it not merely to *an* ancient source, but to what had become *the* ancient source, Ptolemy. Second, he may have taken Placidus at his word as he famously wrote 'I desire no guide but Ptolemy and reason',[29] and therefore concluded that the material should be attributed to Ptolemy. Third, it may be that Partridge acquired his knowledge or Placidian methods from English sources of which there seem to have been several.

In the years 1687 and 1688 there appeared two editions of a work entitled *The Marrow of Astrology*.[30] Both editions consisted of two sections which were later printed separately. The 1687 edition lists both Richard Kirby and John Bishop as authors for the first section, but only Bishop for the second. The 1688 edition lists only Bishop as the author for both sections. It also has a foreword by Henry Coley, successor to William Lilly and a significant astrologer in his own right. Also, added to the 1688 edition was a brief dedicatory letter to Robert Boyle not found in the first edition. Both versions of this work are entirely Placidian in method and, while the authors do not seem to mention Placidus, Henry Coley in his foreword to the 1688 edition does.[31] Also, Coley mentioned others including Partridge who used the Placidian method. He wrote,

> . . . following the dictates of the Learned *Monck* known by the Name of *Placido de Titis* (who as is supposed rightly grounded upon the the Famous *Ptolomy's* Foundation) and from him Dr. *Wright, Thomas More Esq.* Mr *Worral* and others. And this very way of Managing of Nativities, Mr. *John Partridge* doth, and has, very much Espous'd and is now a great Promotor, as the most exact and Rational hitherto

---

[28] Partridge, *Opus Reformatum*, p. v.
[29] Placidus, *Primum Mobile*, Cooper trans., p. 47.
[30] Richard Kirby and John Bishop, *The Marrow of Astrology* (London, 1687) and John Bishop, *The Marrow of Astrology* (London, 1688).
[31] Bishop, *Marrow* (1688), Coley foreword, no pagination.

found out, and in Order thereunto Designs a Treatise thereof which he calls *Defectio, Geniturarum,* [sic] shewing the the deffects of the Old Way, and an Emendation thereof, as you may see in his *Annus Mirabilis,* or *Almanack* for the year 1688 written by his own hand.[32]

Dr. Frances Wright is mentioned by Partridge in the introduction to the *Opus Reformatum* as having taught him the method that he uses in the *Opus.*[33] Another interesting item mentioned in this passage is that according to Coley Partridge was already working in the *Defectio Geniturarum* in 1688. It was not published until 1697 after the *Opus Reformatum* in 1693. In any case it is clear from Coley that the Placidian method was already well established in England by 1687, and that no one, except possibly Coley, was trying very hard to acknowledge Placidus as the source of the method.

The general outline of Partridge's reform is described further in the introduction to the *Opus Reformatum.* His reliance on Ptolemy is outlined as follows:

> I have also throughout that Nativity [of Oliver Cromwell]. . . wholly dissented from the Common Method now practised; and where I have so done, I have also given you the Text of *Ptolomy* for my Justification to prevent my being questioned in print; that those who think my method new, may examine that Author, and see whether I have done him and the Art it self Justice or not.[34]

And a bit further on he wrote,

> I do not pretend, that either the Matter or Method, is either of them new, but only the old ones revived; and, to say the truth, it is so old, that I can safely say, it is forgot, and the whole of it will seem strange to this Age.[35]

In another passage from the introduction Partridge lays out the philosophical basis of the reform.

> For whatever the Common Professors pretend to, either by false Notions, or worse Practice, I own it, and study it no

---

[32] Ibid.

[33] Partridge, *Opus Reformatum*, p. ii.

[34] Ibid., pp. iii–iv.

[35] Ibid., p. v.

> otherways than a Branch of *Natural Philosophy*, and do think
> it is no hard matter to give it a fair Foundation on very
> rationall Principles, and those I think demonstrable too
> without any great Difficulty and Trouble, and they are
> *Motion, Rays,* and *Influence;* and these in that Part of *Astrology*
> that takes notice of *Nativities* in particular; which Part of it I
> have made most generally my Study; and for the other Parts
> of it, let those who have imploy'd themselves therein, take
> the same care to justify it both by Examples and Rules. And I
> do believe that this of *Nativities* being done, will give some
> Reputation to the other Parts or *Astrology* likewise; and this
> at present is fallen under my Consideration, tho I believe
> there are some far more able than myself to do it, if they were
> pleased to take the trouble of such a Work up on them.[36]

These passages contain information on both aspects of the
reform, purge and accommodation. The main points on
which all of his reform are founded are: 1) Astrology is a
branch of natural philosophy; 2) It is founded on the 'Motion,
Rays, and Influence' of the stars; 3) This is clearest in the
doctrine of nativities; 4) Exponents of the other branches will
have to demonstrate the same for those branches. It is
implied that if they do not, those other branches will have to
fall by the wayside. This is essentially what happened to
Interrogations until recently and to a lesser degree Elections.
Any branch of astrology that cannot stand up to the criteria
that Partridge has listed do not deserve to continue as
divisions of a reformed astrology. The rest of the text of the
Opus is taken up with specific methodological and *ad
hominem* attacks on the astrology of his recent
contemporaries, especially Gadbury.

The *Opus* gives the general statement as to what the
reform should consist of. In the *Defectio Geniturarum*
Partridge lays out some specifics as to techniques that could
no longer be considered acceptable at least in his eyes. As
one reads through the list, it is notable how many of the
techniques and methods that Partridge condemns did in fact
disappear after his time, and how closely the list of the
'condemned' matches the list given previously of the
differences in the methodology between late medieval
astrology and the astrology of the nineteenth and twentieth
centuries up to the revival of traditional astrology in the late
twentieth century.

The title *The Defectio Geniturarum* is a parody of the title of

---

[36] Ibid., p. viii.

Gadbury's *Collectio Geniturarum.* For most of Partridge's later career Gadbury was the principal negative reference point for Partridge. Reform for Partridge was very definitely *contra* Gadbury. Much of the *Defectio* is a critique not only of Gadbury's astrology but also his religious views. However, the earlier part of *Defectio* is a critique of and a call for a purge of traditional astrological methods. The specifics of reform are outlined in chapters V to XI. The following table lists the topics which were the subject of this critique.

Antiscions of the Planets	Novenaries
The Part of Fortune	Transits
The Alchochoden	Eclipses
The Almuten	Annual Revolutions
Alfridaries	Climacterical Years
Chronocrators (Decennials)	Profections
Lord of the Orb	Heliocentric Aspects
Algebutar	Heliocentric Directions
Dodecatemoria or Duodenaries	

Chapters V to XI contain a summary of his opinions about all of these.

Chapter V, Of Antiscions of the Planets – Partridge rejects antiscions and contra-antiscions as employed in ancient and medieval astrology. These are a type of parallel and contra-parallel of declination of the ecliptic degrees of planets and points, not of the bodies. They are taken without consideration of latitude. Partridge replaces them with the modern method of parallels and contra-parallels of declination.

Chapter VI, Of the Part of Fortune – He is a bit unclear here, as is Placidus,[37] but it appears that Partridge accepts the doctrine of Placidus who appears to give two methods for computing it neither of which is traditional. Partridge also follows Ptolemy and Placidus and rejects the changed formula for night births. He also rejects all other parts. In this he follows Placidus' reading of Ptolemy.

Chapter VII, Of the Alchocoden – Partridge rejects the method

---

[37] The article on the Part of Fortune in James Wilson *Dictionary of Astrology,* 1819.

of the Alchocoden completely and with it also implicitly rejects the doctrine of minor, mean, and greater years of the planets—a cornerstone of ancient and medieval predictive techniques.

Chapter VIII, Of the Almuten – Here he rejects the idea of the Almuten of the Chart and implicitly rejects all other types of complex almutens as are found in Omar of Tiberias, Alcabitius, Bonatti and even (implicitly) Ptolemy. In none of his work does he seem to use the method of computing Almutens either for the disposition of an individual degree, or for disposition over several degrees.

Chapter IX, Of the Alfridaries, Chronocrators, Lord of Orb, etc. – This chapter sweeps away at a single stroke the entire body of planetary time-lords and the methods associated with them. Modern western astrologers who have studied Hindu astrology have been impressed with the method of *dasas* and have noted that the absence of these or similar techniques in western astrology is one of the greatest differences between Hindu and western astrology. Partridge here rejects the entire group as well as some other doctrines that came into medieval astrology from the Hindus by way of the Arabs. Alfridaries are imaginary. The chronocrator system known as Decennials is rejected on page 83 'What Effects can be expected from this old Arabian Mystery?' But this technique is not Arabic! It is Greek and can be found in Julius Firmicus Maternus in precisely the form in which it was known the Middle Ages.[38] This is illustrative of the fact that many astrologers of this period had little knowledge and understanding of Hellenistic techniques other than those found in Ptolemy. In fact the technique is described in Book III, chapter 9 of Schoener's *De iudiciis* in what is, except for the very beginning, Maternus word for word.[39] The Lord of the Orb is 'groundless in nature…'[40] The Algebutar is treated with some derision but not explicitly called groundless. This method is found in Ptolemy in Book IV in the last chapter called by Robbins 'Of the Division of Times' but the reference is not exactly clear. Here is the passage from the Robbins

---

[38] Julius Firmicus Maternus. *Matheseos libri VIII.* 2 vols., ed. Kroll and Skutch (Stuttgart: Teubner, 1968), book 6, chapters 33–40. In the Teubner 1968 edition pp. 190–207.
[39] Schoener, *De iudiciis*, fols. cxxvii verso–cxxx recto.
[40] Partridge, *Defectio*, p. 84.

translation:

> In the first place, we must give the rulership of the times in each prorogation to the star that is actually upon the prorogatory degree or in aspect to it, or, if this condition does not exist, to the one that most nearly precedes, until we come to another which is in aspect with the next following degree in the order of the signs; then to this as far as the next following, and so on; *and the planets which govern the terms are to be given a part of the rulership.*[41]

Most of the passage refers to the primary direction of the major significators to the planets and aspectual positions of the planets. The portion in italics is the reference to directions through the terms which is the basis of the Algebutar. This, along with decennials, is another example of a technique purged because of its association with the Arabs even though its roots are Hellenistic and this one is even in Ptolemy. Partridge concludes this chapter with a discussion of two techniques which came from the Hindus into Arabic astrology, the dodecatemoria or duodenaries, and novenaries.[42] The former are found in Hellenistic sources but probably came into Arabic astrology from the Hindus, the *dwadasamas*. As described they are clearly not understood by Partridge. They are of course rejected. Novenaries (Hindu *navamsas*) are understood correctly but also rejected.

Chapter X, Of Transits and Eclipses – Here the discussion is limited to the use of these in reference to forecasting life and death. However, the ability to forecast death was generally considered to be the best method of evaluating the usefulness of a predictive technique. John Worsdale in his *Celestial Philosophy* begins immediately by using primary directions on the chart of a child who died violently in infancy.[43] This was the ultimate test. Partridge rejects transits and eclipses, annual revolutions, and profections for predicting death. None of these techniques were commonly used in the early twentieth century. Transits were restored to

---

[41] Claudius Ptolemy, *Tetrabiblios*, trans. F. E. Robbins (Cambridge, MA: Harvard University Press, 1954), p. 451.

[42] Partridge, *Defectio*, pp. 85–86.

[43] John Worsdale, *Celestial Philosophy, or Genethliacal Astronomy, Containing the Only True Method of Calculating Nativities Made Plain and Easy* (London: Longman and Co., 1828), p. 35.

favor more recently. Climacteric years are still not a technique in favor and in this Partridge had a lot of company both from foes of astrology and astrologers.[44] The end result is that for forecasting death (and implicitly for any other accurate forecasting) only proper Ptolemaic (Placidian) primary directions can be used for this purpose.

Chapter XI, Of Heliocentrick Aspects and Directions – Here is something unusual. Heliocentric techniques came into astrology from the Copernican reform. They were obviously not traditional. Partridge completely rejects them. In this Partridge shows that he is not a reformer-modernizer but truly desires to return to a purer, *older* order, that of Ptolemy, though in some respects, like Placidus, he is more Ptolemaic than Ptolemy.

CONCLUSIONS

Partridge was the last of the great seventeenth century English astrologers. 'By the end of the century Partridge had won a position at the head of his profession, . . .'[45] He was also the last to achieve a national reputation until Sibly at the end of the eighteenth century, and at his death he was the *only* major, nationally known astrologer. By this time astrology had gone into near eclipse on the continent and survived for the most part only in England. However, even in England it was also at this point completely disestablished. No one in the ruling elite would confess to taking it seriously. But the surviving English tradition continued among the lower middle classes and became the foundation of the astrological revival of the nineteenth century. As a result Partridge became the conduit of the surviving astrological tradition not only in England but in Europe as well and gained an influence out of all proportion to his learning or abilities. While his might not have been the only influence that was transmitted to posterity from the seventeenth century, his impact was nonetheless large.[46]

---

[44] Thorndike, *H.O.M.E.S.*, vols. 7 and 8. See the entry in the index of vol. 8 under 'climacteric year' for a list of entries in which the issue is discussed. Climacteric years have not made a comeback in the tradition revival of the late twentieth and twenty-first centuries.

[45] See *Dictionary of National Biography*, vol. 15, 1909, entry on John Partridge.

[46] See Curry, *Prophecy and Power*, and Nicholas Campion, *History of*

Worsdale, perhaps not the most easy-going or accommodating of the late eighteenth and early nineteenth century astrologers as regards opinions about his predecessors and contemporaries in astrology, wrote this in the introduction to his *Celestial Philosophy*.

> The Authors of the works I allude to, are Gadbury, Coley, Parker, White and Sibly. These pirates have dishonoured this predictive science by the fallacious innovations, and notorious prevarications which pollute their pages; they have multiplied the most flagrant errors in directional motion and judgment, which ought to have been deposited in the confines of oblivion, for it is plain from their pirated works, that they were deficient in Astronomical calculations. . . A Work entitled, 'an illustration of Astrology', was *pirated* and published by Mr. E. Sibly, about thirty years ago, which has done incalculable injury to this noble science. . . . he has also extracted most of the Nativities from Gadbury's collection; with all the erroneous calculations and judgment of that Author, which have been very ably exposed, and refuted, more than a century ago by Mr. John Partridge, in his valuable English works called Opus Reformatum [sic], and Defectio Geniturarum [sic], the compilation of those volumes will immortalize his name, and exhibit his superior talents in this department of Astronomy, to generations yet unborn.[47]

And a bit further along he wrote as follows:

> The Works of Mr. John Partridge, and Mr. William Lilly, are of more value than all others that have been published in this Kingdom; . . . [48]

Even several of those whom Worsdale excoriated followed the Placidian system, whereas very few did so prior to Partridge. Partridge was the only one of the early English Placidians to have had the prestige to have effected this major change in English astrology.

In the end Partridge began a major revolution in technique and method that affected all of the English language astrology. Only recently has the revival of interest in medieval and early modern astrological traditions begun to bring about the reconnection with astrology's past that

---

Western Astrology. Vol. II, the Medieval and Modern Worlds (London: Continuum, 2009) for detailed accounts of astrology's 'afterlife'.
[47] Worsdale, *Celestial Philosophy*, pp. v–vi.
[48] Ibid., p. vi.

Partridge was instrumental in breaking.

Finally, however, the creation of what has been called until recently 'modern astrology', that is the astrology of the nineteenth and most of the twentieth centuries, was completed on an interpretational and philosophical level by the work of Alan Leo.[49] He and those who followed him moved astrology away from its emphasis on prediction toward the interpretation of character. Leo also led the way toward the introduction of an esoteric element in astrology derived in large part from the Theosophical movement. Both of these elements in turn were continued and expanded by the work of the American astrologers Dane Rudhyar (1895–1985) and Marc Edmund Jones (1888–1980) and the humanistic astrology movement that they inspired. Thus, it was with modern astrology until the revival of 'traditional astrology' in the late twentieth century.[50]

BIBLIOGRAPHY

Bishop, John. *The Marrow of Astrology*. London,1688.

Bonatti, Guido. *Decem continens tractatus astronomie*. Augsburg: Erhardt Ratdolt, 1491.

———. *Book of Astronomy*. Translated by Benjamin Dykes. 2 vols. Golden Valley, MN: The Cazimi Press, 2007.

Bos, Gerrit and Charles Burnett. *Scientific Weather Forecasting in the Middle Ages: The Writings of Al-Kindi*. London: Kegan Paul International, 2000.

Campion, Nicholas. *History of Western Astrology. Volume II, the Medieval and Modern Worlds*. London: Continuum, 2009.

———. 'The Traditional Revival in Modern Astrology: a Preliminary History'. *Astrology Quarterly* 74, no. 1 (Winter 2003): pp. 28–38.

Clark, Stuart. *Thinking with Demons: The Idea of Witchcraft in Early Modern Europe*. Oxford, New York: Oxford University Press, 1997.

Curry, Patrick. *Prophecy and Power: Astrology in Early Modern England*. Cambridge: Polity Press, 1989.

Dictionary of National Biography, vol. 15, edited by Sydney Lee. New

---

[49] Nicholas Campion, *A History of Western Astrology*, Vol. 2, chapters 16 and 17.

[50] Nicholas Campion, 'The Traditional Revival in Modern Astrology: a Preliminary History', *Astrology Quarterly* 74, no. 1 (Winter 2003): pp. 28–38.

York: MacMillan, 1909.

Dorotheus of Sidon. *Carmen Astrologicum*, Edited by David Pingree. Leipzig: Teubner, 1976.

Eade, John Christopher. *The Forgotten Sky: A Guide to Astrology in English Literature*. New York: Oxford University Press, 1984.

Gadbury, John. *Genethlialogia: Or the Doctrine of Nativities*. London, 1658.

Gettings, Fred. *Dictionary of Astrology*. London, Boston and Henley: Routledge and Kegan Paul, 1985.

Giuntini, Francesco. *Speculum astrologiae quod attinet ad iudiciariam rationem nativitatum atque annuarum revolutionum.* Lyons: Sumptibus Philippi Tinghi Florentini, 1573.

Goad, John. *Astro-Meteorologica or Aphorisms and Discourses of the Bodies Celestial, Their Natures and Influences Discovered*. London: Obadiah Blagrave, 1686.

Grafton, Anthony. *Cardano's Cosmos: The Worlds and Works of a Renaissance Astrologer*. Cambridge, MA: Harvard University Press, 1999.

Kepler, Johannes. *Kepler's Astrology: The Baby, the Bath Water, and the Man in the Middle*. Translated by Ken Negus. Amherst, MA: Earth Heart Publications, 2008.

Kirby, Richard and John Bishop. *The Marrow of Astrology*. London, 1687.

Lilly, William. *Christian Astrology Modestly Treated of in Three Books*, first edition. London, 1647.

Marshall, Peter. *The Magic Circle of Rudolf II: Alchemy and Astrology in Renaissance Prague*. New York: Walker and Company, 2006.

Maternus, Julius Firmicus. *Matheseos libri VIII.* 2 vols., Edited by Kroll and Skutch. Stuttgart: Teubner, 1968.

———. *Ancient Astrology—Theory and Practice*. Translated by Jean Rhys Bram. Park Ridge, NJ: Noyes Press, 1976.

Morin, Jean Baptiste. *Astrologia Gallica*. Hagae-Comitis: Adrianus Vlacq, 1661.

North, John David. *Chaucer's Universe*. New York: Oxford University Press, 1988.

Partridge, John. *Partridge's Advice to the Protestants of England*. London, 1678.

———. *Mikropanastron: Or an Astrological Vade Mecum*. London, 1679.

———. *Opus Reformatum: Or Treatise of Astrology in Which the Common Errors of That Art Are Modestly Exposed and Rejected*. London, 1693.

———. *Defectio Geniturarum: Being an Essay Towards the Reviving and Proving the True Old Principles of Astrology*. London, 1697.

Pico della Mirandola. *Disputationes adversus astrologiam divinitricem.* 2 vols. Eduzione Nazionale Dei Classici Del Pensiero Italiano, Edited by Eugenio Garin. Florence: Vallecchi Editore, 1946.

Pingree, David. *From Astral Omens to Astrology: From Babylon to BīKāNer*. Rome: Istituto italiano per l'Africa et l'Oriente, 1997.

Placidus de Titus, Didacus. *Primum Mobile*. Translated by John Cooper. London: Davis and Dickson, 1814.
Ptolemy, Claudius. *Tetrabiblos*. Translated by F. E. Robbins. Cambridge, MA: Harvard University Press, 1954.
Schoener, Johannes. *De iudiciis nativitatum libri tres*. Nuremberg: Iannes Montanus, 1545.
Shumaker, Wayne, ed. and trans. *John Dee on Astronomy = Propaedeumata Aphoristica (1558 and 1568)*. Berkeley, CA: University of California Press, 1978.
Thorndike, Lynn. *History of Magic and Experimental Science*. 8 vols. New York: Columbia University Press, 1923–58.
Wilson, James. *Complete Dictionary of Astrology*. Islington Green: William Hughes, 1819.
Worsdale, John. *Celestial Philosophy, or Genethliacal Astronomy, Containing the Only True Method of Calculating Nativities Made Plain and Easy*. London: Longman and Co., 1828.

PLACIDEAN TEACHINGS IN EARLY NINETEENTH-CENTURY BRITAIN: JOHN WORSDALE AND THOMAS OXLEY

Martin Gansten

ABSTRACT: John Worsdale (1766–ca. 1826) has been described as something of a historical anomaly, perhaps the last representative of a dying astrological tradition, struggling uselessly against the rising tide of modernity. While this may be true with regard to the natural philosophy underpinning his view of how and why astrology works, Worsdale's actual practices place him rather in the vanguard of an emerging modern astrology characterized by a modified Placideanism. Although the first stirrings of Placidean teachings were felt in Britain towards the end of the seventeenth century, they gained firm ground only after the subsequent hiatus of judicial astrology spanning most of the eighteenth century. This paper examines the British adoption and transformation of the doctrines of Placidus, particularly as evinced in the writings of John Worsdale and those of his junior contemporary and occasional critic, Thomas Oxley (1789–1851).

The history of modern astrology arguably begins in Italy, where, in 1650, the Olivetan monk and professor of mathematics Placido de Titi (better known as Placidus, 1603–1668) published his *Physiomathematica sive coelestis philosophia*, 'Physiomathematics or celestial philosophy'.[1] According to his perhaps most famous statement, Placidus 'desired no other guides but Ptolemy and Reason'.[2] Ptolemy's *Tetrabiblos* being a most incomplete guide for a practising astrologer, the proportion of Placidus' own reason in the resulting system was, for better or worse, correspondingly large. The uses he

---

[1] Also known as *Quaestionum physiomathematicarum libri tres*, 'Three books on physiomathematical questions' and first published under the pseudonym Didacus Prittus Pelusiensis—*pace* Lynn Thorndike, who, in *A History of Magic and Experimental Science*, Vol. 8: *The Seventeenth Century* (New York: Macmillan, 1958), pp. 302 f., mistakes the two titles for separate works.

[2] John Cooper, trans., *Primum Mobile [...] by Didacus Placidus de Titus* (London: Davis and Dickson, 1814), p. 47.

made of Ptolemy's work speak of scholastic training and ingenuity, but would have greatly surprised its author.

Placidus was determined to purge astrology of everything 'fictitious' or merely symbolical and establish it firmly on the basis of Aristotelian natural philosophy and physics; but he was not to be honoured as a prophet in his own country. Despite having been thrice censored and approved by the Catholic Church, Placidus' *magnum opus* was placed on its Index of forbidden books in 1687, a decision renewed in 1709. Instead, Placidean teachings found a haven in Protestant England, where they were promulgated towards the end of the seventeenth century, notably by John Partridge (1644–1715).

In 1693, Partridge published his *Opus Reformatum*, in which he rejected the traditional astrological doctrines which he had previously espoused in favour of Ptolemy and Placidus, although the latter is only rarely mentioned by name.[3] More particularly, the book sets out to refute Partridge's former friend Gadbury, who is abused on nearly every page of the book, not only as an incompetent, ignorant and dishonest astrologer, but as a traitor and a turncoat. The background of this bitter attack lay in Gadbury's new-found Catholic sympathies during the religio-political struggle over the English throne in the late seventeenth century. Partridge's own sympathies lay with the Parliament and in particular with Oliver Cromwell, whose nativity and primary directions are discussed extensively in *Opus Reformatum*.[4] He was also favourably disposed towards William Lilly, whose religious and political views (not to mention his long-standing feud with Gadbury) seem to have made up, in Partridge's eyes, for his clinging to erroneous astrological ideas. *Opus Reformatum* was soon followed by *Defectio Geniturarum*, in which Partridge criticized the

---

[3] Cooper, *Primum Mobile*, p. iv, notes: 'It was from this book [by Placidus] that Mr. Partridge took all the best of the matter which he inserted in his *Opus Reformatum* and *Defectio Geniturarum*, though he very rarely acknowledged the obligation'.

[4] Primary direction, known before the seventeenth century simply as 'direction', is an ancient method of astrological prognostication based on the apparent diurnal rotation of the celestial sphere. As the heavenly bodies move across the sky in the hours following a person's birth, each degree of such motion (corresponding to approximately four minutes of time) is equated with one year of life.

analyses of nativities found in earlier writers, particularly on the subject of fatal directions; the main target was once again Gadbury, to whose *Collectio Geniturarum* Partridge's title alludes.

Partridge was by no means the only English astrologer of his day to take the Placidean teachings to heart. Others included Richard Kirby and John Bishop, who a few years before had published *The Marrow of Astrology*—an unacknowledged and somewhat abbreviated translation of Placidus' own work with very little original content added.[5] But there is little doubt that Partridge was the most instrumental in bringing about the Placidean revolution in England—and, by extension, in making Placidus the grandfather of modern western astrology.

Following its unprecedented popularity in the seventeenth century, English astrology all but vanished in the eighteenth; and the newly-discovered teachings of Placidus were forgotten until the very end of the century, when they found a champion in John Worsdale (1766–ca. 1826).[6] Worsdale has been described by Patrick Curry as 'a

---

[5] The work plagiarized was Placidus' *Tabulae Primi Mobilis* (1657), which about a century later was again rendered into English by an unknown translator engaged by a Dr. J. Browne of Islington. The manuscript of this translation was lent out, clandestinely copied by a third party, and published by Manoah Sibly in 1789 as his own under the title *Astronomy and elementary philosophy*. A supposedly improved version was published 25 years later by John Cooper as *Primum Mobile*, giving the name of the original author as Didacus Placidus de Titus [*sic*]. *The Marrow of Astrology* was reissued only a year after its first publication, this time under the sole name of John Bishop and with a preface by Henry Coley, who does name Placidus as the originator of the method taught, if not of large portions of the text itself. Coley mentions 'Dr. *Wright, Thomas Moor Esq.* Mr. *Worral* and [...] Mr. *John Partridge*' as other contemporary English adherents of Placidus, and feels that their endeavours 'ought to be encouraged, and assisted, as Aiming at Truth it self, and not rejected and rediculed, (as some are too forward to do)'.

[6] Worsdale's year of death is given in the *Oxford Dictionary of National Biography* as 1828 or after, and by Patrick Curry in *Prophecy and Power: Astrology in Early Modern England* (Cambridge: Polity, 1989), p. 132, as 'c. 1828', presumably based on the year of publication of Worsdale's last work. However, Ellic Howe in *Astrology: A Recent History Including the Untold Story of its Role in World War II* (New York: Walker, 1968), p. 27, states: 'Celestial Philosophy, or Genethliacal Astronomy [...] was published two years after his death. (It was seen through the press by his son John, who

remarkable, and remarkably late, heir of the Ptolemaic reformers' representing 'the last gasp of anti-scientific naturalism at any learned level'.[7] If we confine our examination to the natural philosophy underpinning Worsdale's astrology, this is no doubt an accurate portrayal; but I would argue that the actual astrological practices of Worsdale simultaneously place him in the vanguard of an emerging modern astrology characterized by a modified Placideanism. I should like here to look at the contributions of Worsdale as well as his junior contemporary Thomas Oxley, with whom he contrasted sharply in many ways, and to examine some major points of difference between them and earlier generations of Placideanists.

Worsdale's first astrological work appeared as early as 1796, but he is best remembered, when at all, for his *Celestial Philosophy or Genethliacal Astronomy*, published posthumously in 1828. Its opening sentence sets the tone: 'This Work contains an exposition of the Errors of all Ancient and Modern Authors, impartially stated [...] including the Names of all piratical Authors, who have dishonored this CELESTIAL SCIENCE by their inexplicable principles and practice'. Worsdale's allegiance to Ptolemy as interpreted by Placidus is evident throughout, although the name of Placidus is never mentioned—most likely due to Worsdale's frenzied anti-Catholic bias, which makes Partridge look positively tolerant. The style is terse and highly technical, except for occasional outbursts condemning 'Infidels, Deists, and Atheists' along with rivalling astrological authors and baby-eating popish priests.

Judging from his works, Worsdale's main interest appears to have been in the prediction of death. His examples are mostly concerned with the correct method of finding the giver of life (hyleg) and its lethal directions, sometimes with ill-concealed satisfaction at the fulfilment of dark forecasts made to disbelievers. Indeed, one historian has spoken of 'the pathological pleasure that Worsdale derived from acquainting clients, or others who had offended him, with the date they might expect to die'.[8]

---

appears to have succeeded to his astrological practice at Lincoln. His decease was not announced, probably to avoid the loss of clients.)'

[7] Curry, *Prophecy*, p. 134.

[8] Howe, *Astrology*, p. 27.

Not much is known about Thomas Oxley (1789–1851). In 1830 he published a work entitled *The Celestial Planispheres, or Astronomical Charts*, a *Supplement* to which appeared in 1833; and in 1848 he published *The Gem of the Astral Sciences, or Mathematics of Celestial Philosophy*. The first book was printed in Liverpool, the latter two in London. *The Gem of the Astral Sciences* describes Oxley as a civil engineer; *The Celestial Planispheres*, as 'many years mathematician in the United States of America'.[9] There is in fact a record of a United States patent for an unspecified invention granted to a Thomas Oxley on 3 March, 1821; he is then listed among 'Aliens who have not resided two Years in the United States'.[10] On the other hand, a series of letters to the Editor of the *Mechanics' Magazine* in 1839, where a Thomas Oxley claims with two colleagues to have anticipated the invention of the Daguerreotype, states that he lived in Liverpool for nearly eight years, including the years 1823–24. If, as seems likely, all of these records refer to the same scientific gentleman, Thomas Oxley's residence in the United States cannot have lasted more than four years.

Oxley was not the first astrologer to promote the use of planispheres for calculating horoscopes or directions, but he did invent his own variant of the instrument, an accomplishment which he liked to compare to Napier's discovery of logarithms. Worsdale, who, like Oxley, found the earlier variety of planispheres wanting, contented himself with giving his opinion on them in his usual frank and unreserved manner:

---

[9] Oxley's interests and inventions were many and varied. As early as 1816, he had published *Facilography, or, A system of easy, expeditious writing: entirely new, applicable to all languages, ancient and modern, in characters completely adapted to conciseness and currency in combination, expressing every word without the omission of a single letter, in half the space and in one third the time required for common running hand, comprised and rendered attainable in six lessons, calculated to facilitate the accounts, correspondence and memorandums of the merchant and man of business, where both accuracy and dispatch are indispensibly requisite, and to expedite the preparations in manuscript, and other exertions of the man of letters*, in which he described himself as 'author of several fugitive pieces, essays, &c. moral and philosophical; and Master of a mathematical and commercial academy'.

[10] *Synoptical Index to the Laws and Treaties of the United States from March 4, 1789, to March 3, 1851* (Boston: Charles C. Little and James Brown, 1852), pp. 138, 542.

> This *paltry thing* at first sight appears *beautiful to behold,* in consequence of the *various Colours* with which the *Signs* and *Planets, &c,* are ornamented; but the more it is attentively surveyed, the more *disgusting* it appears, with all its *visible imperfections* [...] though it is *artfully* contrived to attract the notice of the innocent, and delude the ignorant, and unwary.[11]

Oxley appears to have influenced modern astrology in one highly visible respect, although his influence has rarely been acknowledged: he was prime mover behind the shift from the traditional square horoscope chart to the modern circular format.[12] As early as 1830 he passionately argued his case as follows:

> There is also another very great impediment to the perfect attainment of this science, which is the absurd figure, or diagram almost always used, and very improperly called a figure of the heavens; which figure consists of a square and a number of half squares, or triangles cornered and dovetailed into one another like a mosaic pavement. In the name of reason I would ask in what respect can such a tessalated [*sic*] pavement be compared to a figure of the heavens! The orbits of the planets are nearly circular, the planets themselves are globular, and the lines distinguished by the names of ecliptic and equator, etc., are perfect circles. How excessively absurd then must it be, to represent the figure of the heavens under the similitude of a broken pavement, or of a square of board made up of a number of other squares, cut through their diagonals and clumsily glued together again. Surely it could never have been a man of science who invented so absurd a figure, but some sordid miser, with the view of saving half an inch of paper.[13]

Oxley's lead in employing circular charts was followed by R. J. Morrison (1795–1874), better known by his *nom de plume* Zadkiel, three years afterwards, and in later decades by the

---

[11] John Worsdale, *Celestial Philosophy, or Genethliacal Astronomy* (London: Longman & Co., 1828), pp. 55 f.

[12] Credit for the research underlying this conclusion goes to Philip Graves.

[13] Thomas Oxley, *The Celestial Planispheres, or Astronomical Charts in IV. Parts, illustrated by the Nativities of the Emperor Napoleon and King William IV* (London: Davis and Dickson, 1830), p. 38.

second famous Zadkiel, A. J. Pearce (1840–1923).[14] Others were more conservative in their choice of diagram, and the square format survived in some publications until the turn of the century.

A considerable portion of Oxley's *Celestial Planispheres* is devoted to the discussion of the emperor Napoleon's nativity, a topic almost as popular in its time as that of Adolf Hitler's horoscope would become among twentieth-century practitioners. It was also a subject which brought many of Oxley's and Worsdale's differences into focus. While Oxley agreed that Worsdale had picked the correct time of birth for the emperor—there were several such times proposed by astrological authors in a number of pamphlets—he made it clear that this agreement between them was due to 'very strong scientific reasons' and 'not the *Gentlemanly* language in which he has drawn up his remarks on this Nativity'. To Oxley, who admired Napoleon's enterprising spirit and ability to raise himself from relatively humble beginnings to imperial dignity, Worsdale's flow of invectives directed at the emperor was proof of narrow-minded caste prejudice:

> From what I have seen of Mr. Worsdale's Astrological works, he appears to be what we may call a clever Astrologer, or a Ptolomean; I wish I could compliment him so far as to pronounce him a Mathematician, Philosopher, Politician, or even a man of candor. To be serious, I should be ashamed of a man who could so prostitute his talents by writing such a tirade of falsehood and calumny, on one of the greatest geniuses, and on one of the most meritorious characters that the world ever produced [...] no doubt one of the most detestable traits which Mr. Worsdale can discover in Napoleon is, that Napoleon was a Tyrant without being duly qualified by his ancestors [...] Oh for the good Mr. Worsdale! the liberal minded Mr. Worsdale![15]

Nevertheless, Oxley reproduced some of Worsdale's predictions on Napoleon's overthrow and death, 'published

---

[14] See Zadkiel (pseud.), *The Grammar of Astrology* (London: Sherwood, Gilbert and Piper, 1833); Alfred John Pearce, *The Text-Book of Astrology* (London: Mackie, 1911). Morrison, the first 'Zadkiel' on the English astrological scene, was succeeded after his death by one R. V. Sparkes, who died only a year later, so that Pearce was really the third editor of *Zadkiel's Almanac*. Morrison and Pearce were, however, the more well-known of the three.

[15] Oxley, *Planispheres*, pp. 117 ff.

sixteen years before the latter event transpired! by which [sceptics] may see that there really exists a Predictive Science, founded on regular and methodical rules and calculations'.[16] The two astrologers largely agreed on the nature of these rules. Both followed Placidus and Partridge in their method of dividing the houses and made use of several Placidean innovations.[17] These included the new aspect angles called quintile (72°), biquintile (144°) and sesquisquare (135°), taken from 'the very excellent Kepler', as well as the prognostic techniques of secondary directions and progressions, for which Placidus had sought to establish Ptolemaic authority.[18]

---

[16] Ibid., p. 124. Oxley was less than impressed with Worsdale's mathematical skills, however, and describes with vindictive pleasure his discovery of an error in Worsdale's nativity for Napoleon: 'I said to myself, "I must have committed some great oversight, for surely Mr. Worsdale can never have made so gross a blunder as to put the cusps of the twelfth and sixth houses of the figure four whole degrees wrong!!" The next morning I projected another Planisphere for the same Nativity, the result was exactly the same as the first, and as I had never before found my Planispheres to deceive me, I now concluded that I was right, and that Mr. Worsdale, the pretended Ptolemy of our age, was wrong […]' (Oxley, *Planispheres*, p. 90).

[17] The so-called Placidus system of house division, based on the method of direction or ἄφεσις taken from Ptolemy, had in fact been proposed earlier—it was known to Abraham ibn Ezra in the twelfth century—but had not found wide support; see John David North, *Horoscopes and History* (London: The Warburg Institute, 1986), pp. 20 ff.

[18] Placidus wrote of his new prognostic techniques: 'We call these motions the secondary directions, to distinguish them from the primary and principal; and we are of opinion, that Ptolemy, speaking of annual places, is to be understood of the places of those motions, and when of the menstrual, hints at the places of the progression' (Cooper, *Primum Mobile*, p. 25). Today, secondary directions (equating the motions of the celestial bodies on each day following birth with the corresponding year of life) are generally known to astrologers as *secondary progressions* or simply *progressions*, while the 'progressions' of Placidus (equating each synodic month with one year of life) seem largely to have fallen into oblivion. There is no mention of either technique in Ptolemy, who, in the place referred to by Placidus (*Tetrabiblos* IV.10), was in fact writing about yearly and monthly *profections*. The reference to Kepler occurs in connection with Placidus' argument for a connection between astrology and musical harmonies, also mentioned by Ptolemy; see Cooper, *Primum Mobile*, p. 79.

All aspects were calculated not only in the traditional way along the ecliptic, but by proportions of the planetary semi-arcs, known as aspects *in mundo* or 'in the world'.[19]

Certain features of the Placidean system, however, are conspicuous by their absence from the works of both Worsdale and Oxley. One such feature is the consideration of crepuscular and obscure arcs. To Placidus, light was the medium through which the influence of the heavenly bodies is transmitted to us. This belief led him to devise special procedures in primary directions involving the sun, whose light is visible for some time before its rising and after its setting. When the sun was below the horizon by less than 18° of altitude, it was said by Placidus to be in the crepuscular or twilight space; below 18°, it was in the obscure space. In such cases, Placidus modified the Ptolemaic method of direction.[20] Worsdale does not discuss these suggested modifications, but tacitly ignores them.[21] Oxley, on the other hand, discusses them in some detail, concluding:

> After thus investigating thoroughly all the various circumstances and all the various Positions under which the Sun can be placed, both under the Crepusculine Parallels,

---

[19] The diurnal circle described by a planet is divided into four semi-arcs measured between its points of rising, culmination, setting, and anti-culmination by the degrees of right ascension passing over the meridian during each phase. In calculating Placidean aspects *in mundo*, each semi-arc is taken as the equivalent of 90°. The principle is related to, but not identical with, the aspects in oblique ascension mentioned, for instance, by Antiochus of Athens (2nd century CE?) and alluded to by Ptolemy in *Tetrabiblos* III.11. Placidus tried to establish Ptolemaic authority for his new definition of aspects by arguing that as Venus cannot be more than 48° distant from the Sun in the zodiac, Ptolemy, speaking (in *Tetrabiblos* I.23) of a sextile between the two, must have meant a 'mundane' sextile (see Cooper, *Primum Mobile*, pp. 15 f). In reality, of course, Ptolemy was referring to whole-sign aspects.

[20] When the sun was in the crepuscular space, Placidus wanted the other planet or aspect involved in the direction (the promissor) to be brought not to the corresponding point in its semi-arc, as would normally be the case, but rather to the sun's circle of altitude—a circle parallel to the horizon and also known as a crepuscular arc. When the sun was in the obscure space, Placidus would work only with that part of the sun's semi-arc which was located below the crepuscular space and which he termed the obscure arc.

[21] For instances of directions ignoring the crepuscular or obscure position of the sun, see Worsdale, *Philosophy*, pp. 159 ff., 294 ff.

and also in the obscure spaces, it does appear to me very plain that Placidus's precepts for the application of the Eastern differences are, in many respects not only inconsistent, but impossible.[22]

Oxley's objections are mathematical and empirical; the Placidean principles are not universally applicable, and the standard techniques of astrological forecasting appear to function just as well without such special exceptions. They are not, however, philosophical: Oxley does not touch at all upon the idea of light as the transmittor of astrological influences. Indeed, toward the end of the *Celestial Planispheres* Oxley dismisses the whole notion of such influences in favour of a theory of non-causal covariance.[23] Worsdale, who does not scruple to uphold planetary causality as part of his 'elementary philosophy', nonetheless deviates from the Placidean emphasis on light as its instrument.

Another practice ignored by Worsdale is the use of the so-called *horimaea* (ὡριμαία [sc. ἄφεσις]). Unlike many innovations of Placidus' masquerading as Ptolemaic doctrines, the horimaea is one of two procedures actually given in the *Tetrabiblos* for calculating the length of life—in this case, by the setting of the chief significator of life (the hyleg or apheta) at the western horizon, with the other planets adding or subtracting years according to their own positions.[24] It is not the main procedure for the purpose, and

---

[22] Oxley, *Planispheres*, p. 139.

[23] Ibid., pp. 176 ff. The prevalent astrological language of causality, including the word 'influence', is nevertheless employed by Oxley throughout the work.

[24] *Pace* Curry, *Prophecy*, p. 132, hyleg and apheta are synonyms, and there seems to be no reason for singling out this astrological doctrine as an 'arcane interpretive point without any possible physical rationale'. Certainly it would not have appeared so to either Ptolemy, Placidus or Worsdale, although it has been less in vogue since the twentieth century. Hyleg (with several variant spellings, such as *hylech, alhileg*, etc.) is a Medieval Latin form of the Arabic *(al)-hīlāj*, which in its turn is derived from Middle Persian *hīlāk*, 'releasing'—a translation of the Greek word ἀφέτης, 'releaser, starter', also directly Latinized as apheta. Several older authors, being unfamiliar with other classical languages than Latin, Greek and Hebrew, mistakenly imagined the word hyleg to be derived from Hebrew *hālakh* 'go'; see John Partridge, *Opus Reformatum* (London: Awnsham and John Churchill, 1693), p. 137; John

Placidus devotes comparatively little space to it. Worsdale's first book contains a brief summary of the method but no examples; his *magnum opus*, published some thirty years later, is wholly silent on the matter despite the inclusion of several horoscopes in which the horimaea would have been of relevance.[25] Oxley similarly gives only a very short summary of Ptolemy's doctrine, with no attempt at applying it to any actual nativity. Indeed, the outlines presented by both authors are so brief as to be rather obscure, and it is a moot point whether either of them fully understood the procedure.[26] Instead, they focus exclusively on the other method, which is directing the hyleg to the malefic planets and their aspects.

Placidus, who took a scholastic-Aristotelian view of celestial mechanics, believed the daily rotation of the celestial sphere from east to west to be the only true motion of the heavenly bodies. The apparent motion of the planets through the zodiac in the opposite direction was thought to be entirely due to the varying resistance of their own respective spheres: Saturn, the lightest of the planets, follows the diurnal motion with barely any delay at all, whereas the dense and heavy moon lags behind by thirteen degrees per day. According to Placidus, the zodiacal aspects formed by such apparent movements were relevant only when measured between planets: the only true relationship between the heavenly bodies and the horizon or meridian is based on the diurnal motion, and must be measured by aspects *in mundo*. Worsdale upholds this convention, although without expounding on its underlying philosophy; but Oxley challenges it:

Worsdale, *Genethliacal Astrology* (Newark: Ridge, 1798), p. 116; and Oxley, *Planispheres*, p. 265—the latter two almost certainly copying a footnote from Ebeneezer Sibly, *A Complete Illustration of the Celestial Science of Astrology* (London: Green & Co., 1784–1790), p. 463.

[25] See Worsdale, *Astrology*, pp. 122 f. for the mention of *horimaea* (spelled *horimea*); Worsdale, *Philosophy*, pp. 101 ff. for a horoscope which would merit the use of *horimaea*.

[26] More than a century earlier, Partridge had called this technique (which he did not name) 'a thing known to very few of our Age, either Theorically [*sic*] or Practically' (Partridge, *Opus*, p. 94). A worked example, although not very detailed, is found in John Partridge, *Defectio Geniturarum* (London: Benj. Tooke, 1697), pp. 205 f.

> Now let us ask those who are deeply versed in these matters;
> since we see that the Sun and Moon are directed to the
> Aspects of other Planets both in the Zodiac, and in Mundo,
> would it not be equally rational to direct the Ascendant and
> tenth House [that is, the horizon and meridian], to the
> Aspects of the Planets, both in the Zodiac and in Mundo?[27]

In support of this contention Oxley proceeds to cite the
horoscope of King William IV, who, when his ascendant was
directed to Saturn's square in the zodiac at the age of 27
years and 5 months, had the misfortune to break his left
arm.[28]

These alterations to the Placidean teachings were all
simplifications, or instances of what we may call a
streamlining process, eliminating special rules and
exceptions to produce a single mode of directing, a single
doctrine of aspects, and a single procedure for calculating
length of life. But there were also simple differences of
opinion, one instance being the correct calculation of the so-
called Part of Fortune. According to Ptolemy's well-known
definition, this is a point always as far removed from the
ascendant as the moon is from the sun, so that it becomes, as
it were, a 'lunar ascendant' (σεληνιακὸς ὡροσκόπος).[29] The
traditional computation of this distance by degrees of
ecliptical longitude did not satisfy Placidus. 'I willingly
confess', he wrote, 'that, with regard to the ⊕ [Part of
Fortune], I have laboured a long time, and have not been able
hitherto to find any truth in it'.[30] Convinced by his
admiration for Ptolemy that the truth must nevertheless be
there to find, he sought to reinterpret the definition found in
the *Tetrabiblos*.

---

[27] Oxley, *Planispheres*, p. 198.

[28] Oxley gives the King's birth data as 21 August, 1765, at 3:54 A.M.,
the right ascension of the midheaven being 29°15′ and the ascendant
17°28′ of Leo. The accident took place on 21 January, 1793.

[29] *Tetrabiblos* III.11.

[30] Cooper, *Primum Mobile*, p. 308. James Wilson, in *A Complete
Dictionary of Astrology* (London: William Hughes, 1819), pp. 305 f.,
rejecting the concept of the Part entirely, saw in this statement a
strong proof of astrology: '[Placidus] could find truth in the
planetary configurations, because their effects are founded on the
immutable laws of nature, but when he came to investigate the
effects of the ⊕ he could "find no truth in it", because there was
none'.

Placidus' first attempt at finding an alternative Part was to project its position not along the ecliptic, but along the Moon's apparent orbit through the zodiac. He abandoned this model, however, to embrace the one proposed by Adriano Negusanti of Fano, Italy (d. 1685), who wanted the Part to be projected along the Moon's circle of declination. This mode of calculation results in the Part generally occupying a point in space distant not only from the ecliptic, but from the zodiac as a whole; and followers of Placidus therefore generally refused to assign any zodiacal position to it.[31]

In his early writings, Worsdale championed this doctrine of the Part of Fortune 'calculated according to the Rules of the learned PTOLEMY, so amply laid down by that immortal Master of the predictive Science, by giving it the same Latitude, and Declination as the Moon'.[32] Three decades later, however, he wrote: 'Nothing can be more absurd than allowing [the Part of Fortune] to claim the same Latitude and Declination as the Moon'. Instead, Worsdale now advocated a third method of calculating the Part of Fortune *in mundo*, apparently devised by himself.[33] Oxley, on the other hand,

---

[31] Being located outside of the zodiac, the Placidean Part of Fortune cannot receive any zodiacal aspects; and as it is not carried across the sky by the diurnal motion, it is equally unable to form any aspects *in mundo*, and therefore restricted to the passive role of receiving such aspects from other planets. The point that, although an artificial semi-arc may be assigned to the Placidean Part of Fortune from its horizontal and meridian distance in order to determine its house position, the Part does not in fact describe such an arc by diurnal motion, was lost on some later astrologers; see Sepharial (pseud.), *Directional Astrology* (London : William Rider & Son, 1915), pp. 81 f.

[32] Worsdale, *Astrology*, pp. 212 f. Placidus' method will in fact give the Part the same declination as the moon but not the same latitude. Although Worsdale was of course mistaken in ascribing the doctrine to Ptolemy, perhaps the most surprising part of his statement is the use of the word 'amply'. As noted by William Lilly in *Christian Astrology* (London: John Macock, 1647), p. 553, 'Ptolomey [...] in all his writings was extream short'.

[33] See Worsdale, *Philosophy*, pp. 16 ff., 128 ff. The method consists in computing the oblique ascensions or descensions of the sun and moon under their own poles and projecting the difference from the eastern horizon along the celestial equator. The point reached is the oblique ascension or descension of the Part of Fortune, which is then reassigned to the ecliptic and given the right ascension and declination of its ecliptical degree, despite Worsdale's assertion that

affirms that Placidus alone had understood Ptolemy's intentions, but adds:

> It has hitherto been generally believed, that if the Part of Fortune was found according to its Mundane Position, that its place in the Zodiac could not be known, this I have heard asserted by very expert artists, but I have here shown the method, by which this can be done with very great exactness.[34]

This desire to assign every point a place in the zodiac is another example of the streamlining tendency.

Finally, certain changes made to the Placidean system were the result of misunderstanding. Placidus had advocated the method of proportional semi-arcs for house division as well as for directions. As the calculations were cumbersome and time-consuming, he also published tables which could be used to approximate the semi-arc system by means of poles and circles of position—concepts familiar to astrologers of his day.[35] By frequently repeated misrepresentations, this method came to be accepted by many as the true Placidean system, and was used exclusively by both Worsdale and Oxley.[36] Other misconceptions with more far-reaching consequences include the gradual reinterpretation of the concept of 'converse' directions, a topic which requires a separate investigation and to which I hope to return in the near future.

Thus we see that the second wave of Placidean teachings in Britain, following the hiatus that spanned most of the eighteenth century, was characterized by a tendency towards simple and uniform principles. The lack of a continuous tradition inevitably led to some misunderstandings of astro-

---

it 'can only be directed in Mundo'.

[34] Oxley, *Planispheres*, p. 160. Oxley appears to have misunderstood the common objection. Although it is certainly possible to project the place of any celestial object, real or imagined, onto the ecliptic, the Placidean Part of Fortune will nevertheless remain an extra-zodiacal point in the great majority of cases.

[35] A circle of position is a pseudo-horizon passing through a celestial body, the zenith of this horizon being known as the pole of the body in question.

[36] Among the more well-known proponents of the method in the nineteenth and twentieth centuries were R. J. Morrison (Zadkiel I), W. R. Old (Sepharial) and E. C. Kühr.

logical doctrine, but also made it possible to dislodge astrological techniques from theoretical frameworks no longer felt to be relevant. The works of Worsdale and Oxley, and of their junior contemporaries such as 'Raphael' (Robert Cross Smith, 1795–1832) and 'Zadkiel' (Richard James Morrison, 1795–1874), confirmed this simplified version of Placidus's system as the standard of modern astrology—a transitional stage preparatory to the Theosophical reinvention of the art at the end of the nineteenth century.

BIBLIOGRAPHY

Bishop, John, and Kirby, Richard. *The Marrow of Astrology*. London: Joseph Streater, 1687.

Cooper, John. *Primum Mobile [...] by Didacus Placidus de Titus*. London: Davis and Dickson, 1814.

Curry, Patrick. *Prophecy and power : astrology in early modern England*. Cambridge: Polity, 1989.

Howe, Ellic. *Astrology: A recent history including the untold story of its role in World War II*. New York: Walker, 1968. Original title: *Urania's Children*, 1967.

Lilly, William. *Christian Astrology*. London: John Macock, 1647.

North, John David. *Horoscopes and History*. London: The Warburg Institute, 1986.

Oxley, Thomas. *The Celestial Planispheres, or Astronomical Charts in IV. Parts, illustrated by the Nativities of the Emperor Napoleon and King William IV*. London: Davis and Dickson, 1830.

————. *A Supplement, or only True Key to the Use and Construction of the Celestial Planispheres, for working Nativities and resolving Astronomical Problems by the Scale and Compasses*. London: Davis and Dickson, 1833.

————. *The Gem of the Astral Sciences, or Mathematics of Celestial Philosophy, with improved Formulæ and all the Rules of Calculations used therein [...]*. London: Simpkin, Marshall & Co., 1848.

Partridge, John. *Opus Reformatum*. London: Awnsham and John Churchill, 1693.

————. *Defectio Geniturarum*. London: Benj. Tooke, 1697.

Pearce, Alfred John. *The Text-Book of Astrology*. London: Mackie, 1911.

Placidus de Titis. *Physiomathematica, sive Coelestis Philosophia*. Mediolanum [Milan]: Io. Baptista Maltesta, 1650.

————. *Tabulae primi mobilis*. Patavium [Padua]: Pauli Frambotti, 1657.

Ptolemy, Claudius. *Tetrabiblos: Claudii Ptolemaei opera quae exstant omnia*. Vol. III., bk. 1: Ἀποτελεσματικά, ed. Wolfgang Hübner. Leipzig: B. G. Teubner, 1998.

Sepharial [Walter Richard Old]. *Directional Astrology*. London: William Rider & Son, 1915.

Sibly, Ebeneezer. *A Complete Illustration of the Celestial Science of Astrology*. London: Green & Co., 1784–1790.

Sibly, Manoah. *Astronomy and elementary philosophy*. London: W. Justins, 1789.

Synoptical Index to the Laws and Treaties of the United States from March 4, 1789, to March 3, 1851. Boston: Charles C. Little and James Brown, 1852.

Thorndike, Lynn. *A History of Magic and Experimental Science*. Vol. 8: *The Seventeenth Century*. New York: Macmillan, 1958.

Wilson, James. *A Complete Dictionary of Astrology*. London: William Hughes, 1819.

Worsdale, John. *Genethliacal Astrology*. Newark: Ridge, 1798 [1796].

———. *Celestial Philosophy, or Genethliacal Astronomy*. London: Longman & Co., 1828.

Zadkiel [Richard James Morrison]. *The Grammar of Astrology*. London: Sherwood, Gilbert and Piper, 1833.

USING THE STARS:
ASTROLOGY AT THE COURT
OF PETER THE GREAT

Robert Collis

ABSTRACT: Astrology exerted a strong influence at the court of Peter the Great, yet it has received scant attention from either Russian or Western historians. My article explores two particular ways in which astrology had an impact upon various aspects of Petrine court culture. First, I analyse the manner in which official court panegyrics repeatedly utilised astrological symbolism in order to extol the reign of Peter the Great. Secondly, I study the prominent role played by astrology in Russian calendars published between 1708 and 1725. The promotion (and distribution) of pocket calendars among his courtiers and military officers, which were replete with astrological prognostications, enabled the Russian monarch to inculcate his vision of reform and Russian power among his servitors. Thus, far from shunning astrology, I argue that Peter the Great actively embraced the ancient practice as a means to promote both his own power and the status of his realm.

In a recent work entitled *The Petrine Revolution in Russian Culture*, the American historian James Cracraft argues that Peter the Great (1672–1725) oversaw a period 'of intensive Europeanization'. Cracraft elaborates by referring to 'the transmission of values as well as whole technologies, styles as well as beliefs and knowledges, from one quite distinct cultural matrix to another'.[1] Inherent in this argument is the assumption that Europe embodied a homogenous cultural and scientific model—founded on the pillars of reason and rationality. Accordingly, Cracraft includes chapters on the development of the Russian navy, military modernization, bureaucratic revolution, linguistic reform and the promotion of science and literature.

This prevailing paradigm regarding the Petrine reform programme is endorsed by W. F. Ryan, who has written the

---

[1] James Cracraft, *The Petrine Revolution in Russian Culture* (Cambridge, MA: The Belknap Press of Harvard University Press, 2004), p. 309.

only English-language historical study of magic in Russia. He writes, for example, that 'Peter the Great [...] had a robust enthusiasm for almost anything Western, in particular in the areas of technology, both civil and military, administration and manners' and that this 'practicality belonged more to the Enlightenment than to the seventeenth century and there are few traces in him or his court of the occult interests of his father'.[2]

However, Peter's 'robust enthusiasm' for European culture and science included the promotion of various forms of Western, or more accurately German, Polish and Ukrainian, astrological practice and motifs at his court. This does not contradict Cracraft's argument that Peter the Great instigated cultural transfer from Europe; rather it suggests that a more nuanced and broader understanding of European culture and society itself would help to explain the complex nature of the reforms instigated by the Russian monarch.

In this paper, the extent to which the court of Peter the Great embraced strands of European astrological thought will be examined in two ways. Firstly, I will provide a brief overview of how astrological motifs were extensively used by clergymen from the Ukraine, Belarus and southern Russia in official panegyrics in praise of Peter the Great. Secondly, I will outline how Peter the Great actively encouraged the publication of Russian almanacs and calendars after 1708, which were replete with astrological information and predictions. Significantly, these almanacs rank as the first Russian versions of an older Western European publishing tradition that dates back to the fifteenth century.

THE USE OF ASTROLOGICAL MOTIFS IN PANEGYRICS TO PETER THE GREAT

To mark the christening of Peter the Great in June 1672, the leading court cleric Simeon Polotskii (1629–1680) wrote a panegyric saturated with astrological motifs. The clergyman made a highly favourable interpretation, for example, of the fact that the new tsarevich was born during the conjunction of Mars and Jupiter, as well as pronouncing that the 'four-

---

[2] W. F. Ryan, *The Bathhouse at Midnight: An Historical Survey of Magic and Divination in Russia* (Stroud: Sutton Publishing, 1999), p. 23.

cornered aspect of the planets' signified glory.[3] Hence, the new Romanov heir is foreseen as a ruler who will capture Constantinople from the Turks.

Polotskii was born in Belarus and educated at the renowned Kiev Academy. He had been invited to Moscow by Tsar Aleksei (1629–1676)—Peter the Great's father—in 1664 and quickly established himself as a fine exponent of baroque literary motifs, as well as founding a Latin school. The cleric was arguably the finest graduate of the Kiev Academy, which promoted a wide study of the liberal arts.[4] When in Moscow, Polotskii developed a form of baroque literature new to the Russian court that freely drew on astrological tropes. As early as 1665, the cleric composed a

[3] I. F. Golubev, 'Zabytye virshi Simeona Polotskogo', *Trudy otdela drevnerusskoi literatury* 24 (1969): pp. 254–59. Also see P. N. Krekshin, 'Zapiski novgorodskago dvorianina Petra Nikiforovicha Krekshina', in *Zapiski Russkikh liudei. Sobytiia vremen Petra Veilkago* (Newtonville, MA: Oriental Research Partners, 1980), p. 12. For further discussion of Polotskii in relation to Peter the Great's horoscope, see G. F. Miller, 'Rozhdenie gosudaria imperatora Petra Velikogo', *Opyt trudov Vol'nogo rossiiskogo sobraniia* (Moscow, 1780), pp. 87–105; N. A. Polevoi, 'Astrologicheskie predveshchaniia pri rozhdenii Petra Velikogo', *Russkii vestnik*, no. 2 (1842): pp. 258–80; M. P. Pogodin, 'Goroskop Petra Velikogo', *Moskvitianin* 1 (1842): pp. 58–65; D. Sviatskii, 'Zvezda Petra I', *Mirovedenie*, no. 3 (1927): pp. 168–87; A. P. Bogdanov and R. A. Simonov, 'Prognosticheskie pis'ma doktora Andreasa Engel'gardta tsariu Alekseiu Mikhailovichu', in *Estestvenno-nauchye predstavleniia drevnei Rusi*, ed. R. A. Simonov (Moscow: Nauka, 1988), pp. 151–203; V. I. Pluzhnikov and R. A. Simonov, 'Goroskop Petra I', *Trudy otdela drevnerusskoi literatury* 43 (1990): pp. 82–100; Galina Bednenko, 'Goroskop Petra Velikogo', *Goroskop*, no. 1 (1997): pp. 37–39. For an analysis of the astrological influences on Polotskii, see A. N. Robinson, 'Simeon Polotskii—Astrolog', in *Problemy izucheniia kul'turnogo naslediia*, ed. D. S. Likhachev (Moscow, 1985), pp. 177–84. For examples of the astrological poetry of Polotskii, see, for example, 'Beseda so planity' ('Conversation with the Planets'); '4 Preobladaiushchikh temperamenta' ('The 4 Predominant Temperaments'); 'Znaki semi planet i kharakter ikh vozdeistviia' (The Signs of the Seven Planets and the Character of their Influence') in S. Polotskii, *Virshi*, ed. V. K. Bylinin and L. U. Zvonareva (Minsk: Mastatskaia litaratura, 1990), pp. 86, 117, 123.

[4] For more on Polotskii in general, see Leonid, arkhimandrit, 'K biografii Simeona Polotskogo', *Drevniaia i novaia Rossiia* 1, no. 4 (1876): p. 398; I. A. Tatarskii, *Simeon Polotskii: Ego zhizn' i deiatel'nost'* (Moscow, 1886).

star-shaped poem to mark the birth of Tsarevich Simeon
Alekseevich (1665–1669) (see fig. 6.1).

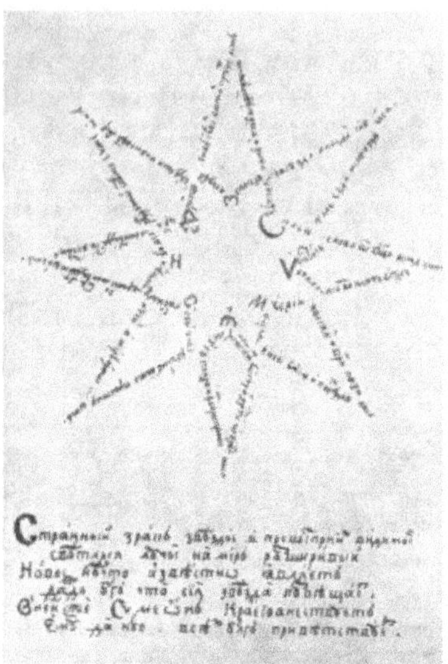

*Fig. 6.1: A star-shaped poem written by Simeon Polotskii to celebrate the
birth of Tsarevich Simeon in 1665. Source: V. A. Chemeritskii,
'Belorusskaia Literatura (XVII v.)', Istoriia vsemirnoi literatury 6
(Moscow, 1987), p. 373.*

Polotskii died in 1680, but his influence on the court of
Peter the Great was to be immense. Indeed, the style of
baroque panegyrics he developed at court, which were laced
with astrological themes, was continued by a succession of
Ukrainian and southern Russian clerics well into the
eighteenth century.

The legacy bequeathed by Polotskii is evident, for
example, in an emblematic poem written by the cleric Karion
Istomin (ca. 1640s–ca. 1720s), from Kursk in southern Russia,
in order to mark the marriage of Peter the Great to Evdokiia
Lopukhina in January 1690.[5] In this richly detailed work,
Istomin draws on astrology in order to predict a long and
happy marriage for the couple. The cleric justifies his use of
astrology by citing Isaiah 51:6, which states: 'Lift up your

---

[5] For more on Istomin, see E. B. Pokrovskaia, 'Karion Istomin—
pevets mudrosti' in Karion Istomin, *Kniga liubvi znak v chesten brak*
(Moscow: Izdatel'stvo "Kniga", 1989), pp. 43–64.

eyes to the heavens and look upon the earth beneath'. He proceeds to state that 'Astronomers look with cunning at the heavens [in order] to find out about their needs in the world'. Istomin then proclaims that the royal wedding had been predetermined by the heavenly stars and that the young couple will 'live for a century united in love'. These words are accompanied by an illustration depicting two individuals observing the sun and moon through telescopes (see fig. 6.2).

Fig. 6.2: Illustrated plate from Karion Istomin's Kniga liubvi znak v chesten brak (1690), pl. 9.

The corresponding text explains that the solar and lunar depictions represent the tsar and tsarina respectively.[6] Despite the woeful inaccuracy of Istomin's predictions—only nine years later Peter confined his wife to a nunnery—the emblematic poem testifies to the continued tradition of using astrological tropes in baroque panegyrics in order to extol the Russian monarch.

In 1700, Peter the Great followed in his father's footsteps by inviting a leading Ukrainian cleric—Stefan Iavorskii (1658–1722)—from the Kiev Academy to Moscow.[7] Iavorskii became the head of the Russian Orthodox Church, and as with Polotskii before him, the Ukrainian quickly garnered a reputation as the pre-eminent exponent of baroque panegyrics. Indeed, for the next two decades Iavorskii was commissioned to write a series of panegyrics to mark special court occasions, many of which were underpinned with a mixture of astrological motifs, biblical prophecy, and mysticism.

Between 1703–1706, for example, Iavorskii delivered a series of New Year sermons, in which he developed the theme of Ezekiel's chariot ascending to heaven. In addition to this main theme, which was influenced by Merkavah mysticism, Iavorskii also drew on astrology to interpret events of the preceding year and pronounced annual prognostications. In the sermon he delivered on New Year's Day 1705, for example, he pronounced that the Russian capture of Narva from the Swedes the previous August had occurred 'when the sun was radiating in the sign of the heavenly virgin'. Iavorskii then added that astrologers interpret the virgin as subduing the lion in the celestial zodiac, and was thus able to tame the ferocious Swedish lion on the field of battle. After these observations, Iavorskii prognosticated about the upcoming year by attaching great prophetic significance to the correlation of names, letters and numbers. Thus, the cleric proclaimed that 'this fifth year

---

[6] Istomin, *Kniga*, p. 77.

[7] For more on Iavorskii, see Iurii Samarin, *Stefan Iavorskii i Feofan Prokopovich kak propovedniki* (Moscow, 1844); Viktor Zhivov, *Iz tserkovnoi istorii vremen Petra Velikogo: issledovaniia i materially* (Moscow: Novoe literaturnoe obozrenie, 2004); Robert Collis, *The Petrine Instauration: Religion, Esotericism and Science at the Court of Peter the Great, 1689–1725* (Turku: Annales Universitatis Turkuensis, 2007), pp. 187–241.

begins from the name of Jesus', which he states has five letters. Moreover, he added that 'the most Holy name Maria also has five letters'. Accordingly, Iavorskii announced that 'there shall be for us genuine pleasure in this year'.[8] The tsar's liking for Iavorskii's New Year prognostications is testified in a letter to a courtier in 1707, in which the monarch expresses the hope that 'in this year the prophecy of Iavorskii will be realized'.

Iavorskii's most extensive use of astrological themes occurs in a panegyric written to mark Peter the Great's birthday, on 30 May 1709. After extolling the tsar as a 'true pupil of Plato', the cleric proceeds to describe how rulers in antiquity invited astrologers to 'interpret the day, hour, month, planet and heavenly sign when a child is born' and that 'from the celestial signs of the type of horoscope and the type of ascendance, they could foretell and prophesize about the birth of adolescents, about what kind of disposition they shall have and about their kind of behaviour'. Following on from this prologue, Iavorskii then turns to Peter's birthday, from which he draws favourable omens.[9]

The cleric continued to be called upon by the monarch to deliver such panegyrics up until his death in 1722. Hence, in August 1720, Iavorskii gave a sermon to mark the Assumption of the Virgin Mary. On this occasion he once again read significance into the way in which the zodiacal sign of the Virgin is located between the Lion (Leo) and Libra. The cleric recalled how the victories enjoyed by the Russian Fleet against the Swedish navy in 1714 and 1719 both occurred in July, 'when the Lion appeared in its zodiacal sign'. Thus the Virgin, according to Iavorskii, was able to victoriously tame the Swedish lion by barring its open mouth.[10]

It is remarkable that for around sixty years, between 1665 and 1725, Orthodox clerics from the Western borders of Russia's territory employed astrological themes in official panegyrics, which extolled the monarchs, as well as the Russian state. In this regard, Stefan Iavorskii was the undoubted heir to Simeon Polotskii in the manner he

---

[8] Stefan Iavorskii, 'Slova Stefana Iavorskago, mitropolita riazanskgao i muromskago', *Trudy kievskoi dukhnovnoi akademii* 3 (July 1874): p. 119.

[9] I. A. Chistovich, ed., 'Neizdannye propovedi Stefana Iavorskago', *Khristianskoe chtenie*, Vol. 2, (1867), pp. 114–17.

[10] Chistovich, 'Neizdannye', Vol. 1, p. 422.

employed a rich variety of astrological tropes in his literary and oratorical works. Both Aleksei Mikhailovich and Peter the Great were fully aware of the unique characteristics of Ukrainian theological training, which was greatly influenced by Uniate forms of Catholicism in the Polish-Lithuanian Commonwealth. Whilst the Ukrainian clerics at the Russian Court adhered to Orthodox dogma and ritual practice, they also introduced expressions of baroque aestheticism into Russia that did not contradict the theological tenets of the Eastern Church. Crucially, this included aspects of esotericism that could be used as a potent form of symbolism in order to extol the Russian monarchy.

THE PETRINE ALMANAC

Significantly, the arrival of Polotskii at the Muscovite court in 1664 also coincided with the onset of a marked interest by Tsar Aleksei in Polish and German almanacs. Hence, in this year, one first notes the translation of a Polish almanac.[11] However, the volume of such translations increased substantially in the late 1680s and the early 1690s, that is, when Peter the Great came of age. It is extremely noteworthy that the almanacs translated at this time, which included the works of the Poles Stanislaw Slowakowicz (1634–1702), Adam Stanislaw Pecherzynski (fl. 1695–1707) and Tomasz Franciszek Orminski (d. 1735) and the German Johann Henrich Voigt (1613–1691), contained political prognostications concerning Russia.[12] Evidently a mixture of curiosity

---

[11] A. I. Sobolevskii, *Perevodnaia literatura Moskovskoi Rusi XIV–XVII vekov. Bibliograficheskie materially* (St. Petersburg, 1903), p. 142.

[12] On Orminski, see Joannes Ambrosius Wadowski, *Anacephaleosis Professorum Academiae Zamoscensis* (Warsaw, 1899–1900), p.65. On Pecherzynski, see Karol Józef Teofil Estericher, ed., *Bibliografia Polska*, Vol. 24 (Cracow, 1912), pp. 174–76. For more on Slowakowicz, see Estericher, *Bibliografia Polska*, Vol. 9, p. 10. Voigt was a resident of Stade, which between 1645–1712 was part of the Swedish-controlled province of Bremen-Verden-Wildeshausen. Significantly, Voigt received a yearly pension from the Swedish Crown and was commissioned to write a series of works for his paymasters. Thus, apart from annual calendars, he also wrote *Ordnung und Nachfolge aller Könige in Schweden* and *König Caroli XI Genealogiam und Stamm-Register von Carolo Magno herstammende*. Voigt also traveled to Stockholm in 1686, where he was honoured with a royal audience with King Charles XI. Thus, it was in Voigt's interest to include (negative) prognostications about Sweden's great

and apprehension motivated the Russian authorities to translate such works. The power of foreign almanacs to incite unease among the tsarist authorities is strikingly illustrated by the example of Voigt's almanac for 1682, which contained the prediction that 'neither will Moscow escape her ill-fortune'. A contemporary German resident in Russia, Georg Adam Schleusing, noted that the Muscovite authorities had taken the trouble to translate Voigt's work as his prediction of ill-fortune was interpreted as being fulfilled in the Streltsy Guards Revolt of that year.[13] In 1699, the Austrian envoy in Moscow, Johann-Georg Korb, noted that it was still deemed a criminal offence 'to introduce the calendar of Vogt the astronomer into Muscovy' because he 'presaged rebellion to the Muscovites'.[14] Yet, despite the ban on Voigt's calendars, Peter the Great ordered translations of the almanac to be made throughout the 1690s, along with a host of other similar works by Poles and Germans.[15]

Up until 1708, the Foreign Office continued to translate Polish and German almanacs for Peter the Great. The translation of such almanacs enabled Peter and his officials to be informed about the nature of foreign predictions concerning Russia. However, translations alone clearly did not provide the Russian authorities with the means to control the negative impact of inauspicious predictions. Consequently, in 1708 the tsar ordered the publication of a Russian

---

eastern rival. For a biography of Voigt and a list of his principal works, see Franz Wolpmann, *Die in ihrer Unruhe gestillete Seele Davids* (Stade, 1691), pp. 33–44. Peter the Great also commissioned a translation of William Hanemann's *Verwunderlich-Englischer Wahrsager, oder ausfürliches Prognosticon* in 1704. The Russian tsar owned a sizeable collection of foreign calendars and almanacs (in the original language and in translation) and are listed in his personal library collection. See *Biblioteka Petra I: ukazatel' spravochnik*, ed. E. I. Bobrova (Leningrad, 1978), pp. 24 (no. 37), 29 (nos. 84–86), 38 (no. 167), 50 (nos. 271–73), 71–72 (nos. 487–98), 85 (no. 676), 124 (nos. 1121–22), 126 (no. 1151), 127 (nos. 1166–68), 130 (no. 1215).

[13] Georg Adam Schleusing, *Neu-entdecktes Sibyrien oder Siewerien* (Jena, 1688), pp. 151–52.

[14] Johann-Georg Korb, *Diary of an Austrian Secretary of Legation at the Court of Czar Peter the Great*, Vol. 2, trans. and ed. The Count Mac Donnell (London: Bradbury & Evans, 1863), pp. 196–97.

[15] For analysis of the German and Polish almanacs translated in Russia in the 1690s, see P. Pekarskii, *Nauka i literature v Rossii pri Petr Velikom*, Vol. 1 (St. Petersburg, 1862), pp. 286–89; Sobolevskii, *Perevodnaia*, pp. 135–37; Collis, *Petrine Instauration*, pp. 421–24.

calendar—the *kalendar' ili mesiatseslov*—that was printed in Moscow and which continued to be published annually for the remainder of his reign.[16]

The Russian monarch took an extremely active role in the publication of these first Russian calendars and ensured that they were distributed to members of the court and military officials. Indeed, it should be stressed that Peter envisaged the calendars in a highly practical manner—consistent with the overarching nature of his personality—in which court and military officials used the pocket almanac on a daily basis to plan and organize all aspects of their lives in line with new tendencies in the sphere of official culture: from the observance of religious and state festivals, to matters of personal health and well-being, as well as providing his elite with a readily available (and authorized) source of knowledge on astronomical phenomena and astrological predictions.

The calendars featured an abundance of astrological information. Thus, after listing key chronological events relevant to Russian history, the calendars provided information regarding the signs of the zodiac and the seven planets. Every month contained predictions regarding the weather, and the publications also contained prognostications mainly related to military affairs and health matters. The calendar for 1713, for example, which was printed in Moscow in December 1712, asserted that the position of the planets portended peace for 1713, as well as stating that general health would also be better than in the preceding year. The only exception to this standard format was the first calendar printed in St. Petersburg at the close of 1713 (for the following year), which excluded all prognostications. However, any permanent shift away from astrological predictions in the calendar were curtailed by Peter the Great himself. On 23 November 1714 (OS) the tsar wrote to Ivan Musin-Pushkin (1661–1729), who oversaw the publication of the calendars, and informed him that prognostications were to be printed in the forthcoming issues.[17]

---

[16] From 1714 the *kalendar'* was also published in St. Petersburg. See, A. Pokrovskii, 'Kalendari i sviattsy'' *Biblioteka Moskovskoi Sinodal'noi tipografii* 5 (1911), p. XLV.

[17] I. I. Golikov, *Deianiia Petra Velikago, mudrago preobrazitelia Rossii*, Vol. 5 (Moscow, 1838), p. 591. The date is given according to the Old Style (OS), that is, according to the Julian Calendar, which in the

Each annual calendar also contained information related to the human body as a microcosm of the cosmos, which designated zodiacal significance to specific internal and external parts of the body. As Katharina Volk has noted, this doctrine—known as *melothesia*—was espoused by Marcus Manilius (fl. 1st century CE) in his influential work *Astronomicon*.[18] Thus, the illustration of the *homo signorum* present in the 1721 edition of the Russian calendar (see fig. 6.3) is entirely in keeping with this classical astrological tradition. The sheet provides astrological information relating to conducive times for bloodletting of veins and vessels (*O krovopuskanii zhilnom i rozhechnom*) and when to take medicine (*kogda lekarstvo prinimat*) during January 1721.

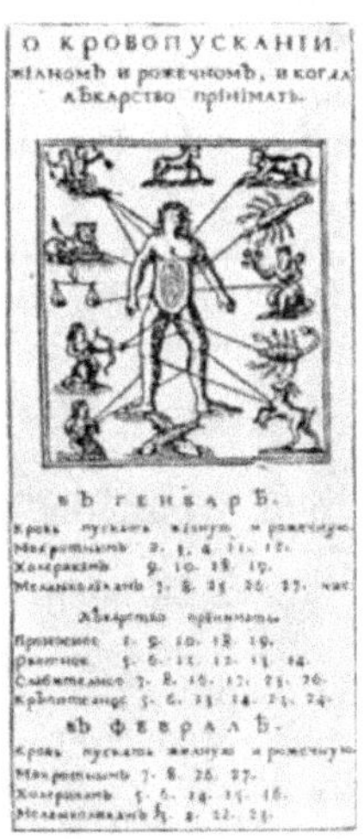

Fig. 6.3: From the 1721 Kalendar ili Mesiatsoslov. *Source: A. D. Petrov, ed.,* Sobranie knig izdannikh v tsarstvovanie Petra Velikago *(St. Petersburg, 1913).*

Underneath the illustration of the *homo signorum*, one can see designated dates for bloodletting dependent upon whether a person has a moist, choleric or melancholic temperament. The chart also provides the best days in the month to take medicine that would induce diarrhoea and sickness.

---

eighteenth century was eleven days behind the New Style Gregorian calendar.

[18] Katharina Volk, *Manilius and his Intellectual Background* (Oxford: Oxford University Press, 2009), p. 111.

In short, the Russian calendars emulated the style and content of the Polish and German publications that had been translated in Moscow since the 1660s. Indeed, up until the death of Peter the Great in 1725, the Russian calendars continued to directly draw on the prognostications of Voigt and on Paul Halcke (1662–1731), who hailed from Buxtehude in the district of Stade.[19] The latter was a founding member of the Hamburg Mathematical Society, which was established in 1690 by Heinrich Meissner and Valentin Heins and also included the noted Pietist mystic Johann Jakob Zimmermann.[20] The attraction of such a method was that the Russian authorities could now choose favourable prognostications by foreign practitioners, whilst at the same time augmenting these predictions with matters more relevant to the Russian audience.

However, the official state calendars were not the only publications of their type in the Russian Empire during the reign of Peter the Great. Remarkably, a number of Orthodox monasteries produced almanacs replete with astrological information. In either 1696 or 1697, for example, the monks of Antoniev-Siiskii Monastery, near Kholmogory in

---

[19] The calendars for 1715, 1718, 1721, 1722 and 1723, for example, used information from Voigt, whilst the Moscow edition of 1717 featured translated extracts from Halcke. See Pekarskii, *Nauka*, Vol. 2, pp. 310, 369, 439. It is interesting to note that Halcke lived and worked in the district of Stade, as he very much followed in the astronomical/astrological tradition championed in the area up until 1691 by Voigt. For more on the astronomical and astrological work of Hamburg-area mathematicians, such as Voigt and Halcke, see Jochen Schramm, *Sterne über Hamburg: die Geschichte der Astronomie in Hamburg* (Hamburg: Kultur und Geschichtskontor, 1996). A number of other German almanacs were translated into Russian during the reign of Peter the Great, with strong links to Voigt and Halcke. Thus, a calendar by Wolfgang Heinrich Adelungk (1649–1710) was translated into Russian in 1706. See, Pekarskii, *Nauka*, Vol. 1, p. 288. Also see Collis, *Petrine Instauration*, p. 423. Later, calendars by Hermann Wahn (1678–1747) and Nicolaus Rohlfs (1695–1750), who (as with Halcke) lived in Buxtehude. For more on the translations of calendars by Wahn and Rohlfs in Russia, see Pokrovskii, 'Kalendari', p. XXVII.

[20] J. F. Bubendey, 'Geschichte der Mathematischen Gesellschaft in Hamburg 1690–1890', *Mitteilungen der Mathematischen Gesellschaft in Hamburg* 2, no. 1 (1890): pp. 8–33. For more on Zimmerman, see Donald F. Durnbaugh, 'Work and Hope: The Spirituality of the Radical Pietist Communitarians', *Church History* 39, no. 1 (March 1970): pp. 79–90.

Arkhangel'sk Province, produced a so-called *Koliadnik*, which provided meteorological predictions and monthly horoscopes.[21]

The most prominent and widely distributed church almanac was the annual *Kalendar ili mesiatsoslov* produced by the Kiev Caves Monastery. The 1717 edition of the calendar contained political prognostications on an almost weekly basis concerning the on-going Great Northern War being waged by Russia against Sweden. Thus, the calendar predicts that 'the enemy [Sweden] will want to destroy three towers with open gates' in reference to the Polish town of Torun. Moreover, the calendar was also awash with meteorological predictions.[22]

Furthermore, in the secular sphere a series of six so-called *Bruce Calendars* were printed by the Civil Typographers between 1709 and 1715. These single-sheet calendars were jointly produced by Jacob Bruce (1669–1735)—hence the title—who acted as the director of the initiative and Vasilii Onufrievich Kiprianov (fl. 1705–1723), who was the head librarian of the country and in 1706 became the head of the Civil Typographers.[23] Bruce, who was of Scottish descent, ranks as one of the foremost champions of learning and the advancement of astronomy in Russia in the first quarter of the eighteenth century. At the turn of the eighteenth century he established the country's first observatory in Moscow and played a key role in setting up the Mathematics and Navigation School in the city—the first of its kind in Russia. What is more, he was a much-valued servitor of Peter the Great, occupying key positions in the military, the diplomatic field and various prestigious civil posts.[24]

The *Bruce Calendars* complemented the annual state calendars by presenting astronomical and astrological information in a format that was designed to be referred to less frequently, but could be admired in aesthetic terms. The six

---

[21] А. E. Viktorov, *Opisi rukopisnykh sobranii v knigokhranilishchakh severnoi Rossii* (St. Petersburg, 1890), p. 99. For more on the *koliadnik* in Russia, see Ryan, *Bathhouse*, p. 380.

[22] Pekarskii, *Nauka*, Vol. 2, p. 358.

[23] Three full sets of the *Bruce Calendars* are extant in Russia at The State Hermitage Museum (St. Petersburg), The Library of the Academy of Sciences (St. Petersburg) and the Pushkin State Museum of Fine Arts (Moscow).

[24] For more on Bruce, see Collis, *Petrine Instauration*, pp. 45–106.

sheets are all characterized by a remarkable degree of ornate design, emblematic imagery, religious symbols and classical astrological motifs, all redolent of the highpoint in Russian baroque culture.[25] In structural terms, each of the first four sheets, which were published in 1709 and 1710, address different aspects of astronomical, astrological and religious knowledge: the first sheet provides information on the entry of the sun into the twelve signs of the zodiac according to Moscow's latitude; the second sheet gives a comprehensive list of saints' days and religious festivals, alongside astronomical calculations regarding the dates of Easter between 1709–1784; the third sheet provides a series of astrological predictions based on the planets regarding the seasons; and the fourth sheet offers astrological information regarding the course of the Moon in the zodiac. The final two sheets each provide brief summaries of the respective information printed in the preceding four sheets.

The first sheet is simply entitled 'A New Published Plate' (*Novo siia tablitsa izdana*). Below the heading one can see two cherubims holding a shield with a two-headed eagle (the Russian State emblem), and above them is a banner inscribed with a quote from Psalm 21: 'O lord; and in thy salvation how greatly shall he rejoice!' A depiction of Moscow can be seen below the shield, either side of which are models of the universe according to the Ptolemaic system. The main body of the sheet provides twelve vertical columns with symbols and emblems of the zodiac, accompanied by a brief description of the qualities of each sign. Thus, Pisces is stated as being 'cold and dry' by nature and is accompanied by an emblem depicting two fishermen, as well as a kitchen garden to the left that is bathed in sunshine (see fig. 6.5).

---

[25] All descriptions of the *Bruce Calendars* are based on the sheets stored at The Pushkin State Museum of Fine Arts (Moscow). For an in-depth description of the six sheets, see A. N. Filimon, *Iakov Brius* (Moscow: Chistye vody, 2003), pp. 417–50.

Fig. 6.4: 'A New Published Plate' (Novo siia tablitsa izdana) (1709). Source: Photograph by Natal'ia Antonova and Inna Regentova. Reproduced with kind permission of the The State Hermitage Museum, St. Petersburg.

Fig. 6.5: The Emblematic depiction of Pisces, accompanied by relevant astrological and astronomical information, as found in 'A New Published Plate' (1709). Source: Photogragh by Natal'ia Antonova and Inna Regentova. Reproduced with kind permission of the The State Hermitage Museum, St. Petersburg.

The astronomical data provided in each of the twelve columns relates to the daily sunrise, sunset and the lengths of day and night according to Moscow's latitude.

The second sheet, as mentioned, is predominantly religious in tone and content, providing a list of saints' days and religious festivals, as well as astronomical calculations regarding the paschal calendar. The inclusion of a baroque-style triangular representation of God, below the title banner, is a noteworthy feature in a Russian context, as such an aesthetic depiction was alien to the Orthodox tradition. Below the Imperial two-headed eagle, one can also note the depiction of the Peter and Paul Fortress in St. Petersburg.

Whilst the first two sheets do embrace astrological imagery and provide brief descriptions of the qualities of the twelve signs of the zodiac and the seven planets respectively, the emphasis in each sheet is on the provison of astronomical data regarding the sun and in relation to the Orthodox calendar respectively. However, the third sheet—entitled 'The Omens of All the Seasons According to the Planets' (*Predznamenovanie vremeni na vsiakoi god po planetam*)—concentrates on providing astrological predictions based on the qualities of the planets and when they will have most influence during the course of each year.

Fig. 6.6: 'Kalendar povsemstvennyi ili mesiatseslov na vse leta Gospodnie' (Everyday Calendar for the Entire Year of the Lord) *(1709). Source: Photogragh by Natal'ia Antonova and Inna Regentova. Reproduced with kind permission of the The State Hermitage Museum, St. Petersburg.*

Astrological verses are inscribed on either side of the ornate banner displaying the title. To the left can be read: 'The seven planets show their influence to us, they narrate the quality of every year [and] they change various things. They [the planets] are administered in the four seasons'. The verse to the right reads: 'As in spring, so in summer, as also in autumn and in the depths of winter, finally they proclaim all afflictions [with regard to] what happens to man'. The top third of the sheet is also replete with a fine panoply of astrological symbols, with the twelve signs of the zodiac encompassing allegorical depictions of the four seasons (see fig. 6.7).

Fig. 6.7: 'The Omens of All the Seasons According to the Planets (1710). Source: The State Hermitage Museum, St. Petersburg. Source: Photogragh by Natal'ia Antonova and Inna Regentova. Reproduced with kind permission of the The State Hermitage Museum, St. Petersburg.

The main body of the sheet is split into seven principal columns at the top, each illustrated by a human depiction of the planets in the spirit of the *Planetenkinder* tradition.[26] Furthermore, a lefthand column is divided into fourteen sections, with the first providing general information on the qualities of the planets. This is then followed by sections on how the ruling planet influences the four seasons, as well as its impact on sowing crops in the spring and autumn. One also finds sections devoted to how the ruling planet affects plants and trees, vines and wine, as well as meterological influences. Moreover, it is also possible to discern the influence of ruling planets on reptiles and fish, as well as the impact on human health and afflictions. Lastly, the paschal number of each planet is given, alongside information relating to the years in which it correlates to solar cycles.

In a Russian context, this sheet provides remarkable evidence of the attraction of astrological predictions and symbolism amongst leading Petrine courtiers. Moreover, it is highly significant that the source of all the astrological information is drawn verbatim from a table found in the first volume of *Specula Physico-Mathematico-Historica*, a work published in 1696 by Johann Zahn (ca. 1641–1707), of the Premonstrate Order in Würzburg.[27] Zahn was very much in the mold of the encyclpaedic polymath Athanasius Kircher (1602–1680).[28] However, unlike Kircher, Zahn was an enthusiastic advocate of astrology. Thus, in the monumental three-volumes of his *Specula*, Zahn's section on astrology repeatedly cites the work of Agrippa, Cardano, Paracelsus, Robert Fludd, and Antonio Francisco de Bonattis, among others, in order to expound his approach towards the celestial art.

---

[26] For more on the *Planetenkinder* tradition, see Dieter Blume, *Regenten des Himmels: Astrologische Bilder im Mittelalter und Renaissance* (Berlin: Akademie, 2000).

[27] The table is entitled 'Tabula Significationum & Electionum Oeconominarum ex Planeta validiore, ac Dominatore per Annum', in Johann Zahn, *Specula Physico-Mathematico-Historica*, Vol. 1 (Augsburg, 1696), p. 300.

[28] On the influence of Kircher in Russia, see Collis, *Petrine Instauration*, pp. 256–59. Also see a discussion of Collis's work on Kircher in Russia in Joscelyn Godwin, *Athanasius Kircher's Theatre of the World* (London: Thames & Hudson, 2009), p. 253.

Fig. 6.8: Frontispiece to the first volume of Johann Zahn's Specula
Physico-Mathematico-Historica *(Augsburg, 1696).*

Zahn hardly warrants a footnote in contemporary accounts
of natural philosophy in the late seventeenth century, yet the
enthusiastic embrace of his astrological predictions in
Moscow in 1710 illustrates his widespread influence at the
time. Moreover, the baroque aesthetic of his astrological
oeuvre is not only replicated in the *Bruce Calendars*, but is
also in broad accord with the wider cultural inclinations of
the Petrine court.

The fourth sheet, entitled 'Daily Predictions of Influences
According to the Course of the Moon in the Zodiac'
(*Predznamenovanie deistv na kazhdyi den' po techeniiu Luny v
zodii*), is in the same vein as the preceding publication. Verses
on an astrological theme adorn the banner on both sides of
the main heading. The upper third of the sheet contains an
illustration of the twelve signs of the zodiac in the shape of
an arch, underneath which is a depiction of the moon. The
main body of the sheet is then divided into three tables, with
the first containing information on the lunar cycle throughout the twelve zodiacal signs. The second table is split into
the twelve signs of the zodiac, and has data relating to the

lunar cycle and days, in combination with the relevant zodiacal sign. Lastly, the third table then provides extensive descriptions that recommend whether it is good, bad or inconsequential to undertake specific actions, which correlate to the signs of the zodiac. In other words, the sheet provides information vis-à-vis the position of the moon in relation to the signs of the zodiac and the corresponding possible influences on an extraordinary range of human activities. A small sample will suffice to give a flavour of the intriguing nature of the astrological advice (see fig. 6.9). For example, it provides medical help, suggesting the best times to take medicines or buy precious stones, as well as advice on when it is best to conduct alchemical experiments or to inquire about secret arts. Practical advice is also dispensed, as regards shaving, when to buy produce or move home, various agricultural matters and on military affairs, such as when best to release prisoners in order to lessen the chance of them seeking revenge. In short, the sheet offers a cornucopia of astrological advice for an esoterically-minded Russian courtier.

It is once again fascinating to note that a German source is used verbatim for all the astrological information. In this instance the sheet cites the influence of 'Martin Albert, a Theophrastic and Spagyric Medic and Metallist from Chemnitz'. In other words, a Paracelsian physician, whose tables on the passage of the moon through the twelve signs of the zodiac appeared in the third book of *Magia Naturalis* by Wolfgang Hildebrand (fl. 1610–1631), which was first published in 1610 and continued to be republished into the eighteenth century (see fig. 6.10).[29]

---

[29] For the original astrological tables by Martin Albert, see Wolfgang Hildebrand, *Neu-vermehrt, Vortrefflich, Ausserlessen Curieuses Kunst und Wunderbuch*, Bk 3 (Frankfurt am Mayn, 1704), pp. 514–17. For more on Hildebrand, see Laura Balbiani, 'Wolfgang Hildebrand e la fortuna editoriale della *Magia Naturalis*', *L'analisi linguistica e letteraria* 5 (1997): pp. 153–86.

Fig. 6.9: The fourth sheet of the Bruce Calendars entitled
Predznamenovanie deistv na kazhdyi den' po techeniiu luny v zodii
(Daily Predictions of Influences According to the Course of the
Moon in the Zodiac) (1710). *Photogragh by Natal'ia Antonova and Inna
Regentova. Reproduced with kind permission of the The State Hermitage
Museuem, St. Petersburg.*

Fig. 6.10: Frontispiece to Wolfgang Hildebrand's Neu-vermehrt,
Vortrefflich, Ausserlessen Curieuses Kunst und Wunderbuch
(Frankfurt am Mayn, 1704).

The inclusion of lengthy citations on astrology from
Zahn and Hildebrand points to the considerable input of
Jacob Bruce on the composition of the *Bruce Calendars*. Not
only did Bruce own copies of key works by both German
authors, but he also possessed the most extensive collection
of German and English astrological tomes in early
eighteenth-century Russia.[30]

The publication of the *Bruce Calendars* was endorsed by
the Russian monarch. This is testified by the fact that both
the fifth and sixth sheets, published in 1715, contain depictions of Peter the Great. In the sixth sheet, for example, the
tsar can be seen at the base, wearing a suit of armour
adorned with astrological symbols and standing beside a
globe, around which can also be seen representations of the
twelve signs of the zodiac. Saturn can also be seen standing

---

[30] For a discussion of Bruce's library collection, including his
ownership of works by Zahn and Hildebrand, see Collis, *Petrine
Instauration*, pp. 73–78. For an incomplete catalogue of Bruce's
library, see *Biblioteka Ia. V. Briusa*, ed. E. A. Savel'eva (Leningrad:
BAN, 1989). For additional catalogue listings, see *Materialy dlia
istorii Imperatorskoi Akademii Nauk, 1742–1743*, Vol. 5 (St. Petersburg,
1889), pp. 152–245.

to the right of the monarch, as well as a depiction of the Peter and Paul Fortress above the globe. It is significant that this illustration is based on an almost identical image that adorns the base of Paul Halcke's *Verbesserter Hamburgische Curiositäten Auss das 1715*, published several months before the *Bruce Calendars*.

Fig. 6.11: *Image from the frontispiece of Paul Halcke's* Verbesserter Hamburgische Curiositäten Auss das 1715 *(Hamburg, 1714).*

As mentioned, the calendars produced by Halcke in Hamburg were a key source of astronomical and astrological information for the annual *kalendar' ili mesiatseslov* publications that were printed after 1708. Thus, once again a German source was used as a template with minor alterations to accommodate the Russian context.

CONCLUSION

To conclude, it is worth citing R. A. Simonov, the leading historian of astrology in Russia, who states that 'the tsar reformer was a complicated and contradictory character [who] was not an opponent of astrology'.[31] However, I would go further and state that Peter the Great actively embraced aspects of astrological thinking in order to promote his personage and reform programme. Furthermore, as part of his broader reform of the Russian calendar, the tsar encouraged leading servitors to embrace an astrological worldview in their daily lives, based on the promotion of pocketbook almanacs and lavish instructional prints. Moreover, it is worth emphasizing that clergymen, who were mostly from the Ukraine, such as Iavorskii, and leading scientific figures, such as Jacob Bruce, formed the vanguard of Peter the Great's servitors, who were charged with

---

[31] R. A. Simonov, 'Rossiiskie pridvornye "matematiki" XVI–XVII vekov', *Voprosy istorii* 1 (1986): p. 83.

assimilating foreign aspects of astrological culture into the official and everyday sphere of Russian Court life. In other words, the Russian monarch championed forms of astrological practice that cut across religious and scientific divides that were becoming increasingly prevalent and acute in many Western European countries, particularly in France and England.

In this regard, it is significant that the Russian tsar specifically drew on Polish and German forms of astrological prognostication, which were then adapted to the demands of life at the Russian Court. Such a transfer of ideas was entirely in keeping with Peter the Great's wider borrowing of Western cultural practices and technological innovations, yet it has long been a neglected aspect of Petrine Russia.

BIBLIOGRAPHY

Balbiani, Laura. 'Wolfgang Hildebrand e la fortuna editoriale della *Magia Naturalis' L'analisi linguistica e letteraria* 5 (1997): pp. 153–86.

Bobrova, E. I., ed. *Biblioteka Petra I: ukazatel' spravochnik.* Leningrad, 1978.

Bubendey, J. F. 'Geschichte der Mathematischen Gesellschaft in Hamburg 1690–1890'. *Mitteilungen der Mathematischen Gesellschaft in Hamburg* 2, no. 1 (Leipzig: B. G. Teubner, 1890).

Chistovich, I. A., ed. 'Neizdannye propovedi Stefana Iavorskago'. *Khristianskoe chtenie.* Vols. 1 and 2 (1867): pp. 259–79, 414–29, 814–37.

Collis, Robert. *The Petrine Instauration: Religion, Esotericism and Science at the Court of Peter the Great, 1689–1725.* Turku: Annales Universitatis Turkuensis, 2007.

Cracraft, James. *The Petrine Revolution in Russian Culture.* Cambridge, MA: The Belknap Press of Harvard University Press, 2004.

Filimon, A. N. *Iakov Brius.* Moscow: Chistye vody, 2003.

Golikov, I. I. *Deianiia Petra Velikago, mudrago preobrazitelia Rossii.* Vol. 5. Moscow, 1838.

Golubev, I. F. 'Zabytye virshi Simeona Polotskogo'. *Trudy otdela drevnerusskoi literatury* 24 (1969): pp. 254–59.

Hildebrand, Wolfgang. *Neu-vermehrt, Vortrefflich, Ausserlessen Curieuses Kunst und Wunderbuch.* Frankfurt am Mayn, 1704.

Iavorskii, Stefan. 'Slova Stefana Iavorskago, mitropolita riazanskgao i muromskago'. *Trudy kievskoi dukhnovnoi akademii* 3 (July 1874): pp. 72–121.

Istomin, Karion. *Kniga liubvi znak v chesten brak.* Moscow: Izdatel'stvo "Kniga", 1989.

Korb, Johann-Georg. *Diary of an Austrian Secretary of Legation at the Court of Czar Peter the Great.* Vol. 2. Translated and edited by The Count Mac Donnell. London: Bradbury & Evans, 1863.

Pekarskii, P. *Nauka i literature v Rossii pri Petr Velikom.* Vols. 1 and 2. St. Petersburg, 1862.

Petrov, A. D. *Sobranie knig izdannikh v tsarstvovanie Petra Velikago.* St. Petersburg, 1913.

Pokrovskii, A. A. 'Kalendari i sviattsy'. *Biblioteka Moskovskoi Sinodal'noi tipografii* 5 (1911): pp. I-XLVI.

Ryan, W. F. *The Bathhouse at Midnight: An Historical Survey of Magic and Divination in Russia.* Stroud: Sutton Publishing, 1999.

Samarin, Iurii. *Stefan Iavorskii i Feofan Prokopovich kak propovedniki.* Moscow, 1844.

Schleusing, Georg Adam. *Neu-entdecktes Sibyrien oder Siewerien.* Jena, 1688.

Simonov, R. A. 'Rossiiskie pridvornye "matematiki" XVI–XVII vekov'. *Voprosy istorii* 1 (1986): pp. 76–84.

Sobolevskii, A. I. *Perevodnaia literatura Moskovskoi Rusi XIV– XVII vekov. Bibliograficheskie materially.* St. Petersburg, 1903.

Viktorov, A. E. *Opisi rukopisnykh sobranii v knigokhranilishchakh severnoi Rossii.* St. Petersburg, 1890.

Volk, Katharina. *Manilius and his Intellectual Background.* Oxford: Oxford University Press, 2009.

Wolpmann, Franz. *Die in ihrer Unruhe gestillete Seele Davids.* Stade, 1691.

Zahn, Johann. *Specula Physico-Mathematico-Historica.* Vol. 1. Augsburg, 1696.

STONEHENGE TO THE SPHINX: ESOTERIC THEORY AND PRACTICE IN TWENTIETH-CENTURY ASTROARCHAEOLOGY

Nicholas Goodrick-Clarke

ABSTRACT: Modern archaeoastronomy chiefly relies on alignment-orientated statistically-led methods, thereby claiming empirical scientific status for its studies of ancient astronomies. Scant prehistoric ethnographic data in the Old World has inhibited cultural astronomy, whereas native Indian customs and beliefs have facilitated studies of cultural astronomy in New World pyramid cultures. However, the old stones of Europe have spoken. Beginning in the late Renaissance, antiquaries and philosophers have applied various forms of cultural astronomy and astroarchaeology to present ideal or lost societies from Atlantis to Druidic England. Since the late nineteenth century, esotericists have used cultural astronomy to elicit hidden secrets from Stonehenge or to discover 'pre-sand' Egypt. This paper examines the ideas of romantic and nationalist cultural astronomers and cosmographers who interpreted prehistoric sites in early twentieth-century Germany. Despite German defeat in 1945, their legacy acquired a universalist coloration and resurfaced across the western world in the 1960s onward. I examine these ideas with respect to their philosophical sources, and identify their political and religious inspiration in modernity since 1800. Golden age myths, ancient wisdom-traditions, prophecy and apocalyptic feature in powerful echoes of Platonic, Gnostic, and neo-Hermetic thought.

Investigations of ancient monuments and their possible relationship with the sun, moon and other astronomical data reach back some three centuries in European modernity. Broadly speaking, two major classes of ancient monuments are especially prominent in these speculations, the megaliths of north-western Europe and the pyramids of ancient Egypt. Just as Sir Norman Lockyer (1836–1920), the founder of modern astroarchaeology first studied astronomical alignments in Greece, the Levant and Egypt in the 1890s, before turning his attention to Stonehenge, our story begins with antiquaries who focused their attention on the monuments in their own countries and ends with the more generalized speculations of recent archaeoastronomers whose researches concern Egypt and exotic cultures. I will argue that this progress from regional to exotic, from the particular to the universal has both historical and cultural causes, as well as political reasons. In conclusion, I will indicate that a certain current in archaeoastronomy and astroarchaeology reflects major *topoi* in the theory and practice of Western esotericism.

Archaeoastronomy has been recently defined as the study of how past people 'have understood the phenomena in the sky and what role the sky played in their cultures',[1] while Clive Ruggles has observed that archaeoastronomy should not be understood as a study of ancient astronomy in any modern sense, but as an investigation into past cultures' symbol-laden interpretations of phenomena in the sky.[2] Modern archaeoastronomy chiefly relies on alignment-orientated statistically-led methods, thereby claiming empirical scientific status for its studies of ancient astronomies. Scant prehistoric ethnographic data in the Old World has inhibited cultural astronomy, whereas native Indian customs and beliefs have facilitated studies of cultural astronomy in New World pyramid cultures.

THE DISCOVERY OF STONEHENGE

However, the old stones of Europe have spoken. The discovery of ancient monuments in Britain, France and Germany offered an obvious field for speculation as to their origin and purpose. Thus archaeoastronomy in Europe began with the mysteries posed by the ancient monuments, which have remained a central reference in most subsequent studies, thus introducing the cognate term 'astro-archaeology'. Stonehenge and Avebury in southern England, not least on account of their massive proportions and marvellous reputation, provided the initial focus. In the first

---

[1] Rolf M. Sinclair, 'The Nature of Archaeoastronomy', in *Current Studies in Archaeastronomy: Conversations across Time and Space*, ed. John W. Fountain and Rolf M. Sinclair [Fifth Oxford International Symposium on Archaeoastronomy] (Durham, NC: Carolina Academic Press, 2005), pp. 3–13.
[2] Clive Ruggles, *Ancient Astronomy* (Chicago: ABC-Clio, 2005), p. 19.

century BCE Diodorus Siculus wrote his extensive world history *Bibliotheca historica*, in which he referred to the mysterious island of Hyperborea, whose inhabitants had built a sacred precinct to Apollo and a temple spherical in shape.[3] This text has frequently been taken to signify Stonehenge in recent literature, but Diodorus' fifth volume remained unknown to European writers until translated into Latin by Poggio Bracciolini at Bologna in 1472. The first European accounts of Stonehenge included Henry of Huntingdon's *Historia Anglorum* and Geoffrey of Monmouth's *History of the Kings of Britain* in the twelfth century. Geoffrey's story described the monument as a memorial to the numerous British nobles slain by the invading Saxon army of Hengist and Horsa in the fifth century CE. The Romano-British leader Aurelius Ambrosius avenged the defeat and commissioned the legendary Merlin to transport the Dance of the Giants, a collection of stones with magical properies from Ireland, orginally taken by giants from Africa, to England where they were erected at Stonehenge. This story was current for nearly five hundred years, repeated in the poetry of Alexander Neckham (1157–1217), in Langtoft's chronicles (*c.* 1300), and in a variant version by Polydore Vergil in his *Anglia Historia* (1534) that the monument was the sepulchre of Ambrosius.[4]

During the Renaissance the English nation-state evinced a closer concern with sovereignty and its historical identity, and attention turned to the countryside and the cultural heritage of England. The poet and antiquary John Leland (1506–1552) wrote several topographies based on itineraries across England and Wales, the Elizabethan magus John Dee (1527–1609) busied himself with the British founding legends of Brutus and Arthur, itineraries and possible excavations, while the chronicler Raphael Holinshed (1529–1580) produced his three-voume *Chronicles of England, Scotlande and Irelande* (1577), which served William Shakespeare (1564–1616) in the composition of his history plays. William Camden (1551–1623) published *Britannia* (1586), the first topographical survey of the islands of Great Britain and

---

[3] Hecateus of Abdera *c.* 350 BCE, quoted by Diodorus Siculus, *Histories* V, cited in Rodney Castleden, *The Stonehenge People: An Exploration of Life in Neolithic Britain 4700–2000BC* (London: Routledge & Kegan Paul, 1987), p. 138.

[4] T. D. Kendrick, *The Druids: A Study in Keltic Prehistory* (London: Frank Cass, 1927), p. 4.

Ireland, and the first detailed historical account of the reign of Elizabeth I of England.

By the early seventeenth century public and scholarly attention had lit upon the ancient monuments. In 1620, while staying with Philip, Earl of Pembroke at his seat, nearby Wilton House, King James I watched an excavation organised by the Duke of Buckingham in the middle of Stonehenge. His curiosity aroused, the king instructed Inigo Jones (1573–1652), the surveyor-general of the royal buildings and pioneering Palladian architect, to prepare a report on the monument, posthumously published as *The most notable Antiquity of Great Britain, vulgarly called Stone-Heng on Salisbury Plain* (1655). His conclusion that Stonehenge was not built by the ancient Britons, but was a Roman temple of the Tuscan order to the sky god Coelus, reads rather like a justification for Jones' introduction of neo-classical architectural principles to Britain, than an appraisal of the site itself. This hypothesis of Roman origins was controversial as Edmund Bolton had in 1624 claimed that the monument marked the tomb of the British queen Boadicea. On the basis of a comparison with Danish megaliths suggested by Ole Wormius, Walter Charleton (1619–1707) then identified Stonehenge as a ninth-century Danish monument in his *Chorea Gigantum* (1663). The debate continued with polemical works published by Inigo Jones' son-in-law John Webb as *A Vindication of Stone-Heng Restored* (1665) and John Gibbon's *A Fools Bolt soon shott at Stonage* (1665).

THE DRUIDS AND THE STONE CIRCLES

The most important of the early Stonehenge antiquarians was certainly John Aubrey (1626–1697), an influential and well-connected figure, fellow of the Royal Society and friend of the king. Born at Easton Percy near Malmesbury, John Aubrey is best known for his gossipy *Brief Lives*, but he should be equally celebrated for his discovery of Britain's stone circles. In 1649, while out hunting he chanced upon the wonders of Avebury and became fascinated by the stones. Surmising that the stones were clearly some form of temple, but where neither Roman, Saxon nor Dane had been, he concluded that they must have been previously erected when the only priesthood in Britain were the Druids. Stuart Piggott has documented how the Druids themselves had exercised the imagination of classical writers in variants of hard and soft primitivism and these alternative images of the ancient Celtic priesthood also coloured the European reception of its ancestral forbears from the Renaissance onwards.[5] In his 1659 sketch of ancient Wiltshire, Aubrey was the first antiquary to link Stonehenge and Avebury with the Druids: 'I come by comparative arguments to give clear evidence that these monuments (Avebury, Stonehenge, and the like) were Pagan temples… and have also with humble submission to better judgment, offered a probability that they were Temples of the Druids.'[6] In 1663 he revisited Stonehenge for the benefit of King Charles II and again elaborated on the Druidical origin of the stone circles. 'Their religion is at large described by Caesar. Their priests were Druids. Some of their temples I pretend to have restored, as Avebury, Stonehenge, &c., as also British sepulchres'.[7]

Over the years John Aubrey compiled the first, objective compilation of pre-Roman monuments in Britain from the Merry Maidens in Cornwall to the moon-aligned recumbent circles of Northern Scotland. Between lay famous rings like the Rollright Stones in Oxfordshire and Long Meg and her Daughters in the Lake District. For years he was 'never off horseback' searching and his scribbled notes formed the foundation of stone circle studies.[8] Aubrey influenced Dr. Robert Plot (1640–1696), the historian of Staffordshire and Oxfordshire, first professor of chemistry at Oxford, and keeper of the Ashmolean Museum, and also probably John Toland (1670–1722), who wrote a history of the Druids, acknowledging Aubrey's views.[9] Aubrey's own study, *Templa Druidum* was relegated to a chapter-heading in his major work, *Monumenta Britannia*, but this remained unpublished, although Edmund Gibson printed extracts

---

[5] Stuart Piggott, *The Druids* (London: Thames & Hudson, 1968), pp. 123–30.

[6] John Aubrey, *Topographical Collections*, ed. J. E. Jackson (Devizes, 1862), p. 317, cited in Kendrick, *The Druids*, p. 8.

[7] Peter Lancaster Brown, *Megaliths, Myths and Men: An introduction to astro-archaeology* (Poole: Blandford Press, 1976), p. 54; Piggott, *The Druids*, p. 134.

[8] Aubrey Burl, *John Aubrey and Stone Circles: Britain's First Archaeologist from Avebury to Stonehenge* (Amberley, 2010).

[9] Kendrick, *The Druids*, p. 9.

from the *Templa Druidum* in his 1695 edition of Camden's *Britannia*.[10]

This historical review of speculation concerning the origin and purpose of Stonehenge and Avebury highlights the intellectual stages in the emergence of esoteric astro-archaeology. In the Renaissance the Druids were recognized as pre-Roman ancestors in Britain, France and also Germany, but were still portrayed as savage and cruel in such works as Elias Schedius' *De Dis Germanis* (1648) and Esaias Pufendorf, *Dissertation de Druidibus* (1650). Although he linked the Druids with Stonehenge and Avebury, Aubrey himself still evinced the mood of hard primitivism, an attitude evident in the state of nature described by his friend and Malmesbury neighbour Thomas Hobbes in *Leviathan* (1651).

Aubrey's enthusiasm for the stone circles and tentative suggestion of their origin in the ancient Celtic priesthood bequeathed a persistent identification of the megalithic monuments with Druidry that has endured in the lay reception of Stonehenge up to the present. In 1718 Aubrey's manuscript *Monumenta* was seen and noted by William Stukeley (1687–1765), a young Lincolnshire doctor with strong antiquarian interests, who made his first visit to Stonehenge in May 1719, later visiting the hardly known Avebury the same year. Over the next five years he visited both Stonehenge and Avebury frequently in the summer months, surveying, sketching, and exploring the wider landscape around them.[11] By profession a doctor, Stukeley's wide range of scientific interests secured him a fellowship of the Royal Society and he became the first secretary of the Society of Antiquaries, while his books identify him as the finest contemporary field-archaeologist in England. Only with the advent of Druids-as-wished for in the pre-Romantic era does one find the genesis of a nexus between megalithic monuments and gentle Druids representing a wise priest-hood. By the time he published the results of his extensive field observations as *Stonehenge* (1740) and *Abury* (1743), his speculations on the monuments had absorbed his romantic notions of the Druids, patriarchal religion and a belief that the Anglican Church was the heir to God's original and

---

[10] Piggott, *The Druids*, pp. 135–36.

[11] Neil Mortimer, *Stukeley Illustrated: William Stukeley's Rediscovery of Britain's Ancient Sites* (Sutton Mallet: Green Magic, 2003), pp. 10–12, 41–44.

universal religion. Stukeley's work was hugely influential in two respects: first, his graphical representations of the stone circles at Avebury as serpent temples of 'Dracontia' (an idea taken from Pliny about the Druids of Gaul using a magical snake's egg) together with engravings of Druids cemented the Druidical association of the megalithic monuments for posterity. Stukeley's competent empirical field-archaeology was mixed with a soft primitivist, typically pre-Romantic, notion of the Druids as wise priests of a proto-Christian religion, whose concepts anticipated the doctrine of the Trinity. Besides making the strong association with Druids, Stukeley was the first antiquarian to make an astronomical reference to Stonehenge, noting that its principal axis pointed to the north-east and the rising of the sun on midsummer day.[12]

Stukeley's lead on the Druidical Stonehenge was taken up by John Wood's *Choir Gaure Vulgarly called Stonehenge, on Salisbury Plain* (1747) and John Smith's *Choir Gaur the Grand Orrery of the Ancient Druids* (1771), and the latter added his own astronomical theories by dividing the vallum circle into 360 equal parts to show that the monument was a calendar of stones rather than a device to show planetary motions. Smith supposed that thirty stones in one of the circles multiplied by twelve, there being twelve signs in the Greek zodiac, yielded the number of 360 days in the ancient solar year.

While the Romantic reception of the Druids would follow its own career in literature, art and historiography, the British megalithic monuments next attracted archaeologists with metrological and astronomical concerns during the nineteenth century. These included Sir Norman Lockyer, William, Flinders Petrie and Charles Piazzi Smyth, all of whom had also been involved in surveys of the Eygyptian pyramids in the 1880s. The intersection of megalithic studies with Egyptomania is a moot concern of astroarchaeology, to which I will return at the close of this paper in the context of Western esotericism.

MODERN EGYPTOLOGY AND PYRAMIDOLOGY

The beginning of modern Egyptology is traditionally dated to Napoleon Bonaparte's military expedition to Egypt (1798–1801). The invading French army was accompanied by the

---

[12] Brown, *Megaliths, Myths and Men*, pp. 56–57.

engineer Jean-Marie Coutelle (1748–1835) and the architect Jean-Baptiste Lepère (1761–1844) who made a detailed survey of the monuments at Giza, Saqqaura and the Memphis sites. One highly significant discovery was the Rosetta Stone, which enabled François Champollion (1790–1829) to decipher the hieroglyphs in 1822. Returning from the campaign, Dominique Vivant, Baron de Denon (1747–1825) established the *Musée Napoleon*, now the Louvre, and published his popular *Voyage dans la Basse et al Haute Égypte pendant les campagnes du general Bonaparte* (1802), which was translated into English and also German.[13] Between 1809 and 1829 the French government published a nineteen-volume work called *Description de l'Égypt* (1809–1829). A major German contribution to Egyptology was made by Karl Richard Lepsius (1810–84) with his *Denkmäler aus Ægypten und Æthiopien* in twelve volumes (1849–59).[14] The era of unauthorized excavations ended with Egyptologists formally recognised once the Turkish viceroy Said Pasha appointed Auguste Mariette (1821–81) director of all works relating to Egypt's antiquities in 1850.[15]

Besides this current of archaeology, esoteric speculations continued with Alexandre Lenoir's *Nouvelle explication des hieroglyphs* (1809) and A. P. J. Devismes' *Nouvelles recherches sur l'origine et la destination des pyramides d'Égypte* (1812). Gérard de Nerval's *Voyage en Orient* (1850) encouraged new avenues for the boldest speculations regarding the esoteric powers of the Egyptian priests. Metrology was a key theme in the early study of Egyptian monuments. Already in 1637 John Greaves, professor of geometry at Gresham College, London made his first of several studies in Egypt and Italy, making numerous measurements of buildings and monuments, including the Great Pyramid. These activities caused him to be deprived of his Gresham professorship for having neglected his duties, but it did fuel many centuries of interest in metrology of the ancient cultures by Sir Isaac Newton and the French Academy.

The theme of the Great Pyramid arose as a widespread current in popular European thought and literature with the

---

[13] James Stevens Curl, *The Egyptian Revival: Ancient Egypt as the Inspiration for Design Motifs in the West* (New York: Routledge, 2000), pp. 204–5; John Ray, *The Rosetta Stone and the Rebirth of Modern Egypt* (Cambridge, MA: Harvard University Press, 2007), p. 32.
[14] Curl, *The Egyptian Revival*, p. 318.
[15] Ray, *The Rosetta Stone*, p. 113.

publication of *The Great Pyramid* (1859) by John Taylor (1781–1864). He claimed that Noah constructed the pyramid on the English inch-based measurement system, a boon to English critics of the French revolutionary metric system, which led in turn to the patriotic idea that Noah had later traveled to England bringing his measurement system with him. Taylor's suggestions were further developed by Charles Piazzi Smyth (1819–1900), the royal astronomer of Scotland, who integrated Taylor's work into British Israelism, a widespread religious denomination that identified the various European nations as descendants of each of the twelve tribes of Israel.[16] Taylor's theories inspired Smyth, also an archaeologist, to travel to Egypt to study and measure the pyramid, subsequently publishing his book *Our Inheritance in the Great Pyramid* (1864), claiming that the measurements he obtained from the Great Pyramid of Giza indicated a unit of length, the pyramid inch, equivalent to 1.001 British inches, that could have been the standard of measurement by the pyramid's architects. From this he extrapolated a number of other measurements, including the pyramid pint, the sacred cubit, and the pyramid scale of temperature. Smyth claimed that the inch was a God-given measure handed down through the centuries from the time of Israel, and that the architects of the pyramid could only have been directed by the hand of God. To support this Smyth said that, in measuring the pyramid, he found the number of inches in the perimeter of the base equaled 1000 times the number of days in a year, and found a numeric relationship between the height of the pyramid in inches to the distance from Earth to the Sun, measured in statute miles.

STONEHENGE AND MODERN ARCHAEASTRONOMY

The religio-metrological theories of Smyth and Taylor were widely known in British non-conformist circles beyond British Israelism. William Petrie (1821–1908), a member of the Plymouth Brethren, a civil engineer and professional surveyor, regarded Smyth's theories as a powerful reconciliation of science and religion. He trained his son William Flinders Petrie (1853–1942) early in surveying skills and

---

[16] Michael Barkun, *Religion and the Racist Right: The Origins of the Christian Identity Movement* (Chapel Hill, NC: University of North Carolina Press, 1997), pp. 12–14.

encouraged his archaeological interests. Influenced by Smyth's metrological ideas, Flinders Petrie surveyed local Kent sites, proceeding to Stonehenge in 1872 (*aet.* 19), publishing his findings as *Inductive Metrology, or the recovery of ancient measures from the monuments* (1877) and *Stonehenge* (1880). He then progressed to Egypt, where from 1880 to 1882 he conducted the first triangulation survey of the Giza pyramids and the Sphinx. His work *The Pyramids and the Temples of Gizeh* (1887) provided a landmark in the history of Egyptology. Despite Petrie's disappointment in Smyth's pyramid-inch theories, he was henceforth immersed in the archaeology of Egypt and spent the rest of his career on this subject with the exception of brief periods he spent excavating in Palestine.

Sir Norman Lockyer (1836–1920), an English astronomer and physicist, and founder and editor of the journal *Nature* (est. 1896), developed a scientific approach to the investigation of prehistoric astronomy, and launched the modern interest in the subject. Proceeding from early surveys of the orientation of Greek, Levantine and Egyptian temples in the 1880s to work at Stonehenge in 1901, Lockyer inaugurated the scientific study of astroarchaeology. His books on this subject, *The Dawn of Astronomy* (1894) and *Stonehenge and other British Stone Monuments Astronomically Considered* (1906), were widely published and widely read in the late nineteenth and early years of the twentieth century. Lockyer concluded that early British megalithic sites were mostly orientated to the rising or setting sun at the quarter days, in November, February, May and August, or to stars which rose before the sun at those times of year. He believed that customs changed over the centuries, and later megalithic sites were orientated mainly towards the solstices. Henry Boyle Somerville (1863–1936), an Irishman trained in hydrographic survey and a captain in the Royal Navy, encountered Lockyer's books in 1908 and thereafter spent much time surveying the coastlines of Scotland and Ireland. Boyle Somerville suggested that many megalithic alignments were towards the extreme rising and setting positions of the moon, and was the first to produce accurate scale plans of many important sites.

Alexander Thom (1894–1985), a Scotsman and professor of engineering at Oxford, discovered an interest in megalithic astronomy in the late 1930s, subsequently undertaking surveys of hundreds of stone circle sites in Scotland,

England, Wales, and Brittany. The subsequent analysis of the results led him to believe that an eight, or even sixteen-month solar calendar was in use in prehistoric times. He also confirmed the megalith builders' interest in the movements of the moon, and particularly in the extreme positions of the moon's 18.6 year cycle, the major and minor standstills. Most importantly for the metrological aspect of astroarchaeology, Thom came to the conclusion that there must have been a common unit of measurement was in use in prehistoric times, which he named the 'megalithic yard' of 2.72 feet (0.83 metres).[17] Thom's later work was published as *Megalithic Sites in Britain* (1967), *Megalithic Lunar Observatories* (1971), and *Megalithic Remains in Britain and Britanny* (1978), the last title co-authored with his son Archie after they had completed a detalied survey of the Carnac stone rows from 1970 to 1974. In 1988 Clive Ruggles edited a memorial volume to Thom containing many papers about his work from numerous professional astronomers and archaeologists relating to Thom's work in geometry (the methods used to set out the megalithic rings), mensuration or metrology (the possible use of standard units of measurement in setting out the rings or rows), and astronomy (the connection between the structures aligned upon the horizon and the rising and setting positions of the sun, moon or stars).[18]

Gerald Stanley Hawkins (1928–2003), an English astronomer and author best known for his work in the field of archaeoastronomy became professor of astronomy at Boston University in 1957. He wrote widely on numerous subjects, including tektites, meteors, and the steady-state universe theory. Hawkins applied the technological resources of the university to studying the astronomical alignments of ancient megalithic sites. He fed the positions of standing stones and other features at Stonehenge into an early IBM 7090 computer to model solar and lunar movements. Hawkins argued that the various features at Stonehenge were arranged in such a way as to predict a variety of astronomical events in *Stonehenge Decoded* (1965). Hawkins' work appeared to offer fresh mathematical and astronomical evidence for interpreting Stonehenge as a giant prehistoric

---

[17] Alexander Thom, 'A Statistical Examination of the Megalithic Sites in Britain', *Journal of the Royal Statistical Society* Series A (General) 118, no. 3 (1955): pp. 275–95.

[18] *Records in Stone: Papers in Memory of Alexander Thom*, ed. C. L. N. Ruggles (Cambridge: Cambridge University Press, 1988).

observatory as opposed to a primitive temple. The archaeological community was sceptical and the eminent prehistorian Richard Atkinson denounced the book, which was correspondingly popular amongst the members of 1960s counterculture, who shared a similar view of the 'wisdom of the ancients' suggested by Alexander Thom's surveys.

Hawkins' and Thom's work implied a different picture of the nature and organisation of Neolithic and Early Bronze Age society to that which archaeologists generally saw. Euan MacKie, curator of the Hunterian Museum at Glasgow University, then attempted to redraw this image of the prehistoric past on the basis of his interests in archaeological methodology and the relevance of Darwinian theory to the physical and social evolution of humanity, particularly to great periods of change like the origins of agriculture and cities. MacKie has argued that Thom's archaeoastronomical discoveries demonstrated the existence of a prehistoric class of wise men or 'astronomer-priests' who had great authority and directed the erection of the stones and built up an expertise in empirical astronomy. This view was in contrast to the common interpretation of Neolithic society as mainly consisting of dispersed, isolated and egalitarian farming groups.[19] MacKie left open the question of whether these priesthoods were autochthonous or migrant Oriental religious technicians from the Near East, a thesis that echoed earlier diffusionist theories and the more recent work of Walter Burkert on Oriental influences on archaic Greek culture.[20]

GERMAN *VÖLKISCH* IDEOLOGY AND OTTO SIGFRID REUTER'S ARCHAEOASTRONOMY

If the English antiquaries had celebrated the ancient monuments (and their putative prehistoric priests) in successive ages of ascendant Renaissance statehood, the English Civil War and Restoration, or Pre-Romanticism, German antiquarianism followed a different course owing to other historical circumstances. Jost Hermand reminds us that

---

[19] Euan MacKie, *The Megalith Builders* (London: Phaidon Press, 1977), pp. 190–99.
[20] Ibid., pp. 170–71, 196; Walter Burkert, *The Orientalizing Revolution: The Near Eastern Influence on Greek Culture in the Early Archaic Age* (Cambridge, MA: Harvard University Press, 1992).

throughout German history from the sixteenth century until the present 'the ideal of a "Teutonic" race has surfaced whenever notions of a distinct volkish identity, national origin or innate German character were at issue'.[21] Ancient Germans were known through a sole surviving copy of Tacitus' *Germania,* which was published in Italy in 1455 in a Catholic polemic to show how beneficial the Roman Catholic Church had been for the barabarous Germans. However, Tacitus' work actually strove to demonstrate the ancient Germans' qualities of loyalty, courage, virtue, nobility, simplicity, and love of freedom as an admonition to the Romans whom he ferared were given to luxury, licence, and decandence. A later generation of German humanists including Conrad Celtis, Ulrich von Hutten, and Philipp Melanchthon writing between 1500 and 1540 found these virtues provided modern Germans with a history and identity that supported the Lutheran break with Rome, while emphasising values of thrift, cleanliness and simplicity espoused by the emergent merchant class of the sixteenth century. In the late eighteenth century ancient Germans returned in a sentimental guise to German literature and thought (the *Göttinger Hain,* Klopstock, Ossian, Johann Gottfried Herder, and the *Sturm und Drang*), as the emergent middle classes celebrated authenticity, originality, freedom, and unspoilt virtue while seeking to distance themelves culturally and politically from a Francophile, French-speaking, French-imitating absolutist nobility. During the Wars of Liberation against Napoleonic France, the anti-French discourse of German identity was trumpeted by such champions of nationalism as Johann Gottlieb Fichte (1762–1814), Ernst Moritz Arndt (1769–1860), and Friedrich Ludwig Jahn (1778–1852). At this time nationalism was decidly democratic, even republican, a cause among radical students after the Congress of Vienna (1815), which restored the old conservative-aristocratic regime across Europe.[22]

German nationalism was itself frustrated by the mosaic of small particularist principalities and duchies alongside the larger states of Prussia and Austria, just as its democratic tendency was checked by the failure of the revolutions of

---

[21] Jost Hermand, *Old Dreams of a New Reich: Volkish Utopias and National Socialism* (Bloomington: Indiana University Press, 1992), p. 2.

[22] Hermand, *Old Dreams of a New Reich,* pp. 5–23.

1848. Slow progress towards unification encouraged Germans to conceive of national identity less in politically effective institutions as in cultural terms. Once Bismarck's defeat of Denmark (1864), Austria (1866), and France (1871) brought German unification under Prussian leadership in the Second Reich, belligerent, annexationist, and Pan-German attitudes colonised nationalist ideology. An idealized Romantic image of medieval Germany was invoked to prove her claim to unity, while Norse sagas and Germanic prehistory often supplied a mythological theme in nationalist sentiment. A 'progressive reaction' heralded a new kind of *völkisch* ideology, so named after the quasi-metaphysical atttributes of the German *Volk,* combining anti-liberalism, racial anti-Semitism, and even occultism in a platform of defensive German identity from the 1870s onwards.[23]

The *völkisch* ideology with its interest in racial theories about Aryans, ancient Teutons, Germanic gods and myths provided an intellectual-cultural legitimation for national identity, chauvinist militarism, and racial supremacism against the perceived encirclement by the perennial French enemy and the Slavs in the German Reich, and against the growing political assertion of the subject nationalities of polyglot Habsburg empire in Austria-Hungary. German archaeoastronomy and astroarchaeology took strength from this *völkisch* movement already well established after 1900 in numerous orders, leagues, societies, and youth groups, well provided with books and periodicals in this vein.[24]

Otto Sigfrid Reuter (1876–1949) was a prominent researcher into ancient German culture and also a dedicated pioneer of the *völkisch,* neopagan German Faith Movement, founding the Deutschgläubige(-religiöse) Gemeinschaft and the Deutscher Orden in 1911. Born at Leer (East Friesland), the son of a maritime navigation instructor, Reuter studied humanities in Altona and Leipzig before joining the Reich Post and Telegraph service, eventually working as director of telegraphs at Bremen. He had studied under the nationalist archaeologist Gustav Kossinna (1858–1931) and soon linked these interests to the old Norse sagas. His first book, *Sigfrid oder Christus?!* (1910), anonymously authored by 'a German'

---

[23] George L. Mosse, *The Crisis of German Ideology: Intellectual Origins of the Third Reich* (London: Weidenfeld & Nicolson, 1966), pp. 4–6.
[24] Uwe Puschner, *Die völkische Bewegung im wilhelmischen Kaiserreich; Sprache-Rasse-Religion* (Darmstadt: Wissenschaftliche Buchgesell-schaft, 2001), pp. 9–26.

outlined his neopagan concerns, with a first chapter on race and religion, describing how the ancient Germans were converted on pain of death to Christianity. After the First World War, Reuter published a learned work on the Edda, ancient Aryan religion, cosmology, and science. *Das Rätsel der Edda und der arische Urglaube* in two volumes (1921, 1923) contained numerous charts relating to astronomical calculations, calendars, and cosmology. The chapters of the first volume covered the excavations of Boghazköi / The World-Tree / The Rainbow Bridge / Ancient Germanic Constellations / Interpreting Nordic Rock Paintings / The heavenly number (The Gates of Valhalla—The world-picture of the Edda—Revelation of Revelation) / The Queen of Heaven and her necklace / The origin of Germanic prophecy and the Apocalypse / The hour of destruction. The work drew from old Hindu religious texts Indian and ancient Norse epics in support of their common Indo-European heritage, thus following a tradition in 'Aryan' studies that reached back to the mainstream anthropological and philological scholarship of the nineteenth century. Reuter found that various numbers in the Edda, for example the number of the *Einheerer* (guardians of Odin), corresponded to the yugas or world-ages in Hindu Puranic mythology; on Ragnarök, the Last Day, 800 *Einheerer* ride forth from the 540 gates of Valhalla to defeat Fenris-Wolf and Loki. Their product is 432,000, the number of years in the Kali Yuga, the last 'iron' age of the world prior to its destruction. The second volume included chapters on figures in Germanic sagas and myth, Aryan calendars, and the doctrine of the ages.[25] His major work was *Germanische Himmelskunde* (1934), which comprised more than 760 pages of analysis including a reconstruction of the old Saxon constellations, astronomical aspects in the layout of German villages, and the Vikings' navigational techniques by the sky. He also demonstrated the triumph of the Germanic eight-fold division of the sky or

---

[25] Otto Sigfrid Reuter, *Das Rätsdel der Edda und der arische Urglaube*, 2 vols (Bad Berka; Verlag Deutsche Gemeinschaft, 1923), II: Altertum und Gegenwart / Argo / Die Gaumensperre des Wolfes / Die himmlische Mühle / Yggdrasil und die heilige Palme / Idafeld / Nordische Felsbilder—Fußsohlenbilder / Wandelsterne / Lichthirsch / Die arische Zeitrechnung / Schöpfungssage (Ymir, Audumla) / Odin und der Sturm / Weltalterlehre / Aufbau des Glaubens (Sinnbilder, Baldersage) / Die Vollendung der Schöpfung.

landscape over the traditional Christian medieval twelve-fold division, lunar and solar observations, Nordic traditions, and old customs in surveying. He also rediscovered and researched the obscure writings of the medieval Icelandic astronomer Oddi Helgason (1070–1140).

GERMAN ASTROARCHAEOLOGY

Lockyer's work was godfather to another astroarchaeological current which flourished in the wake of the *völkisch* (nationalist-racialist) ideology prevailing in Germany before the First World War. If German archaeoastromy had a *völkisch* motive in Reuter's work, the publication of the second edition of Norman Lockyer's *Stonehenge* in 1909 was also influential. In 1913 a German engineer Albrecht wrote a favourable article on Lockyer's observations at Stonehenge and Salisbury in *Das Weltall* (1914–15), the astronomical journal edited by Friedrich Simon Archenhold (1861–1939), director of the national observatory at Treptow near Berlin. In 1920 a German priest Father Joseph Leugering applied Albrecht's speculations on Lockyer's lines around Stonehenge to his own landscape in Westphalia, finding alignments of ancient sites which appeared to be at multiples and submultiples of a fixed measure, the old Germanic *Raste*, equivalent to 44 kilometres. Johann Leugering would later publish his study *Hümling-Emsland* (1936), while his associate Dr. Josef Heinsch, a lawyer and regional planner extended Leugering's studies into a coherent system of sacred geography. Heinsch investigated numerous locations in Germany, the district around Chartres, the Stonehenge area, and sites in Bohemia to conclude that ancient sites were often linked by a 'solar year line', oriented 6 degrees either north or south of east. These sites, he claimed, joined solar and lunar sites and from these pairs of sites solar lines radiated out at fixed orientations. In the Salisbury-Stonehenge area he discovered sixteen solar year lines. To quote Heinsch,

> Pre-Christian sacred and cultural structures can be understood only by adopting the viewpoint of the ancients. For them everything mundane was bound up with the divine. All human thoughts and actions were subordinated to the energizing influence of the all-powerful divine forces. Their philosophy and wisdom culminated in the knowledge that 'as above, so below', and in the attempt to bring all their activities and ambitions into harmony with higher nature,

the divine will. This ancient belief in the unity of all life and the analogy and reflection of the great in the small finds its [...] representation in the imagery of microcosm-macrocosm.[26]

In 1933 a medieval geometrical mosaic pavement was discovered beneath the quire of Xanten Cathedral in Westphalia, northwestern Germany which displayed a square marked with lines and diagonals. Heinsch surveyed the mosaic and found it had the same midsummer sunrise alignment as the Avenue at Stonehenge. Heinsch was impressed by the Xanten mosaic pavement's resemblance to the ancient cosmographic diagrams in Norse, Chinese, and Mexican cosmology. He also found that the orientations of the mosaic's Germanic eight- and sixteen-fold division pointed to important churches, mountains and other significant features within the wider region.[27] Heinsch's articles referred to the work of German archaeoastronomers Prof. Hopmann (Leipzig), Prof. Miller (Postdam), and the theories of Otto Sigfrid Reuter and Wilhelm Teudt and were published in *Hagal,* the journal devoted to runological and Norse-Germanic researches, the organ of the Edda Gesellschaft, originally founded by the *völkisch* journalist and Ariosophist, Rudolf John Gorsleben in 1925 and subsequently edited by Werner von Bülow.[28]

If Heinsch had been inspired by Lockyer's work at Stonehenge, he was even more strongly influenced by the work of Wilhelm Teudt, whose studies of the sacred geography of the Externsteine and the wider Teutoburger Forest area ensured him an enduring place in the gallery of nationalist astroarchaeologists. Wilhelm Teudt (1868–1942) was born in Bergkirchen (Schaumburg-Lippe) and studied evangelical theology in Berlin, Leipzig, Tübingen, and Bonn, becoming a pastor in his native principality in 1885 and the

---

[26] Josef Heinsch, *The Xanten Mosaic-Cosmogram,* trans. Michael Behrend (Bar Hill, Cambridge: Fenris-Wolf, 1979). Originally published in *Der Grafschafter* 23 (September 1933), and again in *Hagal* (March 1935).

[27] Ibid., back cover; Josef Heinsch, 'On the Rediscovery of Prechristian Geomancy', *Journal of Geomancy* 3, no. 2 (1979): pp. 38–41. Originally published in *Hagal* (May 1935).

[28] Nicholas Goodrick-Clarke, *The Occult Roots of Nazism: The Ariosophists of Germany and Austria 1890–1935* (London: I. B. Tauris, 2004), pp. 155–60.

director of the home mission at Frankfurt am Main in 1895. However, in 1908 Teudt resigned from the pastorate, becoming secretary of the Kepler League for the Advancement of Science (est. 1907), an anti-Darwinian society of evangelical academics. In 1909 Teudt published an attack on Ernst Haeckel's evolutionary theories. Following the French occupation of the Ruhr after the First World War, Teudt moved to Detmold, where he started the Cheruskerbund, a Lippe unit of the paramilitary Org. Escherich Freikorps. From the mid-1920s Teudt devoted himself to *völkisch* Germanic studies, wherein his speciality was the discovery of ancient German cult centres, first publishing articles in the archaeological journal *Mannus*. Teudt gathered a circle of supporters, founding the Vereinigung der Freunde germanischer Vorgeschichte in 1928, which began publishing the journal *Germanien* in 1929. In the same year he published his major work *Germanische Heiligtümer* (1929), which had run to four editions by 1936, although it met with rejection from academic archaeologists from the outset.[29]

Teudt's basic hypothesis was that the ancient Germans had possessed a high culture prior to their contact with the Romans and West Franks. Christianization imposed by Charlemagne in the late eighth century had led to a cultural break; the predominantly wooden architecture and works of art had left no significant remains. Teudt confined his research chiefly to the region south-west of Detmold, celebrated in ancient German history as the site of Arminius (Hermann) the Cheruskan's victory over Varus' Roman armies in 9 CE. Teudt called the region the Osningmark in a clear reference to Ernst Wachler's popular *völkisch* novel *Osning* (1914), which identified the Teutoburger Forest with its Externsteine as a Germanic Olympus, replete with Germanic legend.[30] The Externsteine, a massive stack rock formation rising 100 feet above a lake was identified by Teudt as a Saxon Irminsul cult centre, while its upper chamber (most likely a Christian chapel from Charlemagne's time) was a solar observatory. The Gierke Hof in Osterholz was an ancient academy, while a cursus in the nearby

---

[29] *Wilhelm Teudt im Kampf um die Germanenehre. Eine Auswahl von Teudts Schriften*, ed. Rudolf Bünte (Bielefeld and Leipzig: Velhagen & Klasing, 1940).
[30] Hermand, *Old Dreams for a New Reich*, p. 40.

Langelau served as a racecourse. The tumuli east of the Langelau were regarded as a significant triple hill sanctuary, while the Hünnenkirche in Kohlstädt was of Germanic origin and may have been the tower of the seeress Veleda mentioned by Tacitus.[31]

The entire area is saturated in Germanic myth. The great pagan world-pillar called the Irminsul was supposed to have stood here until it was cut down after Charlemagne's conquest of the Saxons in 772. Nearby stands the brass colossus of the Hermannsdenkmal by Ernst von Bandel, erected as an act of national piety between 1841 and 1875 in memory of the Wars of Liberation against the French.[32] Amongst these historical references to national identity stood the enigmatic crags of the Externsteine—but was it a natural feature or an ancient shrine? Cut into the rock of the Externsteine are a number of passages, chambers and chapels. One of these, perched on top of the Tower Rock, is the notable *sacellum,* officially identified as a Christian rock sanctuary with a small altar and a small circular window reminiscent of Carolingian Romanesque sculpture, which Teudt regarded as a solar observatory. At the foot of the southwest face of the easternmost rock is carved a large relief of the deposition of Christ from the Cross. Joseph of Arimathea is standing on what appears to be a bent Irminsul, symbolizing the triumph of Christianity over the old Germanic religion at this former major pagan Saxon pagan sanctuary following Charlemagne's victory.[33]

After the National Socialist seizure of power in 1933, Teudt was courted by the government and party, which he joined in 1933 or 1935. Suitors included Rudolf Hess's Reichsbund für Volkstum und Heimat, an umbrella agency for folklore, local history and conservation. Alfred Rosenberg's Kampfbund für deutsche Kultur, Hans Reinerth's Reichsbund für Deutsche Vorgeschichte, and Heinrich

---

[31] Wilhelm Teudt, *Germanische Heiligtümer. Beiträge zur Aufdeckung der Vorgeschichte, ausgehend von den Externsteinen, den Lippequellen und der Teutoburg* (Jena: Eugen Diederichs Verlag, 1929).

[32] George L. Mosse, *The Nationalization of the Masses: Political Symbolism and Mass Movements in Germany from the Napoleonic Wars Through the Third Reich* (New York: Howard Fertig, 1975), pp. 58–62.

[33] Wilhelm Teudt, *Germanische Heiligtümer,* 2nd ed. (Jena: Eugen Diederichs, 1931), pp. 47–55. Compare with Wilhelm Teudt, *Die Externsteine als germanisches Heiligtum* (Jena: Eugen Diederichs Verlag, 1934), pp. 37–45.

Himmler's Deutsches Ahnenerbe all vied for Teudt's expertise. Teudt settled for Himmler, not least because many of his own critics had joined forces with Rosenberg. Already in 1933 Teudt called for the area including the Externsteine to be declared a 'holy memorial grove' as the Osninghain.[34] Himmler responded positively to this suggestion and declared the whole Detmold area to be 'an area of outstanding importance to the SS worldview'. In 1936 Teudt's Vereinigung der Freunde germanischer Vorgeschichte was incorporated in the Ahnenerbe and its journal *Germanien* became an Ahnenerbe magazine for a lay readership. Teudt became a departmental leader in the organization. Teudt attained honours for his Germanic research in the Third Reich, being appointed professor and an honorary citizen of Detmold in 1935 and awarded the Goethe Medal for Art and Science in 1940. However, the break with Himmler came in 1938 due to Teudt's disputatious temperament with colleagues, whereupon he founded the Osningmark Society at Detmold in 1939. Teudt's association with National Socialism effectively cost him his resources in the Ahnenerbe and then his reputation after the war. However, his works are still influential in esoteric and neopagan circles in Germany.[35]

Teudt and Heinsch's astroarchaeological studies found a ready echo among German nationalists in the favourable climate of the Third Reich. Following publication of Teudt's first edition in 1929, Herbert Röhrig had extended these astroarchaeological and geomantic studies of Westphalia to his own and Otto Sigfrid Reuter's native East Friesland with a work entitled *Heilige Linien durch Ostfriesland* (1930). Other studies found swift publication in Teudt's journal *Germanien,* now in official Ahnenerbe ownership under the SS. August

---

[34] Wilhelm Teudt, 'Die Osningmark als heiliger Erinnerungshain', *Germanien. Monatshefte für Vorgeschichte* 5 (1933): pp. 183–85.

[35] Uta Halle, *'Die Externsteine sind bis auf weiteres germanisch!' Prähistorisch Archäologie im Dritten Reich* (Bielefeld: Verlag für Regionalgeschichte, 2002); Harald Lönnecker, 'Zwischen Esoterik und Wissenschaft—die Kreise des "völkischen" Germanenkundlers Wilhelm Teudt', *Einst und Jetzt. Jahrbuch des Vereins für Korpsstudentische Geschichtsforschung* 49 (2004): pp. 265–94. Iris Schäferjohann-Bursian, 'Wilhelm Teudt im Detmold der 1920er Jahre—seine Suche nach Orientierung', in *Krieg—Revolution—Republik. Detmold 1914–1933*, ed. Hermann Niebuhr and Andreas Ruppert (Bielefeld, 2007).

Meier-Böke understook an investigation of lines through St. Nicholas Church at Lemgo, while Kurt Gerlach (1889–1976) extended the study of 'holy lines' into a concept of 'power lines' which explained the Germanic influence and domination of traditionally Slav areas of settlement such as Bohemia. Gerlach's lines lent an archaeoastronomical interpretation and legitimation to Germany's current colonisation of Central Eastern Europe and the annexation of Slav-settled lands after the absorbtion of the Sudetenland in 1938 followed by the establishment of the Protectorate of Bohemia and Moravia in March 1939.[36]

During the 1930s SS-sponsored astroarchaeology adopted the more far-fetched amateur theories of Herman Wirth (1885–1981), Karl Maria Wiligut (1886–1946) and Günther Kirchhoff (1892–1975). Wirth was a Dutch-German prehistorian with a fascination for petroglyphic symbolism in Nordic and American rock art, who speculated about the common Atlantean ancestry of Eskimos, Central American pyramid-builders, ancient Egyptians and Germans, who impressed Himmler so much as to be appointed the the first director the Ahnenerbe from 1935. He incorporated many ideas from archaeastronomy into his massive works on Nordic prehistory.[37] Karl Maria Wiligut, also known as Weisthor, also came from the fringe world of *völkisch*-occult prehistory, gained Himmler's favour, and was appointed to his personal staff to give his opinion on runes, ancient Germanic traditions, prayers, mantras and clairvoyant practices in archaeology. In 1936 Weisthor and his colleague Kirchhoff undertook a major survey of prehistoric sites and natural features in the Black Forest, submitting a formal 87-page report to the SS on their findings, which included cultural artifacts, crosses, inscriptions, as well as natural and

---

[36] August Meier-Böke, 'Die Ortung von Lemgo in Lippe', *Germanien* 9 (1937); Kurt Gerlach, ‚Frühdeutsche Landmessungen', *Germanien* (1940): pp. 259–69, 302–11.

[37] Herman Wirth, *Der Aufgang der Menschheit: Untersuchungen zur Geschichte der Religion, Symbolik und Schrift der Atlantisch-Nordischen Rasse* (Jena: Eugen Diederichs Verlag, 1928); Herman Wirth, *Die Heilige Urschrift der Menschheit; Symbolgeschichtliche Untersuchungen diesseits und jenseits des Nordatlantik*, serial issue (Leipzig: Koehler & Amelang, 1931–1936). For Wirth see Michael H. Kater, *Das 'Ahnenerbe' der SS 1935–1945* (Stuttgart: Deutscher Verlagsanstalt, 1974); Heather Pringle, *The Master Race: Himmler's Scholars and the Holocaust* (London: Fourth Estate, 2006), pp. 54–62.

man-made formations in the forest. Weisthor made at least five such surveys around Germany for the SS, discovering a cruciform ancient Germanic religious complex around Goslar, a city which possessed particular mythological and religious significance to him and Walter Darré, the Reichsminister for Agriculture.[38] Kirchhoff anticipated Gerlach's lines across Europe by extending the concept of 'holy lines' to the notion of enormous geodetic energy-lines linking Vienna with Giza, Urga and Lhasa across whole continents with a likely eye to Pan-German claims of Eurasian sovereignty.[39]

LEY LINES: GEOMANCY OR ARCHAEOASTRONOMY?

Boyle Somerville, Thom, MacKie and Ruggles today all explore the scientific and technical aspects of metrology and archaeoastronomy, using sober empirical observations at the archaeological sites combined with advanced surveying instrumentation, mathematical calculation and astronomical data. Primarily addressed to the inspiration and motive for such studies, the German astroarchaeological tradition clearly invoked the wisdom of the ancients with regard to the achievements of ancient Germans and their superior culture, prescient evidence for the German power in the present. As the Germans freely mixed geomantic notions with astro-archaeology, I return here to the concept of ley lines, a current of research most probably stimulated by Lockyer's initial studies in astroarchaeology at the beginning of the twentieth century.

Ley lines are alleged alignments of a number of places of geographical interest, such as ancient monuments and megaliths that are thought by certain adherents to dowsing and New Age beliefs to have spiritual power. Their existence was suggested in 1921 by the amateur archaeologist and photographer Alfred Watkins (1855–1935) of Hereford in his book *The Old Straight Track* (1925). On 30 June 1921, Watkins visited Blackwardine in Herefordshire, and while riding in the vicinity he noted that many of the footpaths there seemed to connect one hilltop to another in a straight line. Taking up a map, he noticed places in alignment: 'The whole thing

---

[38] Goodrick-Clarke, *The Occult Roots of Nazism*, pp. 184–86.
[39] Ibid.

came to me in a flash'.[40] Nigel Pennick and Paul Devereux have listed later nineteenth-century antiquaries and writers who suggested linear patterns in the landscape, including William Henry Black, C. W. Dymond, G. H. Piper, Thomas Codrington, Francis J. Bennett, and Hilaire Belloc, some of whose work was known to Watkins. At the same time Sir Norman Lockyer and F. C. Penrose were studying the astronomical alignments of 'sun temples' in Greece, Egypt, Babylonia and Britain, and in the second edition of *Stonehenge* (1909), Lockyer showed the triangle of alignments that linked Stonehenge with Castle Ditches and Sidbury, Old Sarum, Salisbury Cathedral spire and Clearbury, also noted by Bennett.[41] Watkins called the lines 'leys' because so many of them passed through locations whose names included the suffix '-ley'.[42] Watkins books *Early British Trackways* (1922) and *The Old Straight Track* (1925) generally met with skepticism from professional archaeologists. Watkins never attributed any supernatural significance to leys; he believed that they were simply pathways that had been used for trade or ceremonial purposes, very ancient in origin, possibly dating back to the Neolithic, certainly pre-Roman period. His obsession with leys was a natural outgrowth of his interest in landscape photography and love of the British countryside.

While the Germans derived their ideas of 'holy lines' from a reading of Lockyer, as did Watkins in all likelihood, it is interesting to trace the career of Watkins's theories in England as adapted by later writers. Some of his ideas were taken up by the occultist Dion Fortune (1890–1946) who featured them in her novel *The Goat-footed God* (1936). Watkins' ideas went dormant after the outbreak of the Second World War but in the 1960s, ley lines revived with the general interest in counter-cultural ideas and through the works of John Michell (1933–2009), they have become the subject of a variety of magical and esoteric theories. Michell's better known works on this subject include *The Flying Saucer Vision: The Holy Grail Restored* (1967), *The View Over Atlantis* (1969), later revised as *The New View Over Atlantis* (1983), which stimulated renewed interest in ley lines, *City of*

---

[40] Alfred Watkins, *The Old Straight Track: Its Mounds, Beacons, Moats, Sites, and Mark Stones* (London: Methuen, 1925).
[41] Nigel Pennick and Paul Devereux, *Lines on the Landscape: Leys and Other Linear Enigmas* (London: Robert Hale, 1989), pp. 32–37.
[42] Tom Williamson and Liz Bellamy, *Ley Lines in Question* (Tadworth: World's Work, 1983), p. 12.

Revelation (1972), which concerns sacred geometry and metrology, *A Little History of Astro-Archaeology* (1977), *Megalithomania* (1982), and *The Lost Science of Measuring the Earth: Discovering the Sacred Geometry of the Ancients* (2006) with Robin Heath. Michell's books received a broadly positive reception amongst the 'New Age' and 'Earth mysteries' movements. Ronald Hutton has described Michell's research as part of an alternative archaeology that is 'quite unacceptable to orthodox scholarship', while conceding that its real importance resides in its imaginative dimension.[43]

The phenomenonal aspect of ley lines has remained ambiguous. While Watkins appeared to regard them as trackways, later writers suggest that they were lines of energy. Dowsers linked the lines with underground streams and magnetic currents, that is underground, telluric energies, while Michell elaborated a full-blown theory of energy-flows comparable to Chinese dragon-paths (*feng-shui*), carrying divine spiritual energy across the landscape. Tom Graves suggested that the megaliths were 'stone needles' designed to regulate the energy across the earth in a fashion akin to Chinese acupuncture.[44] New Age writers present a broad range of interpretations for the phenomenon. For instance, did the leys mark the path of the current or were they constructed or elaborated to control and direct it? Most of these ideas stemming from Michell's books envisioned a 'golden age', when the country was inhabited by sophisticated philosophers and astronomers of a Stone Age culture who lived in harmony with the environment and one another. Their understanding of geology, botany, and astronomy coupled with the manipulation of the earth-energies enabled them to achieve four harvests a year. Ley power was associated with a range of benefits, in that it could be used to heal, restore fertility, control the weather and to overcome gravity.[45] The American astronomer Edwin C. Krupp commented on the proliferation of astronomical mythologies during the 1970s involving ley lines, the Glastonbury zodiac of Katherine Maltwood, the extraterrestrial links between

---

[43] Ronald Hutton, *The Pagan Religions of the Ancient British Isles: Their Nature and Legacy* (Oxford: Blackwells, 1991), pp. 121–32.
[44] Ibid., p. 122.
[45] Paul Screeton, *Quicksilver Heritage: The Mystic Leys, their heritage of ancient wisdom* (Wellingborough: Thorsons, 1974).

Dogon tribal beliefs in Mali, and the star Sirius, and the ancient astronauts of Erich von Däniken.[46]

NEO-PYRAMIDISM

As the early interest of the English antiqurians in Stonehenge and Avebury gave way to more comparative metrological studies of ancient Egyptian monuments with the advent of Egyptology in the nineteenth century, so the mythic preoccupations of German *völkisch* archaeoastronomy and astroarchaeology in the first half of the twentieth century have returned toward the end of the twentieth century. However, while the national fervour and particularist claims of German astroarchaeology limited their scope to German sites and 'holy lines' in the 1920s through the 1940s, the modern mythology of ancient wisdom and archaeo-astronomy has lit on the Egyptian pyramids and Sphinx again as more universal signifiers, the cosmopolitan property of all mankind. The bridging stimulus for this work came from John Ivimy (b. 1911), who, inspired by Hawkins and Thom's work, compared the European megaliths with sites in Egypt and Mesopotamia in order to discover common ground among the secrets of ancient priesthoods. His seminal work, *The Sphinx and the Megaliths* (1974), advanced views concerning the ancient pre-Christian priesthoods attitudes towards nature, man and God, found new meaning in the old records relating to the Hypoboreans, the identity of the Druids, and the Pythagorean source of their esoteric lore.[47] Pyramidism is a lively field of speculation today, based on the bestselling books of Robert Bauval and Adrian Gilbert, *The Orion Mystery* (1994), Graham Hancock, *Fingerprints of the Gods* (1995, 2001) and *Heaven's Mirror* (1998), Robert Bauval and Graham Hancock, *Keeper of Genesis: A Quest for the Hidden Legacy of Mankind* (1996), Robert Bauval, *Secret Chamber: The Quest for the Hall of Records* (1999). Colin Wilson was not far behind Bauval and Hancock's first books with *From Atlantis to the Sphinx: Recovering the Lost Wisdom of the Ancient World* (1996), and his

---

[46] E. C. Krupp, 'Observatories of the Gods and Other Astronomical Fantasies', in *In Search of Ancient Astronomies*, ed. E. C. Krupp (London: Chatto & Windus, 1979), pp. 219–56.

[47] John Ivimy, *The Sphinx and the Megaliths* (London: Turnstone, 1974).

second volume in the genre, co-authored with Rand Flem-Ath, *The Atlantis Blueprint* (2000).

The constraints of this paper prevent me from offering a further analysis of these works in esoteric archaeology, but it is evident that their inspiration echoes the age-old fascination with the *prisca theologia,* lost knowledge, ancient sages, and the lost continents of diluvial mythology, popular ever since Plato's *Timaeus,* but also to the traditional Hermetic wisdom of correspondence 'as above, so below'. These ideas were revived by the speculations of Theosophy following the lead of Helena Petrovna Blavatsky, Rudolf Steiner, and Charles Webster Leadbeater, whose now largely forgotten books in early twentieth-century esotericism not only indirectly nourished the *völkisch* fabulations of the Ariosophists and Herman Wirth and on Atlantis and Nordic races, but may again be detected in this new genre of ideas involving theories of 'pre-sand' Egypt, heavy rainfall on the Sphinx thereby backdating its erection thousands of years earlier, and its improbable origins to the ruins of a lost civilization two miles beneath the ice of the South Pole.

The Western esoteric traditions have been described by Antoine Faivre as possessing four intrinsic philosophical characteristics: 1) Correspondences; 2) Living nature; 3) Imagination and meditation; 4) the experience of trans-mutation, and two extrinsic or socio-cultural characteristics: 5) concordance between different traditions; and 6) trans-mission. In the earliest Romantic, soft primitivist version of Druid reception, as advanced by Stukeley and Smith one discovers that the Druid's ancestral wisdom, long lost but now 'restored', like the megalithic monuments themselves, touches on a form of astronomy concerned with calendars, planetary motions or prophecy, thus fulfilling the familiar axiom of Hermetic philosophy 'as above, so below' (1). The Druids' possession of an ancient wisdom or *prisca theologia* bears on correspondences between the macrocosm and the microcosm, and on a spiritual knowledge of living nature (2), while their hereditary or initatic caste represents the transmission of such wisdom by a lineage of sages (5).[48]

---

[48] Antoine Faivre, *Access to Western Esotericism* (Albany, NY: State University of New York Press, 1995), pp. 10–15.

Dismissed in the mainstream press as the 'Silly Secret of the Sands',[49] Hancock's *Fingerprints of the Gods* offers a traditional menu of lost continents, ancient wisdom, ancient gods and priesthoods, pyramids, Egyptomania, prophecy, apocalyptic. The Western esoteric traditions are apparent in:

1) ancient wisdom: *prisca theologia*, lineage of sages, here presented as transmission by priesthoods, diffusionism;

2) megaliths/monuments/pyramids/Sphinx as texts/ intermediaries/repositories;

3) eclipse of ancient wisdom/lost knowledge as a *gnostic* narrative of separation, loss, ignorance, alienation, and

4) prophecy, apocalyptic

The same ideas notably played in the eccentric theories of ancient astronauts in the works of Erich von Däniken and Robert Charroux in the 1970s.

Desite the *völkisch* and National Socialist adoption of these ideas for nationalist and racialist ideology in Germany during the first half of the twentieth century, esoteric archaeoastronomy and astroarchaeology have retained their legacy by reacquiring an older universalist coloration, which resurfaced in the romantic counterculture across the Western world in the 1960s onward. Their philosophical sources, political and religious inspiration in modernity since 1800 point toward 'Golden Age' myths, ancient wisdom-traditions, prophecy and apocalyptic in powerful echoes of Platonic, Gnostic, and neo-Hermetic thought.

BIBLIOGRAPHY

Atkinson, R. J. C. *Stonehenge*. 1956. Reprint, London: Hamish Hamilton, 1990.

Aubrey, John. *Topographical Collections*. Edited by John Edward Jackson. Devizes: Henry Bull; London: Longmans, 1862.

Barkun, Michael. *Religion and the Racist Right: The Origins of the Christian Identity Movement*. Chapel Hill, NC: University of North Carolina Press, 1997.

---

[49] 'The Silly Secret of the Sands', Cover Story, *The Sunday Times*, Section 10, 14 May 1995, pp. 10–13.

Bauval, Robert and Adrian Gilbert. *The Orion Mystery: Unlocking the Secrets of the Pyramids*. London: Heinemann, 1994.

Burkert, Walter. *The Orientalizing Revolution: The Near Eastern Influence on Greek Culture in the Early Archaic Age*. Cambridge, MA: Harvard University Press, 1992.

Burl, Aubrey. *The Stone Circles of the British Isles*. New Haven: Yale University Press, 1976.

———. *John Aubrey and Stone Circles: Britain's First Archaeologist from Avebury to Stonehenge*. Stroud: Amberley, 2010.

Castleden, Rodney. *The Stonehenge People: An Exploration of Life in Neolithic Britain 4700–2000BC*. London: Routledge & Kegan Paul, 1987.

Curl, James Stevens. *The Egyptian Revival: Ancient Egypt as the Inspiration for Design Motifs in the West*. New York: Routledge, 2000.

Curran, Brian A., Anthony Grafton, Pamela O. Long and Benjamin Weiss. *Obelisk: A History*. Cambridge, MA: MIT Press, 2009.

Faivre, Antoine. *Access to Western Esotericism*. Albany, NY: State University of New York Press, 1995.

———. 'Egyptomany'. In *Dictionary of Gnosis & Western Esotericism*. Edited by Wouter J. Hanegraaff et al. 2 vols. Leiden: E. J. Brill, 2005: I, pp. 328–30.

Gerlach, Kurt. 'Frühdeutsche Landmessungen'. *Germanien* 10 (1940): pp. 259–69, 302–11.

Goodrick-Clarke, Nicholas. *The Occult Roots of Nazism: Secret Aryan Cults and Their Influence on Nazi Ideology. The Ariosophists of Germany and Austria 1890–1935*. 3rd ed. London: I. B. Tauris, 2004.

———. *The Western Esoteric Traditions: A historical introduction*. New York: Oxford University Press, 2008.

Halle, Uta. *'Die Externsteine sind bis auf weiteres germanisch!': Prähistorische Archäologie im Dritten Reich*. Bielefeld: Verlag für Regionalgeschichte, 2002.

Hancock, Graham. *Fingerprints of the Gods: A Quest for the Beginning and the End*. London: Heinemann, 1995.

Hawkins, Gerald S. *Stonehenge Decoded*. London: Souvenir Press, 1966.

Heinsch, Josef. *The Xanten Mosaic-Cosmogram*. Translated by Michael Behrend. Bar Hill, Cambridge: Fenris-Wolf, 1979. Originally published in *Der Grafschafter*, 23 September 1933, and in *Hagal* (March 1935).

———. 'On the Rediscovery of Prechristian Geomancy'. *Journal of Geomancy* 3, no. 2 (1979): pp. 38–41. Originally published in *Hagal* (May 1935).

Hermand, Jost. *Old Dreams of a New Reich: Volkish Utopias and National Socialism*. Bloomington: Indiana University Press, 1992.

Hutton, Ronald. *The Pagan Religions of the Ancient British Isles: Their Nature and Legacy*. Oxford: Blackwells, 1991.

Ivimy, John. *The Sphinx and the Megaliths*. London: Turnstone, 1974.

Kater, Michael H. *Das 'Ahnenerbe' der SS 1935–1945: Ein Beitrag zur Kulturkritik des Dritten Reichs.* Stuttgart: Deutsche Verlags-Anstalt, 1974.

Kendrick, T. D. *The Druids: A Study in Keltic Prehistory.* London: Frank Cass, 1927.

Krupp, Edwin C., ed. *In Search of Ancient Astronomies.* London: Chatto & Windus, 1979.

Lancaster Brown, Peter. *Megaliths, Myths and Men: An Introduction to Astro-Archaeology.* Poole: Blandford Press, 1976.

Lockyer, J. Norman. *The Dawn of Astronomy.* London: Cassell, 1894.

———. *Stonehenge and Other British Stone Monuments.* 2nd ed. London: Macmillan, 1909.

Lönnecker, Harald. 'Zwischen Esoterik und Wissenschaft—die Kreise des "völkischen" Germanenkundlers Wilhelm Teudt'. *Einst und Jetzt. Jahrbuch des Vereins für Korpsstudentische Geschichtsforschung* 49 (2004): pp. 265–94.

MacKie, Euan. *The Megalith Builders.* London: Phaidon Press, 1977.

Meier-Böke, August. 'Die Ortung von Lemgo in Lippe'. *Germanien* 9 (1937).

Michell, John, *The View over Atlantis.* 1969. Reprint, London: Garnstone Press, 1972.

———. *The New View over Atlantis.* London: Thames & Hudson, 1983.

Mortimer, Neil. *Stukeley Illustrated: William Stukeley's Rediscovery of Britain's Ancient Sites.* Sutton Mallet: Green Magic, 2003.

Mosse, George L. *The Crisis of German Ideology: Intellectual Origins of the Third Reich.* London: Weidenfeld & Nicolson, 1966.

———. *The Nationalization of the Masses: Political Symbolism and Mass Movements in Germany from the Napoleonic Wars Through the Third Reich.* New York: Howard Fertig, 1975.

Pennick, Nigel. *The Ancient Science of Geomancy: Man in Harmony with the Earth.* London: Thames & Hudson, 1979.

———, and Paul Devereux. *Lines on the Landscape: Leys and Other Linear Enigmas.* London: Robert Hale, 1989.

Piggott, Stuart. *The Druids.* London: Thames & Hudson, 1968.

———. *William Stukeley: An Eighteenth-Century Antiquary.* 1950. Reprint, 2nd ed. London: Thames & Hudson, 1985.

Pringle, Heather. *The Master Race: Himmler's Scholars and the Holocaust.* London: Fourth Estate, 2006.

Puschner, Uwe. *Die völkische Bewegung im wilhelmischen Kaiserreich; Sprache-Rasse-Religion.* Darmstadt: Wissen-schaftliche Buchgesellschaft, 2001.

Ray, John. *The Rosetta Stone and the Rebirth of Modern Egypt.* Cambridge, MA: Harvard University Press, 2007.

Reuter, Otto Sigfrid. *Das Rätsdel der Edda und der arische Urglaube.* 2 vols. Bad Berka; Verlag Deutsche Gemeinschaft, 1923.

Ruggles, Clive. *Ancient Astronomy.* Chicago: ABC-Clio, 2005.

———, ed. *Records in Stone: Papers in Memory of Alexander Thom.* Cambridge: Cambridge University Press, 1988.

Schäferjohann-Bursian, Iris. 'Wilhelm Teudt im Detmold der 1920er Jahre—seine Suche nach Orientierung'. In *Krieg–Revolution–Republik: Detmold 1914–1933*. Edited by Hermann Niebuhr and Andreas Ruppert Bielefeld: Aisthesis, 2007.

Screeton, Paul. *Quicksilver Heritage: The Mystic Leys, Their Heritage of Ancient Wisdom*. Wellingborough: Thorsons, 1974.

Sinclair, Rolf M. 'The Nature of Archaeoastronomy'. In *Current Studies in Archaeoastronomy: Conversations across Time and Space*. Edited by John W. Fountain and Rolf M. Sinclair. [Fifth Oxford International Symposium on Archaeoastronomy]. Durham, NC: Carolina Academic Press, 2005: pp. 3–13.

Smyth, Charles Piazzi. *Our Inheritance in the Great Pyramid*. London: W. Isbister, 1864.

Taylor, John. *The Great Pyramid : Why was it built? And who built it?* London: Longman, Green, Longman, and Roberts, 1859.

Teudt, Wilhelm. *Germanische Heiligtümer. Beiträge zur Aufdeckung der Vorgeschichte, ausgehend von den Externsteinen, den Lippequellen und der Teutoburg*. Jena: Eugen Diederichs Verlag, 1929.

———. 'Die Osningmark als heiliger Erinnerungshain'. *Germanien. Monatshefte für Vorgeschichte* (1933): pp. 183–85.

———. *Die Externsteine als germanisches Heiligtum*. Jena: Eugen Diederichs Verlag, 1934.

———. *Wilhelm Teudt im Kampf um die Germanenehre. Eine Auswahl von Teudts Schriften*. Edited by Rudolf Bünte. Bielefeld and Leipzig: Velhagen & Klasing, 1940.

Thom, Alexander. 'A Statistical Examination of the Megalithic Sites in Britain'. *Journal of the Royal Statistical Society* Series A (General) 118, no. 3 (1955): pp. 275–95.

———. *Megalithic Sites in Britain*. Oxford: Oxford University Press, 1967.

———. *Megalithic Lunar Observatories*. Oxford: Oxford University Press, 1971.

——— and A. S. Thom. *Megalithic Remains in Britain and Brittany*. Oxford: Oxford University Press, 1978.

Ucko, Peter and Timothy Champion, eds. *The Wisdom of Egypt: Changing Visions through the Ages*. London: UCL Press, 2003.

Watkins, Alfred. *The Old Straight Track: Its Mounds, Beacons, Mpats, Sites, and Mark Stones*. London: Methuen, 1925.

Williamson, Tom and Liz Bellamy, *Ley Lines in Question*. Tadworth: World's Work, 1983.

Wirth, Herman. *Der Aufgang der Menschheit: Untersuchungen zur Geschichte der Religion, Symbolik und Schrift der Atlantisch-Nordischen Rasse*. Jena: Eugen Diederichs Verlag, 1928.

———. *Die Heilige Urschrift der Menschheit; Symbolgeschichtliche Untersuchungen diesseits und jenseits des Nordatlantik*, serial issue. Leipzig: Koehler & Amelang, 1931–1936.

HOW DO ASTROLOGERS READ CHARTS?

Darrelyn Gunzburg

ABSTRACT: This paper is focused on how meaning is drawn from a natal horoscope based on interviews with contemporary western astrologers who work with natal horoscopes. Some authors of astrological texts suggest that the activity of reading a natal horoscope for a client evokes mystery or the divine. Many astrologers think that reading a chart is a ritual. This paper proposes a different approach, that of creativity, and suggests that reading a natal horoscope is a secular creative endeavour. A glossary of astrological terms is included at the end of the paper.

Reading a natal horoscope forms the central core of a contemporary western astrologer's consultation for a client. A horoscope contains planets in signs and houses and each planet has the potential to form a geometrical relationship with every other planet in a unique, non-repeating way. Claudius Ptolemy (ca.90–ca.168) defined the natal horoscope as one that was concerned with 'the destiny and disposition of every human' thus being reflective of life experiences:

> When, therefore, a thorough knowledge of the motions of the stars, and of the Sun and Moon, shall have been acquired, and when the situations of the place, the time, and all the configurations actually existing at that place and time, shall also be duly known; and such knowledge be yet further improved by an acquaintance with the natures of the heavenly bodies—not of what they are composed, but of the effective influences they possess [...]—when all these qualifications for prescience may be possessed by any individual, there seems no obstacle to deprive him of the insight, offered at once by nature and his own judgement, into [...] prognostication concerning the destiny and disposition of every human being.[1]

---

[1] Ptolemy, *Tetrabiblios*, ed. J. M. Ashmand (Mokelumne Hill, CA: Health Research, 1969), p. 6.

The dilemma for students when reading natal horoscopes is that they approach astrology thinking it is simply a matter of learning the parts—the algorithm of a planet in a sign and a house and its geometrical relationship with other planets—in order to give meaning to the whole. This is unavoidably reinforced initially by those who teach it, for in order to make sense of the whole, a student must first learn the parts. Indeed a perusal of the literature on how to extract meaning from a natal horoscope, from authors such as Derek and Julia Parker, Rob Hand, Alan Oken, and Sue Tompkins, shows that what these authors of astrology books write in order to teach students how to read an astrological chart touches mainly on a methodology which lists the components of the chart—the meanings of the planets, signs, houses, planets through the signs, planets in the houses, aspects, keywords, and so on. Informal discussions with these astrologers reinforces that they know that reading natal horoscopes is more than just reading the parts, yet they struggle to articulate in writing how to extract the meaning of the whole chart. As with acquiring skills such as the ability to throw a clay pot or to play a piece of music, reading a chart requires praxis to complete the learning, a deed not easily written down.

Peter R. Webster explored a similar issue in 1990 with regard to music teaching as opposed to music learning. Webster noted that much of the literature on music education focused on how one could teach music creatively, whereas he advocated shifting the emphasis to teaching creative thinking, considering how the mind works with musical material to produce creative results.[2] From his research he concluded that creative thinking 'is a dynamic mental process that alternates between divergent (imaginative) and convergent (factual) thinking, moving in stages over time. It is enabled by internal musical skills and outside conditions and results in a final musical product which is new for the creator.'[3]

This space of the 'new' appears to be one that is experienced by astrologers when reading charts. In talking with practicing astrologers, most agree that when they read a chart for a client at its best something happens in the

---

[2] Peter R. Webster, 'Creativity as Creative Thinking', *Music Educators Journal* 76, no. 9 (1990), p. 22.
[3] Ibid., p. 28.

consultation space that is unutterable and inarticulate. Darby Costello, an author of astrological texts, astrology teacher and consultant who has been practicing and teaching astrology since the early 1980s, in an interview with me in July 2007, expressed her experience of reading charts as 'The person hands me the key to their inner landscape and I go into their inner landscape with my particular eye and I say "look at this!"'

Some authors have endeavoured to define what occurs in the consultation space. Sue Tompkins writes that 'it is the job of the astrologer to look at things from a wider perspective, perhaps from an inner, magical or soul perspective—rather as a priest, shaman or psychotherapist might.'[4] Demetra George calls it 'space for the presence of the transcendent.'[5] Roy Willis and Patrick Curry describe it as an occurrence 'in which the unknown [...] is invited to speak to the inquiry at hand.'[6] Geoffrey Cornelius defines it as 'entering into a dialogue with the divine.'[7] Stephen Arroyo observes that 'It's important to keep focused on the purpose of the consultation when you're with a client, to guide you through the innumerable combinations of symbols in every chart. Otherwise the chart might start doing a little dance in front of your eyes.'[8] Liz Greene distinguishes how 'Much of what we do for a client has nothing to do with the specific configurations we are looking at, but rather, with the fact that the chart, and ultimately God or the gods through the patterns of the chart, affirm the right of the person to be what he or she is.'[9]

---

[4] Sue Tompkins, *A Contemporary Astrologer's Handbook: An In-Depth Guide to Interpreting Your Horoscope* (London: Flare Publications, 2006), p. 10.

[5] Demetra George, *Astrology and the Authentic Self* (Lake Worth, FL: Ibis Press, 2009), p. 251.

[6] Roy Willis and Patrick Curry, *Astrology, Science and Culture: Pulling Down the Moon* (Oxford: Berg, 2004), p. 62.

[7] Geoffrey Cornelius, *The Moment of Astrology: Origins in Divination* (London: Arkana Penguin Books, 1994), p. xix. See also, Willis and Curry, *Astrology, Science and Culture*, p. 23.

[8] Stephen Arroyo, *The Practice and Profession of Astrology: Rebuilding Our Lost Connections with the Cosmos* (Reno, NV: CRCS Publications, 1984), p. 21.

[9] Juliet Sharman-Burke and Liz Greene, *The Astrologer, the Counsellor and the Priest* (London: Centre for Psychological Astrology Press, 1997), p. 177.

This paper, however, considers this indefinable space through a different syntax—the syntax of creativity. In 1955 G. A. Kelly in his work on personal construct psychology, defined two terms: 'loose construing' (primary process thinking or to think loosely) and 'tight' construing (or secondary-process thinking).[10] He maintained that insight required the skilful alternation between both, thus forming what he called a creativity cycle. Kelly's work on dreams informed his theory. Loose construing for Kelly meant not anticipating a result. In this space of looseness, new elements could enter the system, as in a dream where objects morph into other objects without loss of logic. In such a state judgements were delayed, and self-consciousness and self-censorship were diminished. People often described themselves in this space as having a changed sense of self, where there was a qualitative alteration to the sense of time and space and where a blurring between self-and-other and self-and-world occurred.

When considering the work of painters in 1963, Rudolph and Margaret Wittkower chronicled one of the hallmarks of the emancipated artist as 'a need for introspection, and introspection necessitates pauses, often of considerable length. The skilled hand of the craftsman may be made to work at will, but the "gift of inspiration" cannot be forced.'[11] They termed this way of working 'creative idleness' and offered in evidence the observation of Matteo Bandello (1485–1561), a contemporary of Leonardo da Vinci (1452–1519), who enjoyed the opportunity of observing the latter paint the *Last Supper*:

> Leonardo had the habit—I have seen and observed him many a time—of going early in the morning and mounting the scaffold, since the *Last Supper* is rather high off the ground, and staying there without putting down his brush from dawn to dusk, forgetting to eat and drink, painting all the time. Then for two, three, or four days he would not touch it and yet he would stay considering, examining, and judging his own figures.[12]

---

[10] G. A. Kelly, *The Psychology of Personal Constructs* (New York: Norton, 1955). I am indebted to Australian acupuncturist Ysha De Donna who directed me in my thinking on 'loose construing'.
[11] Rudolf and Margaret Wittkower, *Born under Saturn. The Character and Conduct of Artists: A Documented History from Antiquity to the French Revolution* (New York: W. W. Norton, 1963), p. 59.
[12] Ibid., p. 60.

Leonardo himself divulged that 'great minds produce more when working less. For with their intellect they search for conceptions and form those perfect ideas which afterwards they merely express and portray with their hands.'[13] One could argue that this is an artist's way of 'loose construing'.

In order to understand whether this is reflective of the experiences of astrologers reading natal horoscopes, through questionnaires and interviews I surveyed professional astrologers, astrologers who were attending conferences, those studying astrology within astrological schools, and those who were subscribers to an astrological magazine. My questions included the astrologer's preparation for reading a chart, their methodology of reading a chart, their phenomenology of reading a chart and the astrologer's outcomes, what they sought to achieve when they read a chart. To date I have received over 130 responses. This gave me a general understanding of the situation.

However, I was interested in observing, hearing, and watching these astrologers as they described their process of preparing and reading a horoscope for a client in the consulting room, the phenomenological experience of how they drew meaning from a horoscope. Using some of the themes from the questionnaires, between 2007–2010 I conducted twenty-three semi-structured interviews with astrologers who were all active within the community of western astrologers. The demographics covered the UK, the Netherlands, South Africa, Turkey and the US. All interviewees defined themselves as professional astrologers in some way, as astrological consultants, teachers of astrology, authors of astrological texts, translators of astrological texts, publishers of astrological texts, publishers of astrological software, entrepreneurs, and astrological business consultants. Of the twenty-three interviews, eight were male and fifteen were female, thus forming a one-third two-thirds divide. All but three of those interviewed were happy for me to use their names. Of the three who wished to remain anonymous, one did not want the interview used at all. The interviews were, on average, an hour in length.

All of the astrologers that I interviewed saw clients face-to-face, arranged consultations by telephone or engaged with clients by Skype. As they collated the paperwork for the

---

[13] Ibid.

client and encountered the chart for the first time, these
astrologers described a method predicated on technique. For
example, 'I'll break down the elements and the modalities
and I'll look for rulerships, things in their dignity, detriment,
all of this. I think that my Faculty[14] training taught me to be
very systematic in that way'; or 'if I'm looking at relationships, so I have a list at the top that reminds me to look at
certain things with the Lord of the 7th and Venus and the Lot
of Marriage and that sort of thing. And it's just a list of items
really'; or 'I look at the progressions. I look at the transits. I
look at the planetary picture, the natal chart'; or 'I begin a
session sometimes with an imbalance of elements or
sometimes a planet which is very accentuated or sometimes I
even begin with the Ascendant sign itself or a planet in the
Ascendant sign'; and so on.[15] However, as the astrologers
prepared the work and looked more closely at the horoscope
something else occurred.

Rob Hand, an author and translator of astrological texts,
and consultant from the US who has been practicing, writing
and teaching astrology since 1972, interviewed in April 2010,
described his initial response to the chart: 'First of all I look
to see if there's anything horrendous that leaps out and grabs
you by the throat, like an angular T-Square or a major planet
on an angle or something like that.'

This kinaesthetic response to the chart, where information
is processed using feelings and physical bodily reactions, a
term originally defined by Richard Bandler and John Grinder
in their seminal work on Neuro-Linguistic Programming,[16]

---

[14] The Faculty of Astrological Studies was founded in London in
1948 and offers training in astrological education.

[15] See Glossary at the end of this paper for an explanation of
astrological terms.

[16] John Grinder and Richard Bandler, *Frogs into Princes: Neuro
Linguistic Programming* (Moab, UT: Real People Press, 1979). See also
Dorothy Young Brockopp, 'What Is NLP?' *The American Journal of
Nursing* 83, no. 7 (1983): pp. 1012–13. 'Kinaesthetic' is defined by
Brockopp as one of 'the three modalities that are most often used in
this culture to access and process information ... [thus] the
kinesthetic person favors messages that reflect feelings or physical
action'. See also Diane G. Arnold and Barbara Swaby,
'Neurolinguistic Applications for the Remediation of Reading
Problems', *The Reading Teacher* 37, no. 9 (1984): p. 832. Arnold and
Swaby applied this term to language. See also Sherrie Barr and
Philip Lewin, 'Learning Movement: Integrating Kinaesthetic Sense
with Cognitive Skills', *Journal of Aesthetic Education* 28, no. 1 (1994):

was echoed by Linea Van Horn, an astrology teacher from the US and professional, full time astrologer since 1998, interviewed in March 2010, who asserted:

> I don't get images, I do not hear anything, and it's tempting to say 'This is all mental' but of course it isn't. [...] There is a viscerality about it that just gets down below the deck and that's a crucial part... it's not a neck up interaction. *(laughs)* I mean, I see the patterns coming off the chart. I don't hear anything.

Dorian Gieseler Greenbaum, an author and translator of astrological texts and consultant from the US who, when interviewed in February 2010, also responded to the chart kinaesthetically: 'It's—it's like 'Hah!!' You sit there and—you see whatever it is you see and somehow I don't know whether it's popping out at you or grabbing you but it's something like that.'

Another style of approach to the chart came from Christeen Skinner, a financial astrologer and consultant from the UK who has been practicing, teaching, and writing about astrology since 1981, whom I interviewed in April 2010. Christeen was trained as a musician, played professionally in orchestras and taught music and thus the way she accessed the chart was through a visual-audio modality: 'I see a chart like an orchestra ...[and] I can see myself as a temporary conductor. I know what the transits are, so how is it playing now? Is it going through its classical movement? Is the person doing scales? Where are they?'

Babs Kirby, an author of astrological texts, astrology teacher, and psychotherapist from the UK who has been practicing, writing and teaching astrology since 1985, interviewed in April 2010, experienced a kinaesthetic-emotional response to the initial encounter with the chart: 'I still hand-draw charts [...] and as I draw the chart, it drops into place. [...] When I see aspects and planets in particular signs and houses there's just a felt sense of what that essence will be about. I think it might be happening in my emotions as well'.

For Lindsay Radermacher, an author of astrological texts, astrology teacher and consultant who has been practicing,

---

p. 93. Barr and Lewin described the kinaesthetic sense in dance as 'a sense of the feel of different movements combined with different qualities'.

writing and teaching astrology since the 1980s, interviewed in April 2010, the initial encounter with the chart was an immensely tactile experience. She spoke of 'the way that you can feel it *(holds arms in front of her with fingers splayed 'feeling' it)* filtering into yourself as you're writing'. Even though Lindsay used a computer to print out charts and other astrologically-connected technical information, she adamantly maintained that she was 'a hand and pen person. I just feel as you're actually drawing and writing, and so on, something is going into you of that person as you write it. [...] Just by drawing Venus or Mercury or something like that.' She added: 'There was a sense of settling down to something that was very important, that was the beginning—… well the beginning of the relationship is the hearing of the voice on the end of the phone but it was something about the relationship starting'.

Karen Hamaker-Zondag, on the other hand, an author of astrological texts, astrology teacher, publisher of astrological texts, and Jungian specialist from The Netherlands who has been practicing astrology since 1975, interviewed in May 2010, maintained a purely visual response: 'That is a difficult question because I look at a lot of things. […] I look at the elements, I look at the crosses, I look at if there are Yods or unaspected planets or duets. […] It's so much you look at, there's not one special thing I focus on'.

By comparison, Madalyn Hillis-Dineen, an astrological consultant since the 1980s and one of the world's leading providers of astrological software from the US, interviewed in January 2010, liked to maintain distance and objectivity so that she wouldn't be subjected to too much sensory input before the client arrived: 'I interact with the screen. I don't print out a whole lot of paper and I look at things […] I don't like to get too in-depth because I don't want to do the reading before the reading'.

From this cross-section of responses, what appeared to be happening in this preparatory period was that the astrologers I interviewed were juggling components, gathering data technically and then waiting for a pattern to emerge rather than imposing a structure upon it, the very 'loose construing' that Kelly defined. In such a state where there was no expectation of results and conclusions were delayed, new elements of the horoscope became apparent. When they appeared, they did so suddenly and rapidly via a strong primary perceptual modality: audio, visual, or kinaesthetic.

Rob Hand, Linea Van Horn, Dorian Gieseler Greenbaum, Babs Kirby and Lindsay Radermacher variously described an initial kinaesthetic response, depicting the chart as an entity, parts of which could 'leap out and grab you by the throat'. Trained as a musician, Christeen Skinner saw and heard the chart as a musician would an orchestra and thus listened for the chart's musical signatures. Karen Hamaker-Zondag and Madalyn Hillis-Dineen maintained an observational, visual acknowledgment of the chart.

Once the consultation began, the pattern for these astrologers that I interviewed was to start every reading for a new client in the same way, often repeating the birth data given to them by the client, informing them of what the session would involve on a formal level, the shape and length it was to take, explaining a little about the concept of the horoscope, and outlining briefly the symbols of astrology. The astrologers that I interviewed described and recognized that this was the way they made a transition into reading the natal horoscope. This loosely-set format was what Daniel Budd would call 'ritual repetition',[17] a secular ritual that provided structure and enabled the astrologers to step into the space of reading a chart.

However, some astrologers, such as Darby Costello, wrestled with how to coherently express what happened next in the consultation: 'Once I've got past the Sun the images just leap off the page. But they're not images, they're—... I don't know. I really don't know what happens. I just know that once there, the chart starts activating something that can be described.' Faye Cossar, a professional consulting business astrologer from New Zealand who has lived in Amsterdam for many years, whom I interviewed in April 2010, grappled with the phenomenological process in a similar way:

> What I notice is it takes me a little while to get into the chart, and then I'm in a 'zone' and off I go. There's that alchemical process in the chart where you *know* you've got it. [...] You know that you're changing something in them in some way.

---

[17] Daniel Budd, 'Been There, Done That: Virtual Vs. Ritual Repetition', *The Jung Page, Reflections on Psychology, Culture and Life* (2006),
http://www.cgjungpage.org/index.php?option=com_content&task=view&id=782&Itemid=40.

> And how you know that is—*(pause)*…I don't know. *(laughs).*
> It's very difficult to describe.

Similarly Dorian Gieseler Greenbaum noted: 'It is definitely *not* intellectual. Even though you might have an intellectual foundation in your work, once you start to do a reading you have to let that go in fact'.

Others were able to identify the process on a visual level and likening reading the chart to reading a text. Rod Suskin, an astrology teacher, author of astrological texts, and consultant from South Africa, who has been practicing and teaching astrology for the last 20 years, interviewed in January 2010, made sense of it as 'The symbols of the planets in the wheel […] will stand out as if they're printed in flashing colours […] as if they become physical focal points, as if they were in a different colour […] it's like looking at a piece of text.' Pam Ciampi, an astrology teacher and consultant from the USA who has been practicing and teaching astrology for the last 30 years, paralleled this viewpoint: 'Something will always step forward, absolutely. It might be an aspect, it might be a planet, and all of a sudden it just goes "whi-i-i-ing!" and I think, "O my god I have to really concentrate on that Mars" or whatever… It's very visual.'

Still others described the process as seeing themes, as did Linea Van Horn: 'You see themes emerging, complexes or themes, things that are tied together, things that say the same thing'; or seeing threads, as did Hakan Kirkoglou, an author of astrological texts, astrology teacher and consultant from Turkey, interviewed in January 2010: 'In the first few minutes in every consultation I try to define why they [the client] are with me. […] And then I make a thread or when we begin to talk with the client the astrological chart itself unfolds and then I can go'.

Such descriptions are reflective of Webster's research on creative thinking, mentioned earlier in this paper, which allows for the interactive movement between divergent (imaginative) and convergent (factual) thinking to create the space for a new dynamic.

Benjamin Dykes, an author of astrological texts, translator of astrological texts, and consultant from the US who has been practicing, writing and teaching astrology since the late 1990s, interviewed in March 2010, described the transition moment—the moment when these astrologers noticed that they had established a transition into reading the natal horoscope—as 'a clarifying moment' or 'an 'aha!' moment' predicated upon something the client said which put all his preparation work into context and directed him to look more fully at certain parts of the chart. 'All of a sudden other techniques and things in the chart became relevant once I knew that that Venus was really of interest to her. And so it was a clarifying moment.'

Considering how artists think may provide evidence that is pertinent to understanding the process that these astrologers have been describing. In Amy Ione's study in the year 2000, 'An Inquiry into Paul Cézanne: The Role of the Artist in Studies of Perception and Consciousness' she commented on Robert Solso's experiments carried out using functional magnetic resonance imaging (fMRI).[18] Solso conducted a study between a practicing artist and a novice in a full-body fMRI Notepad. Both were given faces to draw and then the scans were compared. Ione acknowledges that the test had problems. Firstly it was a case study of two and secondly the variation in brain activity from the novice may simply have reflected their individual way of processing facial information. Nevertheless the results showed that whilst the novice seemed to be copying the face, the artist was 'seeing beyond' them. Ione's conclusion was that:

> The 'seeing' process for everyone takes place in the visual cortex at the back of the brain, which receives nerve signals representing light captured in the retina. At the same time, increased blood flows are evidence of increased brain activity....thanks to photographs of scanned 'slices' of different brains, it is possible to see that, when drawing a face, non-artists in the experiment used only the back of the brain, while Mr Ocean [an artist] used mainly the frontal part of his brain....where you find emotion, previous faces, painting experience, intentions and so on...in essence, the control subjects were simply trying to copy what they saw. But [the artist] was creating an abstracted representation of each photograph. He was *thinking* the portraits.[19]

It can be argued that years of training taught these

---

[18] Robert L. Solso, 'Brain Activities in a Skilled Versus a Novice Artist: An Fmri Study', *Leonardo* 34, no. 1 (2001): pp. 31–34.

[19] Amy Ione, 'An Inquiry into Paul Cézanne: The Role of the Artist in Studies of Perception and Consciousness', *Journal of Consciousness Studies* 7, no. 8–9 (2000): pp. 70–71.

astrologers to 'think in charts' just as the artist thought 'in portraits'. Rob Hand called this 'a clear signal':

> There are broadly speaking two kinds of charts. Charts that have a really clear signal and charts that do not. What I look for is to see if there is a clear signal. Is there any pattern being repeated? Is there any symbol that is so powerful that you have to deal with it in order to understand the chart?

In summary then, from the initial juggling of components, the gathering of data and waiting for a pattern to emerge of the preparation period, once the client was in the space with these astrologers another factor came into play. What had previously been free and unrestricted took on a clarity of shape and structure. The chart patterns became obvious. The astrologers I interviewed described a process based on technique and pattern-seeking that changed once the client was present. After an optimal moment of feedback from the client, what Ben Dykes calls 'a clarifying moment', the chart took on a sharpness, and by the clients' continual responses that the patterns they were seeing in the chart were meaningful to the client, the astrologer could move into tight construing.

It seems that once this bridge into reading the chart had been constructed, a further phenomenon based on focused attention entered the arena. In his seminal work, *The Psychology of Optimal Experience* written in 1990, psychologist Mihály Csíkszentmihályi's pioneering investigation into understanding happiness, creativity, and human fulfilment lead him to recognize that attention shapes the self and is in turn shaped by it:

> Attention determines what will or will not appear in consciousness and…is required to make any other mental events—such as remembering, thinking, feeling and making decisions—happen…Attention is like energy in that without it no work can be done and in doing work it is dissipated. We create ourselves by how we invest this energy. Memories, thoughts, and feelings are all shaped by how we use it. And it is an energy under our control, to do with as we please; hence attention is our most important tool in the task of improving the quality of experience.[20]

---

[20] Mihály Csíkszentmihályi, *Flow: The Psychology of Optimal Experience* (New York: Harper Perennial Modern Classics, 1990), p. 33.

Attention played a key role in Csíkszentmihályi's research on the phenomenology of enjoyment, and he defined enjoyment as containing one or more of the following components: Whatever the task at hand, it contained clear goals. This was in contrast to the routines of everyday life where conflicting demands on a person's time, questioning the necessity of one's actions, and critically evaluating the reasons for carrying them out had a tendency make any one purpose diffuse. For the astrologers that I interviewed the goal was the consultation session.

The task provided immediate feedback. Garry Phillipson, an author of astrological texts and a consulting astrologer, interviewed in September 2007, described it this way:

> One thing I often notice is that, when you get into territory that really registers with the person, something arises which the Buddhists call *pīti*—'pleasurable interest', where you feel a little bit thrilled, that something is afoot. You're hooked in to what's happening and just want to see where it's going. It usually goes along with gooseflesh, hairs standing up on the back of your neck, a tingly feeling. [...]You may have said things that are accurate but they don't seem to have caught the imagination of the person. Then all of a sudden—zing! It's happening and you have this sense that, whether by design or not you've now hit the mother lode. You're now onto something that needs to be talked about.

There was a balance between challenges and skills; the person felt that their abilities were matched to the opportunities of the task. Faye Cossar expressed it this way: 'I try not to do much preparation at length. I usually listen and then find it in the chart and then see what really the consultation's about. I'm much freer with that now I've got more experience [...] I would have been terrified to do that in the beginning. *(laughs)'*.

By concentrating on the task at hand the person was able to navigate between the clarity of goals and constant feedback. Christeen Skinner observed: 'I love watching the reaction. You can really see somebody just flower, it's just fabulous. It's the best job in the world. Who would want to do anything else?'

There was intense concentration on the present, no fear of failure, self-consciousness disappeared, and what remained was clarity of purpose. Sue Tompkins, an author of astrological texts, astrology teacher and consultant from the

UK, interviewed in April 2010 observed: 'I'm not even concentrating but I have certainly forgotten myself. I don't exist. I'm there with this person'.

There was also a feeling that at least temporarily, the person had become part of a larger entity. Madalyn Hillis-Dineen described this feeling thus: 'I feel *so* connected and as if I *do* understand [...] I've come out of my—like having to struggle for the words like I am with you right now and I go into another zone where it all just moves so freely and comfortably and easily.' She went on to note: 'It's like a moment of grace. Spiritual people talk about that moment of grace, or feeling like one with everything. You feel one with the client but at the same token you have to have those boundaries [...] and you're feeling very much like everything is flowing'.

Paradoxically through self-forgetfulness, the sense of self emerged stronger after the experience was over. Jack Fertig, an astrology teacher, an author of astrological texts, and consultant from the US, who has been practicing and teaching astrology since 1977, interviewed in March 2010, expressed it this way:

> I feel enlivened and tired. Have you ever performed on stage? It's that kind of feeling after a show where you feel like energized and exhausted all at once. [....] It's a real good exhausted. Some are better than others, of course, but sometimes I just find myself going, 'Wow! *(breathes out) That* was something! That was really exciting. That was fun. That was—...You know sometimes it's like sky-diving, sometimes it's like giving a speech, sometimes it's like the opening soliloquy of the second act of the *Bacchae*...You come out of the space and come back to the real world feeling exhausted but happy and productive, like, 'Yeah, I've done a good thing here!'

The sense of the duration of time was altered. Clock time no longer marked equal lengths of experienced time, as exemplified by this comment from Karen Hamaker-Zondag: 'You see what time it is but sometimes you don't realize it, that you are so in that whole thing ... that there is something in me that watches the time but it doesn't always come through.' When asked how time passed for her, Darby Costello answered: ' Beautifully. The most beautiful place. No matter how frightened or tormented I am, once I'm there there's nothing else except there. It's another time, it's completely central. [... Then] I get aware of time again. No matter how fascinating [the client].' When I questioned Babs Kirby how she experienced time she responded: '*(Long pause)*....Yes, I suppose time actually goes very quickly and yet it feels a long time all at the same time because it feels like a huge amount of intimacy and intensity has happened in a really actually short amount of time that's felt a very long time'.

The combination of all these elements caused a deep sense of enjoyment so rewarding that a person would expend a great deal of energy simply to feel like this. Lindsay Radermacher interpreted that moment this way: 'It's a gestalt. It speaks as a whole. [...] you've got clues, ideas you might have and how all that little dance works and then something is said and it changes and you *know—(small laugh, pauses)....I* know it's something mysterious, *I* know it's something—*(pause)*...alive.' This sense of aliveness was echoed by Babs Kirby who also worked as a psychotherapist and who compared seeing psychotherapy clients with seeing astrology clients. With the former there was 'a shock process, absorption goes on where I get myself into who they are in some way, and that's happening in a very concentrated way with an astrology client and you've only got the one chance'. She noted that this process could happen incredibly quickly or, at times, not at all, but that when it did happen it felt 'alive'.

Csíkszentmihályi named this state of heightened focus and immersion 'flow', a term coined during his 1975 research interviews when people described their experiences using the metaphor of a water current carrying them along. Csíkszentmihályi's use of flow or becoming absorbed in an activity was thus unrelated to the older phrase, 'go with the flow'. Indeed flow as defined by Csíkszentmihályi helped to integrate the self because in that state of deep concentration consciousness was unusually well ordered. Thoughts, intentions, feelings, and all the senses were focused on the same goal and the experience was one of harmony. Rob Hand expressed it this way:

> When I lecture I'm a different person and in a different way I am also a different person when I do readings. There is actually a shift of consciousness. That's one of the reasons why there's no exhaustion because you're actually operating at a different level than you operate under normal conditions. I have given a number of lectures in which I've said things I didn't know I knew. But I'm not channelling.

> It's just that under the intensity of the experience I see more
> clearly. [....] the intensity of situation causes the mind to
> function differently.

When the flow episode was over, the participants described
the way they felt as more 'together' than before, not only
internally but also with respect to other people and to the
world in general. Linea Van Horn referred to it in this
fashion:

> Something has happened that's good and rich. [...] When
> you have one of these readings where it's really... you meet
> and you—...it's—it's—it's some alchemical thing that I can't
> even describe, and when that happens, everybody feels
> better for it, everybody is enriched and enlivened by it and
> nobody is drained or exhausted by it.

Moreover, although the flow experience appeared to be
effortless, it was far from being so. Csíkszentmihályi put it
this way:

> It often requires strenuous physical exertion, or highly
> disciplined mental activity [such as the capacity to
> manipulate symbolic information.] It does not happen
> without the application of skilled performance. Any lapse in
> concentration will erase it. And yet while it lasts
> consciousness works smoothly, action follows action
> seamlessly.[21]

As Darby Costello put it: 'Preparation is quite fast and on the
surface very casual but inside very, very focused'.

The key element for Csíkszentmihályi was that the
activity was an end to itself. Even if initially undertaken for
other reasons, such as a business practice, as the activity
consumed them it became intrinsically rewarding in and of
itself. The question 'Do you like being in that space?' was
most often met with a 'yes'. Here it is described by Evelyn
Roberts, an astrological entrepreneur living in the UK and
the US who has been practicing astrology since the early
1990s, interviewed in March 2010: 'It's a space that doesn't
exist anywhere else [...] but when I go into the space of
doing a reading it's like something else takes over and [....]
it's a very joyful place for me'.

---

[21] Ibid., p. 54.

Csíkszentmihályi defines such an experience as the *autotelic* experience, derived from two Greek words *auto* meaning self and *telos* meaning goal. When the experience is autotelic the person pays attention to the activity for its own sake, not its consequences. He points out that most enjoyable activities are not natural. They demand an effort that one is initially reluctant to make. However, once the interaction provides feedback to the person's skills, it becomes intrinsically rewarding. When an experience is intrinsically rewarding, life is justified in the present. The flow experience has the potential to make life more rich, intense and meaningful and increase the strength and complexity of the self.

In conclusion, then, reading a chart is more than reading each planetary algorithm as a reductionist exercise. It consists of seeing what the astrologers believe are the alternate possibilities contained within the horoscope. To allow such possibilities to take a more concrete form in a consultation also requires the input of the client and their life experiences. In this way the astrologer assesses for the client how the client is articulating the planetary symbols and the connections they make in the horoscope. The astrologer seeks to understand how the person has made use of the myriad possibilities, so the client's context is important.

However, the process begins before the client arrives. In preparing for a client, drawing up and collating the relevant documents, the astrologers that I interviewed appeared to move into the process of loose construing, gathering data and seeing patterns in ways that allowed them to remain open to the possibilities of the chart. Once the session with the client began, they engaged in a repetition of data, a secular ritual that provided structure and enabled the astrologers to step into the space of reading a chart. Within a relatively short period of time a moment of feedback from the client occurred that changed the phenomenological nature of the consultation. The astrologers then engaged in a pattern-seeking experience which had clear rules and guidelines, required concentration, gained immediate feedback, allowed the self to be put to one side and placed them into a space where time was measured differently. This process offered a sense of self-growth by reflection and, mostly, a feeling of tremendous enjoyment at the end as they emerged from the process. It became an autotelic experience, a sense of flow that made life more rich, intense and meaningful.

There is a great deal more that this research has to reveal but it is clear from these interviews that the phenomenology of how contemporary western astrologers extract meaning from a horoscope is reflective of the creative concepts of loose construing connected with tight construing, followed by flow, forming an autotelic experience. Other astrologers define this experience as mysterious or divine. Yet in the same way as an artist reaches for a special space within which creativity can occur, so this paper argues that astrology can also be considered a creative act, suggesting that reading a natal horoscope is a secular creative endeavour.

GLOSSARY

Ascendant — the point where the ecliptic, the apparent path of the sun through the sky, cuts the plane of the horizon in the east.

Detriment — A planet in detriment is a planet that is opposite its place of rulership. It suggest that the area of life governed by a planet in this place in the horoscope will be unable to fulfil its function in an establishment manner.

Dignity — A method of understanding a planet's ability to fulfil or otherwise the promise it offers in a natal horoscope.

Elements — The twelve signs can be divided into four groups of three signs each by the element they represent: Fire, Earth, Air and Water. Signs in the same element are believed to share basic psychological and temperamental characteristics.

Houses — Formed by dividing up the ecliptic into twelve segments.

Lord of the 7th — Also known as the planet that rules the 7th house. The 7th house is that one-twelfth sector of the local sky just above the western horizon occupied by planets in the two hours just before they set.

Lot of Marriage — A lot is formed by projecting the arc between two points from a third point. The Lot of Marriage is one of the lots that pertain to male-female relationships.

Progressions — Also called secondary progressions, where the movement of the planets over the course of a day represents the movement of the progressed planets over the course of a year.

Signs — The zodiac is divided up into twelve equal segments or divisions called zodiac signs.

T-Square — A geometrical relationship between planets in a chart where two planets are separated by 180 degrees and a third planet sits at a point that is 90 degrees from both of them.

Transits — A chart receives a transit when a planet, in the course of its orbit, reaches a point in the zodiac which was previously occupied by, or geometrically connected to, a point at the time of birth.

BIBLIOGRAPHY

Arroyo, Stephen. *The Practice and Profession of Astrology: Rebuilding Our Lost Connection with the Cosmos*. Reno, NV: CRCS Publications, 1984.

Arnold, Diane G., and Barbara Swaby. 'Neurolinguistic Applications for the Remediation of Reading Problems.' *The Reading Teacher* 37, no. 9 (1984): pp. 831–34.

Barr, Sherrie, and Philip Lewin. 'Learning Movement: Integrating Kinaesthetic Sense with Cognitive Skills.' *Journal of Aesthetic Education* 28, no. 1 (1994): pp. 83–94.

Brady Bernadette. *Predictive Astrology: The Eagle and the Lark*. York Beach, ME: Samuel Weiser, 1992, 1998.

Brockopp, Dorothy Young. 'What Is Nlp?' *The American Journal of Nursing* 83, no. 7 (1983): pp. 1012–14.

Budd, Daniel, 'Been There, Done That: Virtual Vs. Ritual Repetition'. *The Jung Page, Reflections on Psychology Culture and Life* (2006),
http://www.cgjungpage.org/index.php?option=com_content&task=view&id=782&Itemid=40

Cornelius, Geoffrey. *The Moment of Astrology: Origins in Divination*. London: Arkana Penguin Books, 1994.

Csíkszentmihályi, Mihály. *Flow*. New York: Harper Perennial Modern Classics, 1990.

George, Demetra. *Astrology and the Authentic Self*. Lake Worth, FL: Ibis Press, 2009.

Ione, Amy. 'An Inquiry into Paul Cézanne: The Role of the Artist in Studies of Perception and Consciousness'. *Journal of Consciousness Studies* 7, no. 8–9 (2000): pp. 57–74.

Kelly, G. A. *The Psychology of Personal Constructs*. New York: Norton, 1955.

Ptolemy. *Tetrabiblos*. Edited by J. M. Ashmand. Mokelumne Hill, CA: Health Research, 1969.

Sharman-Burke, Juliet and Liz Greene. *The Astrologer, the Counsellor and the Priest*. London: Centre for Psychological Astrology Press, 1997.

Tompkins, Sue. *A Contemporary Astrologer's Handbook: An In-Depth Guide to Interpreting Your Horoscope*. London: Flare Publications, 2006.

Webster, Peter R. 'Creativity as Creative Thinking'. *Music Educators Journal* 76, no. 9 (1990): pp. 22–28.

Willis, Roy and Patrick Curry. *Astrology, Science and Culture: Pulling Down the Moon*. Oxford: Berg, 2004.

Wittkower, Rudolf and Margaret. *Born under Saturn. The Character and Conduct of Artists: A Documented History from Antiquity to the French Revolution*. New York: W. W. Norton, 1963.

READING THE BODY INVISIBLE: SUBTLE BODIES, ASTROLOGY, AND ENERGETIC HEALING

Jay Johnston

ABSTRACT: Traditions of astrological healing continue to attract interest in a variety of ways in contemporary spiritual practice. Overtly through the practice of medical astrology (with its long conceptual heritage) and in more indirect ways through, for example the practice of herbalism in secular contexts and in contemporary pagan religions. Indeed, even models of energetic, or spiritual healing incorporate aspects of celestial influence.

This paper discusses the model of interrelation between self, environment, and cosmos proposed in Wellbeing Spirituality (having developed out of New Age cultural practices) and contemporary pagan groups. In particular it focuses on current popular cultural understandings of the subtle body (including the degree to which it is understood to be comprised of celestial substances). Further, these contemporary practices are considered within the conceptual framework and influence of modern psychology and the secularisation of various astrological and magical traditions found in western esoteric traditions (particularly the Renaissance). That is, how the 'sympathetic' relation of cause and cure is both conceptualised and rendered malleable through the intervention of specific healing rituals.

Health—individual and planetary—is a dominant public discourse of the late-twentieth and early twenty-first centuries. Ranging from specific contagion to emotive effect to global climate dynamics much of our identity (as citizens of western cultures) is formed and defined by the relations we cultivate with the environment that surrounds us: the impact it has on us and we have on it. Hence the profusion of terms like 'balance', 'harmony', 'holistic', 'low-impact', and 'sustainable' in popular culture and especially in the discourse of Wellbeing Spirituality and the complimentary and alternative medicine (CAM) that comprises many of its practices.[1] This chapter is concerned with the most nebulous and expansive of relations presented in this culture, that of subtle bodies and energetic healing. It will consider concepts of self and cosmos as ontologically constituted by a form of spiritual energy and the celestial 'mechanism' through which these relations are established and maintained. Specifically, it will reflect on the contemporary melding of energetic concepts of the body and world with astrological schemas and the processes of manipulation—for example healing techniques or rituals—that are aimed at simultaneously achieving individual and global wellbeing.

Contained in the discussion will be a consideration of the way in which the relations between the concept of subjectivity being employed—the subtle body—and the astrological realm are proposed as interacting, including the type of intersubjective ethics that arises from these relations. That is, that the energetic substance is perceived as both the cause and the cure for individual medical ailments as well as broader environmental issues such as global warming. It seems that there is both personal and communal politics embedded in these particular renderings of celestial substance and planetary activity.

The Subtle Body in Contemporary Culture

The concept that the self is comprised of an energetic anatomy—'auras' or 'sheaths' of spiritual energy or networks of energetic paths—is found in many cultures and historical epochs and is certainly a feature of much New Age and Wellbeing discourse.[2] This is primarily a conceptual legacy of the Theosophical Society (founded 1875 in New York by the now notorious Russian Madame Helena Petrovna Blavatsky and Henry Steel Olcott) however the popularity of 'eastern'

---

[1] Wellbeing Spirituality is the term employed by well-known scholar of New Age religion Paul Heelas to designate specific cultural phenomenon and attitude towards spirituality: 'For participants, spirituality *is* life-itself, the "life-force" or "energy" which flows through all human life (and much else besides), which sustains life' and further that this 'holistic thrust of subjective-life spirituality is intimately bound up with the importance widely attached to healing'. Heelas, *Spiritualities of Life: New Age Romanticism and Consumptive Capitalism* (Oxford: Blackwell, 2008), pp. 27; 34.

[2] For an overview see David V. Tansley, *Subtle Body: Essence and Shadow* (London: Thames and Hudson, 1977).

health modalities like Yoga, Reiki, and Traditional Chinese Medicine have also increased its appeal.

Subtle bodies have also long been a feature of the Western Esoteric tradition (furnished—from among other traditions—by the influence of Neo-Platonism); especially as embodied bridges between the 'earthy' physical world and the ethereal world of spirit. Thus the 'energy' of which they are understood to be made is considered to be a simultaneous form of matter and spirit (matter–consciousness) and much of their popularity is to be found in the way this concept of the self elides dominant mind–body dualisms (especially of the Cartesian variety).[3] Here then is a self that is energetically and ontologically linked to the broader cosmos. It is this energy that is 'operated' on to enact healing and cure, and it is this energy that is 'directed' in contemporary pagan ritual. Therefore it is not surprising to find in the popular literature links between this spiritual substance of self and the influence and ontology of contemporary astrology.

Subtle bodies are often placed in specific relation with astrological energies, whether ontologically (as actually being comprised of a specific celestial substance) or via a relation of sympathetic correspondence. For example, Sasha Fenton associates each of the seven *chakras*[4] (a termed adopted from yogic subtle body schemas) with specific zodiac signs and planet(s).[5] Analysis of this type of correlation is expanded in the next section. The strong influence—which is, unusually, often acknowledged—of Renaissance scholar and physician Marsilio Ficino (1433–1499) is also to be found in contemporary literature.

Ficino, working within the Galenic tradition (wherein the individual is primarily influenced by one of four humors: phlegmatic, melancholic, sanguine, choleric[6]), devoted a

---

[3] For a discussion see Jay Johnston, *Angels of Desire: Esoteric Bodies, Aesthetics and Ethics* (London: Equinox, 2008).

[4] *Chakra*: Sanskrit for 'wheel'. For an account of their conceptualisation in Theosophical discourse see Charles W. Leadbeater, *The Chakras* (Wheaton, IL: Theosophical Publishing House, 1973).

[5] Sasha Fenton, *Simply Chakra* (New York: Sterling/Zambezi, 2009), p. 11.

[6] As Frances Yates summarises: 'Sanguine people were active, hopeful, successful, outward-looking, they made good rulers and men of affairs. Choleric people were irritable, inclined to fighting. Phlegmatic people were tranquil, somewhat lethargic. Melancholy people were sad, poor, unsuccessful, condemned to the most servile

substantial study to the physical, emotional and spiritual effects of Saturn and the melancholia—the philosopher's illness—it reputedly caused.[7] Individuals dominantly affected by Saturn could alleviate their imbalance and illness by taking medicines, undertaking activities, or entering into relations with phenomena that bore the 'signature' of Jupiter. For example, silver, amethyst, white sugar, honey, peacock, calf, and 'constant', 'balanced', 'religious and law abiding' thoughts.[8] These medications and behavioral adjustments were proposed to bring about a change of celestial influence. An invisible sympathy unites these disparate objects and thoughts under Jupiter's ambit.[9]

Ficino's emphasis on emotive states in considering an individual's planetary composition has given this Renaissance scheme broad appeal in contemporary texts on subtle bodies and astrology. Subtle body texts in general— like Anodea Judith's *Eastern Body: Western Mind*[10]—are significantly psychologised with each *chakra* associated with specific emotional states, imbalances, and modes of thought. While texts like Thomas Moore's *The Planets Within: The Astrological Psychology of Marsilio Ficino* bring interpretations of Ficino's work in direct dialogue with contemporary astrological practices.[11]

Here then, are two examples of the types of relations to be found between subtle bodies and astrological systems in Wellbeing literature. Ontological relations: where physical and ephemeral bodies are linked because they are made of the same 'substance'; or relations of association including systems of symbolic correspondence. Both these forms are to be found in the popular material this paper now turns to analyze.

---

and despised occupations'. Frances Yates, *The Occult Philosophy in the Elizabethan Age* (1979; repr., London: Routledge, 2001), p. 59.

[7] Marsilio Ficino, *The Book of Life*, trans. Charles Boer (1489; repr., Woodstock CN: Spring Publications, 1996).

[8] Ibid., pp. 90–91.

[9] For an extended discussion of Ficino and subtle bodies see Johnston, *Angels of Desire*, pp. 114–16.

[10] Anodea Judith, *Eastern Body Western Mind: Psychology and the Chakra System as a Path to Self* (Berkeley, CA: Celestial Arts, 1997).

[11] Thomas Moore, *The Planets Within: The Astrological Psychology of Marsilio Ficino* (1982; repr., Hudson, NY: Lindisfarne Press, 1990).

Natal Charts: Mapping the Subtle Body and its Health

The form of esoteric anatomy presented in texts like Cyndi Dale's *The Subtle Body* is by and large an amalgamation of its rendering in many different cultural sources. This reflects the more general attitude ascribed to New Age religious practices that result from an eclectic approach toward a range of spiritual traditions: what some commentators have termed the 'pick-and-mix' approach (with attendant critique of the politics of appropriation that some borrowings—especially from Indigenous traditions—engender).

Underpinning the diversity of schemas and syncretism is the ontological building block of 'energy'.

> Everything is made of energy: molecules, pathogens, prescription medicines, and even emotions. Each cell pulses electrically, and the body itself emanates electromagnetic fields. The human body is a complex energetic system, composed of hundreds of energetic subsystems. Disease is caused by energetic imbalances; therefore, health can be restored or established by balancing one's energies.[12]

In this basically vitalist system the privileged connection point between the more spiritual realms and the physical body are the *chakras*: hence the emphasis on these energetic 'wheels' in much of the popular literature. It is through these junctures in subtle anatomy that the more refined celestial energies are proposed to enter into a more direct relation with nerve, flesh, organ.

Indeed, *chakras* have been host to many correspondent attributions—sounds, smells, tarot cards, gems, colours—figured as useful and necessary in their activation and 'balancing' all of which s directed towards an individual's healing. This subtle anatomy has been extended to the earth as a whole, when incorporating theories of ley-lines specific places and sites—the pyramids of Giza in Egypt, Uluru in Australia, Stonehenge in Britain are posited as marking the earth's *chakras*.[13] The logic that underpins the efficacy of such

---

[12] Cyndi Dale, *The Subtle Body: An Encyclopedia of Your Energetic Anatomy* (Boulder, CO: Sounds True, 2009), p. xxi.

[13] For discussion of New Age sacred sites see Adrian Ivakhiv, 'Power Trips: Making Sacred Space Through New Age Pilgrimage', pp. 263–86, and Marion I. Bowman, 'Ancient Avalon, New Jerusalem, Heart Chakra of Planet Earth: The Local and the Global

practices and relations is that of the doctrine of signatures; or sympathetic correspondences (such as those operational in Ficino's system briefly outlined above). Not surprisingly then, astrological attributions have also been made.

Fenton in *Simply Chakra* follows contemporary astrological discourse in attributing a dominant role to the sun, moon, and rising sign, considering them as the key influences on an individual's *chakra* 'energy. The diagnosis of an individual's energetic imbalance and resultant physiological disorder is achieved by correlating *chakra* astrological attributions to their natal chart—for example the Crown chakra being associated with Capricorn. Hence, every chakra is assigned a zodiac sign and a 'ruling' planet, although the three 'outer' planets (Fenton describes them as 'new' planets and this of course does not take Pluto's demotion into account) Pluto, Neptune, and Uranus, are not represented. For example, the Base or Root chakra is associated with Aries and Scorpio and the planet Mars; its elemental assignation is earth, number 4, it is gendered masculine, and the physical parts of the body associated with it are the legs and 'base of body' including the genitals and reproductive system. At the opposite end, so to speak, the Crown *chakra* is assigned Capricorn and Aquarius and the planet Saturn; with physical ascriptions being the head and the nervous system.[14]

The twelve zodiac signs do not map neatly over the seven *chakras* and with only two *chakras* below the belly button the lower parts of anatomy have a reduced possibility of representation. Fenton's physiological ascriptions shift significantly from those found in relatively common contemporary astrological texts like Alan Oken's' *Complete Astrology* where Capricorn is more usually associated with the skeleton (especially knees), Aries with the head (especially eyebrows and nose).[15] Indeed Leo and the Sun for example are not associated with the heart and chest region; but with the Solar Plexus *chakra* (the term 'solar' no doubt directing this ascription); Pisces is associated with the Brow chakra (and illnesses like migraine or visual impairments)

---

in Glastonbury', pp. 292–314, in *Handbook of New Age*, ed. D. Kemp and J. R. Lewis (Leiden: Brill, 2007). [See also Nicholas Goodrick-Clarke in this volume, pp. 137–66. –Eds.]

[14] Fenton, *Chakra*, 124–25.

[15] Alan Oken, *Alan Oken's Complete Astrology* (New York: Bantam Books, 1988), pp. 142, fn7; p. 57.

rather than feet whilst Taurus more usually aligned with the throat is attributed to the heart region.

Certainly this example—attribution of Taurus to the heart region—could be influenced by Alice Bailey's *Esoteric Astrology*, one of the texts which comprise the Arcane School's 'blue book' series and are understood to be the work of Bailey's Ascended Master and amanuensis Djwhal Khul.[16] The attributions proposed in this text are reproduced and expanded upon in Alan Oken's *Soul-Centred Astrology: A Key To Your Expending Self*, in which the logic of the association is explained. It relies on the interrelation of Theosophical cosmology (their Seven Planes of Perception) and 'Seven Ray' schemas (individuals express a dominant type of energy which also indicates their level of spiritual development and specific strengths and weaknesses of the personality). Oken writes: "Taurus is only found on the Fourth Ray; the Buddhic is the Fourth plane, and the Human is the Fourth Kingdom. The fourth chakra (through which the Second Ray emanates) is the heart'.[17] Crucial here is the numerological association—Fourth Ray, Fourth Plane, fourth *chakra*—rather than the alignments of rays with *chakras*.

It is perhaps suffice to say that the energy of these planets and zodiac signs that Fenton explicates are understood to correspond and work with the energy of the designated *chakra*. While Oken's text is explicitly founded on a series of differentiated energies, this heritage is not so evidently acknowledged in Fenton's system. However, it is clear that in *Simply Chakra* Fenton is prescribing an esoteric anatomy comprised of differentiated energies and indeed that the natal chart is considered to be the 'blueprint' to an individual's constituting energies. That is, particular planets have a capacity to directly influence the energies of a specific *chakra*: they have a sympathetic association with it. Hence Fenton's example:

> Lily was born with the Sun in Leo, the Moon in Gemini and Cancer rising. Lily is a warmhearted person who is extremely loyal to those she loves, and she is also a hard worker (Sun in Leo; solar plexus chakra). She works in the travel trade, she is on the phone a lot ... She is also extremely

---

[16] Alice A. Bailey, *Esoteric Astrology* (1951; repr., New York: Lucis Publishing Company, 1989).

[17] Alan Oken, *Soul-Centered Astrology: A Key to Your Expanding Self* (Freedom, CA: The Crossing Press, 1990), p. 167.

> fond of her brother ... (Moon in Gemini; throat chakra). She
> loves her beautifully decorated home ... and her family
> means a lot to her (Cancer rising; sacral chakra).
>
> Lily was born with severe problems in her reproductive
> system and cannot have children (sacral chakra). She has
> hypoglycemia, and there is a lot of diabetes in her family
> (solar plexus chakra) ... She suffers from throat problems
> and gets bronchitis after a cold (throat chakra).[18]

The natal chart operates here as a map to operations of the
individual's subtle body. It demonstrates—via physical
illness, personality traits, vocational choices and abilities—
which *chakras* will be dominant and which prone to
imbalance (understood as the cause of physical illness).
Fenton's proposition is once again a reflection of 'esoteric
astrology'—although vastly simplified—as Oken clearly
presents the natal chart as a 'map' of the energetic body and
its health:

> The location of the planets in the natal horoscope, as well as
> their sign positions and geometric aspects, will tell us a great
> deal about the relationship of the chakras, glands, and
> physical organs to one another. The development of the
> energies working through the vital centers may also be
> viewed from the perspective of progressions and transits.[19]

The techniques of healing for what are perceived as innate
physical weaknesses (illustrated by the natal chart) involve
working with objects, states, and materials variously
associated by symbolic relation with the 'unbalanced' *chakra*.
To further explore this type of healing modality a different
genre of publication will be addressed, that which is
associated with contemporary forms of paganism.

ALTERS, SPELLS, AND SUBTLE BODIES:
CONTEMPORARY PAGAN ASTROLOGICAL HEALING

Several contemporary pagan[20] astrological texts focused on
healing are at pains to distinguish their practice from, as they

---

[18] Fenton, *Chakra*, p. 125.

[19] Oken, *Soul-Centered Astrology*, p. 155.

[20] Contemporary paganism is a very diverse practice with many
different groups and traditions. For an overview see Graham
Harvey, *Listening People Speaking Earth: Contemporary Paganism*
(1997; repr., London: Hurst and Company, 2007); Ronald Hutton,

term it, 'New Age' practices (of which Fenton would be an example). For example, Janet and Stewart Farrar and Gavin Bone in *The Healing Craft: Healing Practices for Witches and Pagans* present a critique of the preoccupation with spiritual bodies and energies, which is most clearly articulated as follows:

> While modern medical science has concentrated on the physical body, the New Age movement has made a similar mistake by concentrating entirely on the spiritual. One reason for this polarity has been the New Age movement's theosophical basis. New Age philosophy has inadvertently held on to the concept of original sin, which sees physical matter, and therefore the human body, as spiritually corrupt. A good example of this is their view of the lower chakras, which are seen as the source of black magic by some New Age writers. Pagan healing practices ignore this polarized state, believing that true holistic healing can only occur with the balance of all elemental forces present, and therefore treat the physical and the spiritual equally. This has made pagan healers more likely to work in partnership with modern medical science rather than in opposition, seeing their healing practices as complementary rather than alternative.[21]

Pagan healing as presented by Farrar *et al.* walks the middle ground between an overtly physical or overtly spiritual interpretation of the body (and self). However, similar to Wellbeing discourse they contend that the body 'has a complex energy system governing it'[22] which they view as being fully aligned with the pagan view of the elements (which indeed they consider the basis of the Galenic humors):

> Any imbalance in these elements, or 'humors' as they became known, result in an imbalance in other elements. For example, stress affects and imbalances the element of Water (the emotional realm). Its complimentary element Air (the

---

The Triumph of the Moon: A History of Modern Pagan Witchcraft (Oxford: Oxford University Press, 1999); and Michael F. Strimiska, ed., *Modern Paganism in World Cultures: Comparative Perspectives* (Oxford: ABC CLIO, 2005).
[21] Janet and Stewart Farrar and Gavin Bone, *The Healing Craft: Healing Practices for Witches and Pagans* (Washington: Phoenix Publishing, 1999), p. 29.
[22] Ibid., p. 29.

> psychological processes), initially compensates for this, but if
> the stress continues it will also affect the physical body (the
> element of Earth).[23]

Not represented in the above example is the element of Fire
associated with 'the realm of energy'.[24] This elemental
energetic constitution unites the individual and the world.
Farrar *et al.* claim there is 'no difference between healing the
individual and the world we live in, because in effect it is the
same principle'.[25] Their text is also highly eclectic drawing on
Jungian psychology (especially the concept of universal
archetypes), versions of the Kabbalah, and a subtle body
scheme (employing a basically Theosophical version with
however, eight not seven bodies), and including attendant
astrological associations. The subtle bodies are termed 'auras'
and each aura is assigned an elemental or planetary
correspondence. For example: 'Seventh Plane: Upper Spiritual. Pure or abstract spirit. The divine spark. Substance and
energy directed from the Great Unmanifest. Astrological
symbol the Sun' or 'Second Plane: Lower Astral. Instincts
and Passions. Desire to attract and possess. Astrological
symbol: Mars'.[26]

The associations of mind and emotion Farrar *et al.* give to
each subtle body are as outlined in the Theosophical system.
In the text the authors also clearly adopt the *chakra* system
adding twenty-one minor *chakras* to the major seven, and
they provide information on spiritual/energetic healing
techniques including the 'laying on of hands.' These
additional *chakras* are placed in relationships of correspondence with the western esoteric Kabbalah—in particular
the form found in the Hermetic Order of the Golden Dawn's
publications—and its Sephiroth (understood by Farrer *et al.*
as 'components of the Tree of Life').[27] Each of these
additional *chakras* (which seem to be more like pathways, or
nadi's) are also prescribed Tarot and astro-logical or
elemental associations, for example number fourteen is
'reproductive system—The Empress—Venus'.[28] Similar to
New Age and Wellbeing texts Farrar *et al.* present a very

---

[23] Ibid., p. 30.
[24] Ibid., p. 29.
[25] Ibid., p. 28.
[26] Ibid., p. 89.
[27] Ibid., p. 100.
[28] Ibid., p. 103.

eclectic range of material from Herbalism (including the plants' astrological associations), colour healing, massage, energy healing, shamanic healing techniques, a range of divination practices, lists of healing deities to be evoked through ritual, and spells to be cast.[29] It is to the intertwining of magic and astrology in several contemporary pagan texts that this chapter now turns.

Raven Kaldera, a practicing astrologer and pagan shaman (Northern Tradition), uses western astrology and pagan green magic to introduce a healing practice that incorporates intuition, ritual, and spell-craft. As the back cover text to *Pagan Astrology* further accounts: 'Kaldera includes an extensive compendium of modern magical remedies to counteract negative astrological influences and shows how to use planetary energy to aid Pagan worship and green magic practice thorough spell-casting, love magic, and shamanic stargazing'.[30] Central to this practice is the creation of astrologically aligned altars, whose contents are selected via the logic of energetic correspondences (doctrine of signatures). For example, an alter dedicated to Venus in Scorpio (an often maligned position for the planet) has the following correspondences (including items that are stereotypically associated with strong and/or sordid sexuality):

> Color: light fusia; Animal: weasel; Stone: muscovite; Herbs: coriander, summer savoy; Tree: pawpaw; Items: blackberry or raspberry wine, dark red roses, books on sex magic, books on Tantra, books on sexual psychology, controversial pornography, black lace, black silk gloves, many fine chains, massage oil scented with musk, Obsession perfume.[31]

While, Raven Digitalis—practitioner of eclectic Shadow Magick, pagan Priest and cofounder of Eastern Hellenistic magical system—in *Planetary Spells and Rituals* uses an adapted (and in places vastly different) Theosophical cosmo-

---

[29] Indeed, in the chapter devoted to astrological healing—'Astrology and the Human Body'—they do make direct, if brief, mention Ficino and the *Liber de Vita* (*Book of Life*). Farrar et al., *Healing Craft*, p. 104.
[30] Raven Kaldera, *Pagan Astrology: Spell-Casting, Love Magic and Shamanic Stargazing* (Toronto: Destiny Books, 2009), np.
[31] Ibid., p. 210.

logy to describe the efficacy of spells.[32] In the Theosophical system each of the subtle bodies draws their matter–consciousness from a specific Plane of Perception (of which there are also seven): Physical (including Etheric), Astral (Desire), Manas (Mental), Buddhic (Intuitional), Atmic, Monadic, and Adi (Logos).[33] Significantly he associates the Physical Plane with lunar cycles and the Etheric Plane with planetary energies, writing:

> Etheric Plane Working with the web of near-manifest energy that links all things in existence. The ether exists in all things physical, yet is nonphysical itself (such as the aura of the human body). I view planetary energies as etheric in nature, whereas the planet's actual placements are physical (astronomical), much like the elements themselves (earth, air, fire and water) are physical items that carry an etheric essence.[34]

From this perspective astrological influence is presented as working directly through subtle matter (energy) the very constituent of the subtle body. Regarding the nature of illness, Digitalis further writes:

> Much of the time, ailments of the body are direct reflections of spiritual and emotional imbalances. Because the physical body is the most dense and palpable aspect of our complete self (other bodies include the emotional body, mental body, astral body, etheric body, and so on), illnesses and imbalances can naturally influence other levels and manifest on the physical plane.[35]

This is most definitely a subtle body schema that is being 'expanded' via astrological and magical association. Indeed,

---

[32] Raven Digitalis, *Planetary Spells and Rituals: Practicing Dark and Light Magic Aligned with the Cosmic Bodies* (Woodbury, MN: Llewellyn Publications, 2010).

[33] For further detail on this cosmology see discourses of the Theosophical society and those of Alice A. Bailey's Arcane school: Bailey, *Esoteric Healing* (New York: Lucis Publishing, 1953); Helena P. Blavatsky, *Isis Unveiled. Volume I, Science; Volume II, Theology* (1877; repr., London, Adyar, Wheaton: The Theosophical Publishing House, 1971) and *The Secret Doctrine*, electronic book edition (1888; repr., Quezon City: Theosophical Publishing House, 1995); and M. Temple Richmond, *Sirius* (Mariposa, CA: Source, 1997).

[34] Digitalis, *Planetary Spells*, p. 4.

[35] Ibid., p. 127.

Digitalis' text examines each planet in turn and outlines the type of healing spells associated with them, arguing: 'It's widely accepted that planets influence energy (physical, mental, emotional) beyond simply the moon and the sun, whose effects are obvious and palpable'.[36]

The proposed timing of spells presented is complex with the practitioner advised to take into account a wide range of correspondences: planet, elements, month, moon cycle, day, and hourly associations (an appendix provides a list of correspondences). As to be expected, particular planets oversee a particular genre of spell. Jupiter, for example, is worked-with for the predictable goals of prosperity and wealth, but also to alleviate imbalance caused by 'stagnation' including 'severing fears'. It is also invoked for contemporary shamanic rituals like that of 'soul-retrieval', originally popularised by Sandra Ingerman,[37] which Digitalis describes as a 'practitioner journeying back through time and location in order to reclaim energies that were once left behind' and further as a 'significant and potentially deeply healing ritual'.[38] Such associations are evidence of the continual development of systems of energetic and imaginative correspondence that draw together diverse contemporary spiritual practices.

The most potent planetary association with healing presented by Digitalis is that of Earth. Rituals and spells utilising its energies are directly focused on physical healing and purging impurities from the Astral body.[39] Of the more colourful spells of this type is 'Bullshit of the Holy Cow: Purging Impurities & Astral Pollution':

> The following spell is for leeching toxins from the energetic body, and it will actually aid in leeching impurities from the physical body simultaneously. The odd thing about this spell is that the practitioner is to be covered in cow dung ... one must first realize the immense healing properties of the holy cow's excrement.[40]

---

[36] Ibid.

[37] Sandra Ingerman, *Soul Retrieval: Mending the Fragmented Self* (New York: HarperCollins, 1991).

[38] Digitalis, *Planetary Spells*, p. 180.

[39] Control and cleanliness of the Astral body was also an obsession for Alice Bailey. See Alice A. Bailey, *A Treatise on White Magic* (1934; repr., New York: Lucis Publishing, 1974), pp. 221–22; p. 28.

[40] Digitalis, *Planetary Spells*, p. 130.

Thankfully in the interests of public health he provides instructions for collecting 'safe' bovine excrement. Part of the ritual and healing process involves identifying energetic blockages in the subtle body by use of feeling with the hands, as well as meditating on physical and astral impurities.[41]

PERSONAL HEALING AND PLANETARY HEALTH

What this brief exposition of some of the literature from Wellbeing spirituality and contemporary Paganism has sought to highlight is that both discourses conceptualised the self as constituted by multiple energetic relations: subtle bodies. These are understood to simultaneously effect the individual's spiritual development and their own personal psychological and physical wellbeing as well as that of the broader environment. As the analysis has demonstrated, modern (and Theosophical) astrology has been incorporated into this discourse, providing a system of correspondences and techniques through which these subtle bodies can be known and manipulated.

These healing therapeutics emphasise embodiment and sensuality (the incorporation and use of objects, colours, sounds, smells) which constitutes an aesthetics of body–cosmos alignment. The zodiac and its symbolic correspondences provide a framework through which the ephemeral and energetic constituents of the self can be known. Indeed, the predictable cycles of the planets are put to use to 'control' and 'manipulate' the invisible, and essentially unbounded and unknowable bodies of subtle energy.

BIBLIOGRAPHY

Bailey, Alice A. *A Treatise on White Magic*. 1934. Reprint, New York: Lucis Publishing, 1974.

———. *Esoteric Astrology*. 1951. Reprint, New York: Lucis Publishing Company, 1989.

———. *Esoteric Healing*. New York: Lucis Publishing, 1953.

Blavatsky, Helena P. *Isis Unveiled Volume I, Science; Volume II, Theology*. 1877. Reprinted by London, Adyar, Wheaton: The Theosophical Publishing House, 1971.

---

[41] Ibid., p. 133.

———. *The Secret Doctrine*. 1888. Reprinted in an electronic book edition by Quezon City: Theosophical Publishing House, 1995.

Bowman, Marion I. 'Ancient Avalon, New Jerusalem, Heart Chakra of Planet Earth: The Local and the Global in Glastonbury'. In Kemp and Lewis, eds., *Handbook of New Age*, pp. 292–314.

Dale, Cyndi. *The Subtle Body: An Encyclopedia of Your Energetic Anatomy*. Boulder, CO: Sounds True, 2009.

Digitalis, Raven. *Planetary Spells and Rituals: Practicing Dark and Light Magic Aligned with the Cosmic Bodies*. Woodbury, MN: Llewellyn Publications, 2010.

Farrar, Janet and Stewart, and Gavin Bone. *The Healing Craft: Healing Practices for Witches and Pagans*. Washington: Phoenix Publishing, 1999.

Fenton, Sasha. *Simply Chakra*. New York: Sterling/Zambezi, 2009.

Ficino, Marsilio. *The Book of Life*. 1489. Translated by Charles Boer. Woodstock CN: Spring Publications, 1996.

Harvey, Graham. *Listening People Speaking Earth: Contemporary Paganism*. 1997. Reprint, London: Hurst and Company, 2007.

Heelas, Paul. *Spiritualities of Life: New Age Romanticism and Consumptive Capitalism*. Oxford: Blackwell, 2008.

Hutton, Ronald. *The Triumph of the Moon: A History of Modern Pagan Witchcraft*. Oxford: Oxford University Press, 1999.

Ingerman, Sandra. *Soul Retrieval: Mending the Fragmented Self*. New York: HarperCollins, 1991.

Ivakhiv, Adrian. 'Power Trips: Making Sacred Space Through New Age Pilgrimage'. In Kemp and Lewis, eds., *Handbook of New Age*, pp. 263–86.

Johnston, Jay. *Angels of Desire: Esoteric Bodies, Aesthetics and Ethics*. London: Equinox, 2008.

Judith, Anodea. *Eastern Body Western Mind: Psychology and the Chakra System as a Path to Self*. Berkeley, CA: Celestial Arts, 1997.

Kaldera, Raven. *Pagan Astrology: Spell-Casting, Love Magic and Shamanic Stargazing*. Toronto: Destiny Books, 2009.

Kemp, D., and J. R. Lewis, eds. *Handbook of New Age*. Leiden: Brill, 2007.

Leadbeater, Charles W. *The Chakras*. Wheaton, IL: Theosophical Publishing House, 1973.

Moore, Thomas. *The Planets Within: The Astrological Psychology of Marsilio Ficino*. 1982. Reprint, Hudson, NY: Lindisfarne Press, 1990.

Oken, Alan. *Alan Oken's Complete Astrology*. New York: Bantam Books, 1988.

———. *Soul-Centered Astrology: A Key to Your Expanding Self*. Freedom, CA: The Crossing Press, 1990.

Strimiska, Michael F. ed. *Modern Paganism in World Cultures: Comparative Perspectives*. Oxford: ABC CLIO, 2005.

Tansley, David V. *Subtle Body: Essence and Shadow*. London: Thames and Hudson, 1977.

Temple Richmond, M. *Sirius*. Mariposa, CA: Source, 1997.

Yates, Frances. *The Occult Philosophy in the Elizabethan Age*. 1979.
    Reprint, London: Routledge, 2001.

ASTROLOGY'S PLACE IN HISTORICAL PERIODISATION: MODERN, PREMODERN OR POSTMODERN?

Nicholas Campion

ABSTRACT: External critics of astrology, as well as some internal commentators, have struggled to define astrology's relationship with the modern world. To Enlightenment philosophers and nineteenth-century anthropologists it was premodern, its strange survival in the modern world being an anachronism, posing a problem which could be explained using models of social marginality or psychological inadequacy. To contemporary sociologists it is usually postmodern. In these terms astrology is generally seen as a product either of social marginality or psychological inadequacy, and as a means of providing security for individuals who are unable to cope with the pressures of the modern world. For some who are sympathetic to astrology, though, the escape from modernity into postmodernity is viewed positively, liberating astrology from what are seen as the oppressive and distorting norms of modernity. This paper will suggest that all three positions are based on the notion of a single 'astrology' conforming to a single 'truth' about the nature of modernity, and will critique the 'insecurity' hypothesis. It will suggest that much twenty-first century astrology is modernist in nature and modern in its historical affiliation. Its existence in the modern world therefore ceases to be a problem to be explained. The notions of the modern and the postmodern are also examined and their value as universal descriptions questioned.

There is a view, prevalent amongst sociologists who have looked at the matter, as well as some astrologers, that the modern practice of, or belief in, astrology should be classified as 'postmodern'. For external critics of the discipline, this implies that astrology's survival in the modern west poses an existential problem. For example, in his analysis of the *Los Angeles Times* horoscope column, published in 1953, the Frankfurt School philosopher Theodor Adorno argued that astrology is 'basically discordant with today's universal state of enlightenment'.[1] Adorno held to the view that astrology was fundamentally premodern, a dangerous relic of a superstitious past. In 2001, Alan Smithers, then Sydney Jones Professor of Education and Director of the Centre for Education and Employment Research at the University of Liverpool, commented that 'The continuing hold of astrology on the human psyche is curious', adding the Marxist phrase that it constitutes a 'false consciousness'.[2] For John Bauer and Martin Durant, writing in 1997, such curious discordance could be understood in terms of the decline of modernity, drawing on the notion of the postmodern as what Jameson called 'the cultural logic of late capitalism'.[3] Astrology, Bauer and Durant wrote, is

> one among a number of potential compensatory activities that may be attractive to individuals who are struggling to come to terms with the uncertainties of life in late modernity... belief in astrology is prevalent among particular social groups; groups which, as we have indicated, may be experiencing difficulty in accommodating their religious feelings to life in an uncertain post-industrial culture. Paradoxical as it may seem, therefore, we conclude that popular belief in astrology may be part and parcel of late modernity itself.[4]

Such a view is also found amongst sociologists of religion. For example, Paul Heelas considers that the New Age movement in its counter-cultural aspects, and hence astrology, which he includes as New Age, as an aspect of 'modernity in crisis'.[5] However, he neither defines modernity

---

[1] Theodor Adorno, *The Stars Down to Earth* (1953; repr. London: Routledge, 1994), p. 36.

[2] Alan Smithers, 'Astrology, like literature and music, can invest life with meaning', *The Independent* Wednesday 4 April 2001, http://www.independent.co.uk/news/education/education-news/alan-smithers-astrology-like-literature-and-music-is-capable-of-investing-life-with-meaning-753186.html (accessed 10 Apr. 2010).

[3] Frederic Jameson, *Postmodernism, or, the Cultural Logic of Late Capitalism* (London and New York: Verso, 1991), pp. 55–72.

[4] John Bauer and Martin Durant, 'British Public Perceptions of Astrology: An Approach from the Sociology of Knowledge', *Culture and Cosmos* 1, no. 1 (1997): p. 69.

[5] Paul Heelas, *The New Age Movement: The Celebration of the Self and the Sacralization of Modernity* (Cambridge, MA: Blackwell, 1996), pp. 23, 34, 138.

nor explains why the New Age might not instead be an integral aspect of modernity, rather than a symptom of its historical crisis.

All such sociological opinions are, however, based on problematic assumptions. For example Adorno took the *Los Angeles Times* horoscope column as representative of astrology as a whole, ignoring the astrologers, their clients and readers, and the wide range of astrological literature available at the time. Smithers' assumption that there is a 'false' and hence a 'true' consciousness assumes a world of black-and-white truths which is difficult to sustain from a humanities or social-science perspective: what distinguishes a 'false' consciousness from a 'true' one? Bauer and Durant, meanwhile, offered no evidence for their insecurity hypothesis, which is taken unquestioningly from a prevailing view of the postmodern condition as resulting from a failure to deal with modernity. Neither does Heelas present any evidence in support of the proposition that astrology is New Age and, therefore, postmodern. We are presented, then, in sociological accounts of modern astrology's cultural context with a proposition—that astrology is postmodern—which is essentially evidence-free.

The central theme, then, of most of the literature, is that modern belief in astrology is a phenomenon in urgent need of explanation. However, a counter-argument to the Adorno-Smithers-Bauer-Durant view is to be found within the general literature on the sociology and phenomenology of religion. Andrew Greeley, for example, launched a substantial critique of Adorno and argued that the definition of the paranormal as abnormal is unsustainable.[6] Instead, he claimed that 'the paranormal is normal' and that people who have paranormal experiences are not only 'not kooks... deviants...social misfits' but may actually 'be more emotionally healthy than those who do not have such experiences'.[7] (Astrology is often classified as 'paranormal' in the sense that, as Gray put it, it transcends 'the explanatory power of mainstream science' and is widely included in measures of paranormal belief.[8]) Harvey Irwin has also

---

[6] Andrew M. Greeley, *The Sociology of the Paranormal* (London: Sage Publications, 1975).

[7] Greeley, *Sociology of the Paranormal*, p. 7.

[8] W. D. Gray, *Thinking Critically about New Age Ideas* (California: Wadsworth, 1991), p. 7. See also C. Plug, 'An investigation of superstitious belief and behaviour', *Journal of Behavioural Science* 2,

argued recently that paranormal ideas are widespread, frequently appeal to educated people, and that attempts to label such notions as bizarre or marginal are misleading and unhelpful.[9] Rodney Stark, meanwhile, has argued that Adorno and his colleagues were authoritarian modernists who themselves were concerned with the control of information and ideas in order to suit their own purposes.[10] For their part Caird and Law noted that the tendency to regard adherence to non-conventional religions, in which they included theosophy and spiritualism, as a form of social deviance arises from a flawed model of western religion in which a stable society is said to be currently meeting a unique challenge from new ideological sources which it is obliged to resist.[11] Milton Yinger observed that 'the social *use* of deviation to reconfirm and re-establish boundaries, a theme so powerfully developed by Durkheim, is, I suspect, a prime source of magical beliefs and practices amongst contemporary people', a category in which he included science.[12] As Ninian Smart said of the psychology of religion, there is a sense that the purpose is to explain away the phenomena under consideration, rather than investigate or understand it.[13] The same criticism can be applied to much of the literature on the sociology of astrology.

THE HISTORIOGRAPHY OF MODERNISM

The inquiry should begin with an examination of the historiography of modernism. The difficulties of defining

---

no. 3 (1975): pp. 169–78, as well as, Erich Goode, *Paranormal Beliefs: A Sociological Interpretation* (Illinois: Waveland Press, 2000).

[9] Harvey J. Irwin, *The Psychology of Paranormal Belief: A Researcher's Handbook* (Hatfield: University of Hertfordshire Press, 2009).

[10] Rodney Stark, 'Atheism, Faith, and the Social Scientific Study of Religion', *Journal of Contemporary Religion* 14, no. 1 (1999): p. 56; see also Steven Best and Douglas Kellner, *Postmodern Theory: Critical Interrogations* (London: McMillan, 1991), pp. 3, 37.

[11] Dale Caird and Henry G. Law, 'Non-Conventional Beliefs: Their Structure and Measurement', *Journal for the Scientific Study of Religion* 21, no. 2 (1982): pp. 152–63, here pp. 151–52.

[12] John Milton Yinger, *The Scientific Study of Religion* (New York: MacMillan, 1970), p. 78.

[13] Ninian Smart, *The Phenomenon* (London: MacMillan 1973), p. 37; see also Michael Hill, *Sociology of Religion* (London: Heinemann, 1979), pp. 13–14.

modernism are recognised by some commentators, such as Peter Childs, who argues that the term may be no more than a retrospective imposition on a series of disparate individuals and movements.[14] Some of these problems are rooted in its presumed historical origins, and related arguments such as the proposition that the postmodern, including alternative spiritualities, is at fault for deviating from the Enlightenment inheritance. The challenge to the notion of a single Enlightenment narrative was made by R.G. Collingwood, who questioned the over-simplified view of eighteenth-century intellectual culture as characterised by brave scientists or cool, rational encyclopaedists.[15] The image of the Enlightenment as a single phenomenon marked by a kind of positivist, rational secularism, which underpinned Adorno's critique of astrology is, as Kusukawa and Maclean said of the Scientific Revolution, a 'somewhat dodgy concept'.[16] The European Enlightenment had a diverse nature of its own, including as it did, Emmanuel Swedenborg and large numbers of esoteric freemasons.[17] Joscelyn Godwin inferred, in the use of the term 'Theosophical Enlightenment', that the eighteenth-century advocates of 'alternative spiritualities' were outside the mainstream Enlightenment, so I turn to Dorinda Outram, who has argued that the paganism of the French Enlightenment, which is so important to the foundation of Aquarian and New Age ideas, is part of the Enlightenment, not separate to it.[18] As Gillian Bennett argued, the notion that astrology's existence in the modern world is somehow incompatible with post-Enlightenment rationalism is based on a misunderstanding of popular

---

[14] Peter Childs, *Modernism* (London: Routledge, 2005), p. 13.

[15] R. G. Collingwood, *An Essay on Metaphysics*, revised edition (Oxford: Clarendon Press, 1998),

[16] Nicholas Jardine on S. Kusukawa and I. Maclean, eds., in 'Imagineering the Astronomical Revolution, Essay Review', *Journal for the History of Astronomy* 37, part 4, no. 129 (November 2006): p. 471.

[17] Margaret C. Jacob, *Living the Enlightenment: Freemasonry and Politics in Eighteenth-Century Europe* (Oxford: Oxford University Press, 1991).

[18] Joscelyn Godwin, *The Theosophical Enlightenment* (New York: SUNY Press, 1994); Dorinda Outram, *The Enlightenment* (Cambridge: Cambridge University Press, 1995), pp. 31–46.

belief.[19] In the sense that New Age astrology is a peculiarly twentieth-century innovation, then, following Hanegraaff's arguments on New Age culture's intellectual lineage, it may be seen in part as a product of Enlightenment secularisation.

The problem is partly one of definition, for there is no universally accepted meaning of the terms modern and postmodern. Modernism is often defined as characterised by science, materialism, technology, secularism, and a rejection of religion and spirituality. In Charles Jencks' words it is 'the social condition of living in an urban, fast-changing, progressivist world governed by instrumental reason'.[20] Jencks recognises three 'forces' of the modern movement: 'modernisation, the condition of modernity and cultural Modernism'.[21] The problem is that these three may by no means be compatible. In any case, to Childs, 'Modernism' (along with 'Modern' and 'Modernity') is simply a word.[22] To attach too much significance to a word, as if the thing described *is* the word is therefore fundamentally mistaken. There is a world of difference between saying that such-and-such a thing *may be described* as modern, and to say that it *is* modern. Thus Bauer and Durant's error is to assume that there really *is* a historical condition called late modernity, and that astrology really *does* have certain qualities which make it late modern in character.

Jean-Francois Lyotard, who did so much to define modernism, characterised it as marked by 'grand-narratives', the belief in universal truths, of which an influential example is provided by the Enlightenment narrative of the hero-scholar on a quest for truth.[23] For Raymond Williams, writing as a socialist, modernism in politics is characterised by the global domination of 'late-capitalism', with its emphasis on economic production at the cost of all other values.[24] For both

---

[19] Gillian Bennett, *Traditions of Belief: Women, Folklore and the Supernatural Today* (London: Penguin, 1987) pp. 24–25.

[20] Charles Jencks, *What is Post-Modernism?* (1986; repr. London: Academy Editions, 1996), p. 8.

[21] Charles Jencks, *The Post-modern Reader* (London: Academy Editions, 1992), p. 11.

[22] Childs, *Modernism*, p. 12.

[23] Frederic Jameson, foreword to Jean-Francois Lyotard, *The Postmodern Condition: A Report on Knowledge* (Manchester: Manchester University Press, 1985), p. xxiii.

[24] Raymond Williams, *The Politics of Modernism: Against the New Conformists* (London: Verso, 1989).

Lyotard and Williams, modernism becomes oppressive, restrictive and anti-democratic: it emphasises the collective over the individual and is expressed through the disenchanting consequences of technology.

However, the problem with such views is their ahistorical nature. They can only survive through the careful exclusion of two key qualities of the modernising project. The first is the development of liberal democracy with its emphasis on individual rights and choice. The second is modernism in one vital area: the arts, the prime representative of Jencks' 'third force', cultural Modernism. We should turn again to Raymond Williams, who notes that aspects of culture defined as modern, such as avant-garde art, are taken to be representative of 'modernity' as a whole, while being quite clearly not representative of the entire modern world.[25]

Modernism in the arts prioritised precisely those qualities which are supposedly denied by modernity's materialistic denial of individuality and imagination. Amongst leading artists there is no shortage of examples. We could take Wassily Kandinsky, the founder of abstract painting, a theosophist and mystic, who 'who disliked the values of progress and of science and longed for a regeneration of the world through a new art of pure "inwardness"'.[26] Then there is W. B. Yeats representing poetry. Both Kandinsky and Yeats were devout theosophists, driven by the need to manifest the spiritual truths required for the implementation of Blavatsky's new spiritual world.[27] Amongst modernist musicians, Gustav Holst was deeply influenced by the modernizing astrologer Alan Leo (from whose writings his *Planets Suite* took its inspiration), while André Breton, the founder of surrealism, was a practising astrologer.[28] Even if we were to argue that these four were not typical of modernist artists, which would be a difficult line to take, their very presence sabotages cosy notions of modernism as

---

[25] Williams, *Politics of Modernism*, p. 33.

[26] E. H. Gombrich, *The Story of Art*, 15th edition, revised, (London: Phaidon Press, 1995), p. 370.

[27] Elizabeth Heine, 'W. B. Yeats: Poet and Astrologer', *Culture and Cosmos* 1, no. 2 (Winter/Autumn 1997): pp. 60–75.

[28] Raymond Head, 'Astrology, Modernism and Holst's "The Planets"', *Astrology Quarterly* 65, no. 1 (Winter 1994–95): pp. 40–54; Nicholas Campion, 'Surrealist Cosmology: André Breton and Astrology', *Culture and Cosmos* 6, no. 2 (Autumn/Winter 2002): pp. 45–56.

materialist and alternative spiritualities as postmodern. The term 'modern' then becomes not a defined set of modalities, but a convenient description for use in certain circumstances, when postmodern might do equally as well. As Raymond Head wrote, in his study of the composer Gustav Holst, 'Modernism was not conceived as a style but a loose collection of ideas. It was a term which covered a range of movements and styles that largely rejected history and applied ornament, and which embraced abstraction'.[29] As the literary critic Chris Baldick wrote, 'Modernist writers tended to see themselves as an avant-garde disengaged from bourgeois values, and disturbed their readers by adopting complex and difficult new forms and styles. [They] replaced the logical exposition of thoughts with collages of fragmentary images and complex allusions...'.[30] This is aesthetic modernity, but modernity nonetheless. Yet, surely the fragmentation of the individual is a quality ascribed to postmodernity. As Best and Kellner wrote

> Aesthetic modernity emerged in the new avant-garde modernist movements and bohemian subcultures, which rebelled against the alienating aspects of industrialization and rationalization, while seeking to transform culture and to find creative self-realization in art.[31]

Is there, then, any difference between modernity and postmodernity in art beyond the labels imposed by this critic or that in this or that context? Not necessarily. After all, the crisis in late modernity identified by Bauer and Durant as fundamentally antipathetic to modernity, is for Cinzia Blum, an integral feature of modernism.[32] The issue is not whether there is such a universal phenomena either as modernity or modernism, but that the confusion amongst even the most distinguished theorists is such that to then define such-and-such a contemporary belief or practice as modern, in contrast to others which are not modern, is highly problematic.

---

[29] Victoria & Albert Museum,
http://www.vam.ac.uk/vastatic/microsites/1331_modernism/the_exhibition.html (accessed 17 March 2010).

[30] Chris Baldick, *The Concise Oxford Dictionary of Literary Terms* (New York: Oxford University Press, 1991).

[31] Best and Kellner, *Postmodern Theory*, p. 2.

[32] Cinzia Blum, *The Other Modernism: F. T. Marinetti's Futurist Fiction of Power* (Berkeley: University of California Press, 1996), p. 3.

The Historiography of Postmodernism

The historiography of postmodernism is no less confused than that of modernism, even though it is supposedly one of the guiding philosophies of recent times. According to Thomas Docherty,

> there is hardly a single field of intellectual endeavour which has not been touched by the *spectre* of 'the postmodern'. It leaves its traces in every cultural discipline from architecture to zoology, taking in on the way biology, forestry, geography, history, law literature and the arts in general, medicine, politics, philosophy, sexuality, and so on.[33]

Yet, although the term is widely used, there is little more understanding of what it means than there is of modernism. Charles Jencks considered that postmodernism focuses on the individual rather than the collective: 'Above all', he argued, 'it is characterized by the attempt to place humanity and, in particular human reason, at the centre... [its] root meaning, to be beyond or after the modern, remains common to diverse usage'.[34] Part of the problem is that, for Jencks, postmodernism means the continuation and transcendence of modernism, rather than its end.[35] Under these circumstances almost any attempt to distinguish the modern from the postmodern is doomed. As an example, Jencks argues that postmodernism represents the end of a single world view. But when was there ever such a single world view?

The discussion of postmodernism is as confused as is that of modernism, partly because the former is often simply seen as an alternative to the latter. For example, Inglehart, repeating Jencks, argues that,

> In post modernisation, the core project is to maximise the individual well being, which is increasingly dependent on subjective factors. Human behaviour shifts from being

---

[33] Thomas Docherty, *Postmodernism: A Reader* (Hemel Hempstead: Harvester Wheatsheaf, 1993), p. 1.

[34] Jencks, *The Post-modern Reader*, p.10.

[35] Ibid., p.11

> dominated by the economic imperatives of providing food, clothing and shelter towards the pursuit of quality of life.[36]

However, as noted above, such a view is only possible if political modernization—the development of liberal democracy and human rights—is excluded. Thus modernity is caricatured (falsely) as inimical to the interests of the individual and found wanting.

Such confusion was noted by Charles Jencks, who admitted that 'Most people have heard of Post-Modernism and don't have a clear idea of what it means. They can be forgiven this confusion because Post-Modernists don't always know and, even when they think they do, often find themselves disagreeing'.[37] True, Jencks finds such confusion to be a legitimate consequence of Postmodernism's essential nature: 'One of the reasons it became potent', he argued, 'was its suggestive ambiguity, the way it specified the departure point, but left open the final destination'.[38] Docherty noted the problem—that if the word 'postmodern' is ambiguous, some confusion is inevitable: 'The term itself hovers uncertainly in most current writings between—on the one hand—extremely complex and difficult philosophical senses, and—on the other hand—an extremely simplistic mediation as a nihilistic, cynical tendency in contemporary culture'.[39]

However, the problem is not one of ambiguity, but of a lack of historical sense. Discussions of postmodernism as opposed to modernism take place in a historical vacuum, fictionalising the recent past as authoritarian and materialistic. For example, according to Best and Kellner, 'the postmodern is associated with the pagan, with the absence of rules, criteria, and principles, and with the need for experimentation and producing new discourses and values'.[40] But this, of course, is precisely what characterises modernity, not postmodernity, in the arts. According to Blum, 'Futurism', described as the 'earliest incarnation of the

---

[36] Ronald Inglehart, *Modernization and Postmodernization* (Princeton, NJ: Princeton University Press, 1997), p. 75.

[37] Charles Jencks, *Post-Modernism: The New Classicism in Art and Architecture* (London: Academy Editions, 1987), p. 7.

[38] Jencks, *The Post-modern Reader*, p. 10.

[39] Docherty, *Postmodernism*, p. 1.

[40] Best and Kellner, *Postmodern Theory*, p. 164.

modernist avant-garde', was 'characterised by striking ambivalences and contradictions'.[41]

The Postmodern-Modern dichotomy also collapses when we consider cosmology. Postmodernism supposedly takes a perspectivist viewpoint in contrast with the universalism of modernism, in which the universe is the same from wherever one views it. But if such perspectivism is located in Einsteinian relativity, are we genuinely supposed to argue that Einstein was a postmodernist? And astrologers, who believe in universal laws, are not exactly postmodernists.

Worse for the notion of postmodernism, Eleanor Heartney pointed out that its existence can only be understood in relation to modernism and that its presumed characteristics (incredulity towards metanarratives, a crisis of cultural authority and the shift from production to reproduction) are evidence of an identity crisis so severe that 'its most ardent advocates seem unable to come to any consensus about what, exactly it is'; it feels, she continued, 'like Narcissus' reflection in the water, which disintegrates the moment one reaches out to grasp it'.[42]

To sum up, then we have two problems with the definition of astrology as postmodern. First we have the awkward problem of avowedly modernising astrologers. Are they really suffering from a 'false consciousness'? As phenomenologists should we not take their self-description seriously? The only way to incorporate them into the postmodern world is to argue that the modernising project is actually postmodern, at which point all attempts to distinguish the two finally dissolve. Second, postmodern theory is essentially ahistorical and makes confident statements about the present which are almost devoid of knowledge about the past, to which it is compared. Johannes Wolfart recognised that all the various versions of post-modernism (of which there are as many as there are observers) are united by the belief that history is passing through a transitional phase.[43] Postmodernism is really a form of postmillennialism, a species of historical mythology that is predicated on a peaceful transition to a new world,

---

[41] Blum, *The Other Modernism*, p. 1.

[42] Eleanor Heartney, *Postmodernism* (London: Tate Publishing, 2001), pp. 6–7.

[43] Johannes C. Wolfart, 'Postmodernism', in *Guide to the Study of Religions*, ed. Willi Braun and Russell T. McCutcheon (London: Cassell, 2000), p. 381.

and it makes no more sense to ask whether New Age is postmodern than to consider whether postmodernism is New Age.

Zigmunt Bauman recognised the problem of defining postmodernism as a historical phase when he claimed that the term means different things to different people and 'perhaps more than anything else [it is] a *state of mind*'.[44] Bauman lets us out of the modern/postmodern trap. The release from modernism-postmodernism as successive historical periods does not, though, remove the trap posed by the concept of two discrete modes of thought.

However even the notion of postmodernism is subverted by postmodernists. Lyotard argues that the postmodern 'is undoubtedly a part of the modern...a work can only become modern if it is first postmodern. Postmodernism thus understood is not modernism at its end but in its nascent state'.[45] So Mary Klages can then argue that 'Postmodernism ...doesn't lament the idea of fragmentation, provisionality, or incoherence, but rather celebrates that. The world is meaningless? Let's not pretend that art can make meaning then, let's just play with nonsense'.[46]

ASTROLOGY AS DEVIANT

The question arises then, as to whether astrology's survival in the modern world is anachronistic. This question may be addressed by challenging the positivist argument that 'belief' as a whole, and hence belief in astrology, is itself anachronistic. The argument is fundamentally an epistemological one and concerns the issue of who has the right to pronounce on matters of truth; the positivist view that only modern science can make such declarations was shown to be deeply flawed.

Thus the labelling of astrology as deviant may be no more than a device to confirm what Glock and Stark called the 'humanistic value-orientation'; in other words what Herbrechtsmeier termed the 'imperial' attitudes of modern

---

[44] Zygmunt Bauman, *Intimations of Postmodernity* (London: Routledge, 1992), p. vii.

[45] Lyotard, *Postmodern Condition*, p. 79.

[46] Mary Klages, Colorado University, http://www.colorado.edu/English/courses/ENGL2012Klages/pomo.html (accessed 18 April 2010).

science.[47] It is also an application of what Stenmark termed 'methodological scienticism', the mistaken application of inappropriate scientific methodologies to questions which they cannot answer.[48] The proposition that belief in astrology needs to be explained as if its modern existence is anachronistic is itself the product of what Dean *et al.*, ironically referring to astrologers, described as systematic errors of human judgment.[49] As a result, Stark continued, 'It is now impossible to do credible work in the social scientific study of religion based on the assumption that religiousness is a sign of stupidity, neurosis, poverty, ignorance, false consciousness, or that it represents a flight from modernity'.[50]

The argument that belief in astrology is out of step with modernity is based on questionable *a priori* assumptions, chiefly that astrology is necessarily false, and therefore incompatible with the value modernity supposedly places on scientific truth, and that it appeals to individuals whose insecurity renders them unable to deal with the pressures of modernity.

REASONS FOR BELIEF IN ASTROLOGY: IS ASTROLOGY FALSE?

The argument that astrology is postmodern because it is necessarily false, requires that explanations be established for why people believe in it, in contradiction of all the evidence. A number of different hypotheses are proposed. For example, the cosmologist Stephen Hawking took a functional view, seeing the desire for control as crucial: 'The Human race has always wanted to control the future', he wrote, 'or at least to predict what will happen. That is why astrology is so

---

[47] Charles Y. Glock and Rodney Stark, *Religion and Society in Tension* (Chicago: Rand McNally, 1965), pp. 10–11; William Herbrechtsmeier, 'Buddhism and the Definition of Religion: One More Time', *Journal for the Scientific Study of Religion* 32, no. 1 (1993): p. 15.

[48] Mikael Stenmark, *Scientism: Science, Ethics and Religion* (Aldershot: Ashgate, 2001), pp. 2–3.

[49] Geoffrey Dean, Ivan Kelly, and Arthur Mather, 'Astrology', in *The Encyclopaedia of the Paranormal*, ed. Gordon Stein (New York: Prometheus Books, 1996), pp. 89–90.

[50] Stark, 'Atheism, Faith, and the Social Scientific Study of Religion', pp. 56–57.

popular'.[51] The philosopher Bernulf Kanitscheider advanced what we may call the 'gullibility hypothesis', blaming publicity through the media, an argument which may explain how belief spreads but not why it spreads.[52] Geoffrey Dean and his collaborators, including Ivan Kelly, an educational psychologist at the University of Saskatchewan, proposed four reasons for belief in astrology, all assuming gullibility: 'reading sun signs', 'reading astrology books', 'visiting an astrologer' and 'being an astrologer', their argument being that 'astrology seems to work, so we become believers'.[53] Dean emphasises the personal experience that comes from an experience of astrology 'working', whether through reading horoscope columns, and either visiting, or working as, an astrologer. This much is acknowledged by sceptics. For example, Robert Basil conceded that there is an experiential basis for many New Age beliefs; the distinction, though, is between experience and explanation, and the former does not constitute version of the latter.[54] According to Kelly, although its claims are false, 'many people appear to be attracted to astrology because it seems simple and speaks to their lives'.[55] Astrology, in other words, has an immediate and effective way of communicating personal meaning. Dean and Mather agree, suggesting that 'The great popularity of astrology is due largely to its symbolic and non-scientific nature, for this makes it instantly helpful in understanding, i.e. [sic] in areas of belief'.[56] This line of argument takes us close to the notion of astrology as meaning-making. In this regard we can find an analogy in the novel. In response to the rhetorical question, 'Why Write Novels?', Derek Johns wrote 'the reasons we write fiction… [is that] we are story-

---

[51] Stephen Hawking, *The Universe in a Nutshell* (London: Bantam Press, 2001), p. 103.

[52] Bernulf Kanitscheider, 'A Philosopher looks at Astrology', *Interdisciplinary Science Reviews* 16, no. 3 (1991): pp. 259–60.

[53] Geoffrey Dean, 'Discourse for Key Topic 4: Astrology and Human Judgement', *Correlation* 17, no. 2 (Northern Winter 1998/9): pp. 26–28, 47–51; see also Dean, Kelly and Mather, *Astrology*, pp. 86–88.

[54] Robert Basil, 'New Age Thinking', in *The Encyclopaedia of the Paranormal*, ed. Gordon Stein (New York: Prometheus Books, 1996), p. 458.

[55] I. W. Kelly, 'Why Astrology Doesn't Work', *Psychological Reports* 82 (1998): p. 542.

[56] Geoffrey Dean and Arthur Mather, *Recent Advances in Natal Astrology* (Subiaco, Australia: Analogic, 1977), p. 3.

telling creatures who must shape our experience and share it with others'.[57]

The real debate here, though, is not between an astrology that is scientifically, objectively verifiable in the modern sense (requiring statistically replicable data) on the one hand or, on the other, one that is scientifically false and, depending on one's perspective, either a useful way of constructing meaning or a superstition to be eradicated. It concerns the competing views relating to the personal evaluation of evidence. That is, for an individual who experiences astrology as true, the problem of belief, as framed by the sociologists, disappears, for the belief is not in something which is known to be untrue. Most of the scientific and sceptical literature on astrology is published in small-circulation academic journals and largely unknown outside a tiny circle of interested scholars. It therefore has no impact on general public perceptions of astrology. However, debates on significant arguments concerning certain scientific tests of astrology are widely known amongst students and professionals of astrology, but such people also know that sceptical claims and negative results are contested.[58] Therefore, neither general lay interest in astrology, nor deeper engagement in the practice, involve belief in something which is known to be scientifically untrue. The need to explain belief in the phenomenon is therefore based on mistaken assumptions.

REASONS FOR BELIEF IN ASTROLOGY: PREHISTORIC ERROR

The arguments that astrology is inherently false are rooted in the notion of religion as 'primitive error', which were well summarised by James Thrower.[59] This argument also circulates in critical media comments on astrology.[60] The 'primitive error' hypothesis adopts a scheme of periodisation in which it is assumed that astrology belongs to a primitive,

---

[57] Derek Johns, 'Why Write Novels?', *The Author* (Autumn 2008): p. 95.

[58] Nicholas Campion, *A History of Western Astrology*, Vol. 2, The Medieval and Modern Worlds (London: Continuum, 2009), pp. 265–75.

[59] James Thrower, *Religion: The Classical Theories* (Edinburgh: Edinburgh University Press, 1999), pp. 99–125.

[60] Magnus Linklater, 'An academic dispute that is out of this world', *The Times*, 30 August 2001, p. 12.

prehistoric, phase of human intellectual evolution, and that its survival in the modern world therefore represents a disjunction between those individuals who believe in it and the state of intellectual evolution appropriate to modernity. This is why Smithers could refer to astrology as 'false consciousness'.

The evolutionary position in religion was summarised comprehensively by Jevons, who argued that progressively, over the millennia, as humanity evolved, it used its reason to correct false beliefs and identify true ones so that religion, even though fundamentally false, became progressively less so.[61] The philosophical framework for this hypothesis is inherited from the evolutionist theories of religion as developed by anti-Christian positivists, notably Edward Tylor in 1873, James Frazer in 1890, Emile Durkheim in the 1910s and Bronislaw Malinowski in the 1920s. Broadly speaking, the evolutionist perspective holds that religion originates as 'primitive' totemism, animism, or magic, in which natural forces are animated or anthropomorphised, evolves through polytheism into monotheism and finally, in line with the law of progress, into atheist materialism.[62]

Tylor set the tone for cultural-evolutionist discussions of astrology in strident tones, following his discussion of magic. Forgetting that notions of 'truth' are beyond the remit of the anthropologist, he wrote of astrology,

> Looking at the details here selected as fair examples of symbolic magic, we may well ask the question, is there in this whole monstrous farrago no truth or value whatsoever? It appears that there is practically none, and that the world has been enthralled for ages by a blind belief in processes wholly irrelevant to their supposed results, and which might as well have been taken the opposite way.[63]

Tylor's rhetoric ('monstrous farrago... enthralled... by a blind belief'), though, is hardly scholarly. These are words which spring from a deep and profound anger, rage almost, at a perceived affront to the whole of civilisation which has survived from a primitive stage of human development.

---

[61] Frank Jevons, *Introduction to the History of Religions* (London: Methuen, 1896), pp. 402–3.

[62] E. E. Evans-Pritchard, *Social Anthropology* (London: Cohen and West, 1967), pp. 31–33; Hill, *Sociology of Religion*, pp. 19–43.

[63] Edward Burnett Tylor, *Primitive Culture*, vol. 1 (London: John Murray, 1873), p. 133.

Somehow astrology's survival represented a grand paradox, as if, somewhere in central London men were still living in caves, killing each other with flint axes. Astrology, in this sense, was barbaric. This notion that astrology is an affront to civilised values occurs in the research of such scientists as Miller, who concluded that astrology should be resisted because it is un-American in that its fatalism is inimical to democracy.[64] Such views underpin the anger which drives sceptical hostility to astrology.

Yet the notion of early humans as necessarily intellectually primitive has been thoroughly dismantled by a succession of anthropologists, notably by Evans-Pritchard. The error, as Victor Turner has pointed out, was not only to assume that an absence of Christianity indicated primitive status but that the presence of simple technology is evidence of simple minds.[65] The cultural-evolutionary model is, quite simply, not credible. It fails the first test of any sound hypothesis—it lacks evidence. Yet it remains the preferred model of anti-astrology sceptics.

If it can be argued that magic is a primitive form of religion, and that religion itself results from primitive error, then astrology can be deemed false purely by defining it as magic. For example, Lawrence Jerome, one of the driving forces behind the 1975 'Objections to Astrology' argued that 'astrology is false because it is magic' and that, consequently, 'to bow to the magical "dictates of the stars" is to abandon free will and rationality'.[66]. Statements such as those of the sceptic George Abell, for whom belief in astrology is necessarily 'incredible and absurd', can therefore be understood in their historical context as a manifestation of the positivist proposition that all religious belief is patently false.[67]

---

[64] Jon D. Miller, 'The Public Acceptance of Astrology and other Pseudo-science in the United States', paper presented to the 1992 annual meeting of the American Association for the Advancement of Science, 9 February 1992.

[65] Victor Turner, *The Ritual Process: Structure and Anti-Structure* (New Brunswick and London: Aldine Transaction, 2008), p. 3.

[66] Lawrence Jerome, 'Astrology: Magic or Science?', *The Humanist* 35, pt. 5 (Sept/Oct 1975): pp. 10, 16.

[67] George O. Abell, 'Astrology' in *Science and the Paranormal: Probing the Existence of the Supernatural*, ed. George O. Abell and Barry Singer (London: Junction Books, 1981), pp. 70–94.

However, although the idea that there are such mutually exclusive categories as magic, religion and science, is still popular amongst most sceptics, as well as many scientists and academic theologians, it is generally regarded as untenable amongst historians of ideas. The notion that science both follows magic and religion as part of an inevitable evolutionary process, and is separated from them as an entirely distinct mode of perception, has been critiqued in general terms by Stanley Tambiah, in relation to the sixteenth to eighteenth-centuries by Charles Webster and Frances Yates and, in respect of the twentieth century, by Milton Yinger.[68] Rodney Stark, writing as a sociologist, argued that the evolutionist point of view, based in what he regarded as the erroneous notion of the 'primitive mind', was 'incorrect, extremely misleading, and often simply fabricated', and had been discredited once anthropologists began to conduct rigorous fieldwork rather than rely on theory.[69] Let me make it clear that, to blur the distinctions between magic, religion, and science is not to deny that science may follow distinct evidential procedures which themselves may bring major and beneficial advances in knowledge, but to acknowledge that the boundaries in their historical development overlap. The key to the relationship between the three is magic. Contrary to the views of such anthropologists as Durkheim, who attempted to distinguish between religion and magic, religion contains many magical elements in the form of attempts to manipulate the visible world by engaging with the invisible.[70] Meanwhile, as Charles Webster so persuasively demonstrated, modern science emerged in the sixteenth to eighteenth centuries not as a clean and decisive reaction against magic but as a smooth progression, as notions of experimental method and the evaluation of evidence developed. The terms 'science',

---

[68] Stanley Jeyaraja Tambiah, *Magic, Science, Religion and the Scope of Rationality* (1984; repr. Cambridge: Cambridge University Press, 1990); Charles Webster, *From Paracelsus to Newton: Magic and the Making of Modern Science* (Cambridge: Cambridge University Press, 1982); Frances Yates, *The Occult Philosophy in the Elizabethan Age* (1979; repr. London: Routledge and Kegan Paul, 1983); Frances Yates, *The Rosicrucian Enlightenment* (1972; repr. London: Routledge and Kegan Paul, 1986); Yinger, *The Scientific Study of Religion*, p. 77.

[69] Stark, 'Atheism, Faith, and the Social Scientific Study of Religion', p. 47.

[70] Emile Durkheim, *The Elementary Forms of Religious Life*, trans. Karen E. Fields (1912; repr. New York: The Free Press, 1995).

'magic', and 'religion', are therefore constructs which mean different things to different people in different contexts.

REASONS FOR BELIEF IN ASTROLOGY: THE INSECURITY HYPOTHESIS

Inextricably tied to the notion that astrology represents the survival of magical, primitive religion is the theory that it originates as a means of providing security to people who are naturally insecure, fearful and unable to deal with their environment or responsibilities without a crutch—an argument made extensively in relation to the origins of astrology in the ancient near-east, but now questioned.[71] The assumption that insecurity produces, in stages, fear, low-self-esteem, 'persuasability' (i.e., gullibility) and, ultimately, belief in astrology, has entered the psychological literature as a rationale for contemporary belief in astrology.[72] The astronomer Bart Bok, for example, cited a statement put out by the Society for Psychological Study of Social Issues (SPSSI), which posited personal inadequacy, claiming that,

> The principal reason why people turn to astrology and to kindred superstitions is that they lack in their own lives the resources necessary to solve serious personal problems confronting them. Feeling blocked and bewildered they yield to the pleasant suggestion that a golden key is at hand—a simple solution—an ever present help in time of trouble.[73]

The problem with such assertions is that they are taken as a given. Neither Bok nor the SPSSI had any evidence: they

---

[71] Campion, *A History of Western Astrology*, vol. 2, p. 44.

[72] See for example Peter Glick and Mark Snyder, 'Self-Fulfilling Prophecy: the Psychology of Belief in Astrology', *The Humanist* 46, pt. 3 (May-June 1986): p. 50; I. L. Janis, 'Personality correlates of susceptibility to persuasion', *Journal of Personality* 22 (1954); I. L. Janis, 'Anxiety Indices related to susceptibility to persuasion', *Journal of Abnormal and Social Psychology* 51 (1955); Adorno, *Stars Down to Earth*, p. 3.

[73] Bart J. Bok and Margaret W. Mayall, 'Scientists Look at Astrology', *The Scientific Monthly* 52 (1941): p. 244; see also Bart J. Bok, Lawrence E. Jerome, and Paul Kurtz, 'Objections to Astrology: A Statement by 186 Leading Scientists', *The Humanist* 35, no. 5 (September/October 1975): p. 18.

were taking a faith position.[74] Simply, there had been no studies and hence no evidence to support their proposition, and the political imperative of condemning astrology took priority over the normal evidential requirements of science. In that Bok's position was evidence-free, it was a paradoxical manifestation of 'anti-science' within the scientific community. The problem was identified by Carl Sagan in 1975: when invited to sign that year's manifesto, 'Objections to Astrology', he refused on the grounds that none of the signaturees had any knowledge of astrology, that the experimental data was absent, and that the whole exercise represented an authoritarian and fundamentally dishonest attempt to impose one group's set of values in another.[75] Sagan had no time for astrology, which he dismissed as a 'pseudoscience', yet he regarded the position of the organised sceptics as untenable, on the grounds that to speak as scientists was incompatible with an absence of evidence.[76]

In spite of its wide currency, the 'insecurity' rationale for the development of ancient astrology should not be taken for granted. It has been notably challenged by Ulla Koch-Westonholtz on the grounds that, firstly, it represents the inappropriate projection of modern concerns on to an ancient society and, secondly, that the Babylonian omen literature (from which western astrology is descended) indicates a society which was very certain of its beliefs.[77] Similarly the social-psychologists Harry Gollob and James Dittes questioned the supposed relationship between low self-esteem and belief, arguing that there is no evidence that one leads to the other.[78] Rodney Stark then showed that, far from religion appealing to the inadequate and insecure, religious people enjoy better than average mental and physical

---

[74] Nicholas Campion, 'Do Astrologers Have to Believe in Astrology?', *The Sceptic* 15, no. 2 (Summer 2002): pp. 20–22.

[75] Carl Sagan, *The Demon-Haunted World: Science as a Candle in the Dark* (New York: Random House, 1997), p. 285.

[76] Carl Sagan, *Cosmos: the Story of Cosmic Evolution, Science and Civilisation* (London: Warner Books, 1994), p. 66.

[77] Ulla Koch-Westonholz, *Mesopotamian Astrology* (Copenhagen: Museum Tusculanum Press, 1995), pp. 17–18.

[78] Harry F. Gollob and James E. Dittes, 'Effects of Manipulated Self-Esteem on Persuasability Depending on Threat and Complexity of Communication', *Journal of Personality and Social Psychology* 2, no. 2 (1965): pp. 195–201.

health.[79] And, following Stark, Wade Roof showed that those attracted to New Age beliefs tend to be more educated than the average. Under these circumstances, it becomes difficult to sustain the insecurity argument, and the main arguments for the sociological view of astrology as postmodern collapse.

ASTROLOGERS AND POSTMODERNISM

Patrick Curry published one of the first academic discussions of the topic in 1994, in a paper addressed to historians of astrology. He was addressing a very real issue in the historiography of astrology (one also pertinent to sociological treatments of the subject): the imposition of a historical narrative in which astrology is an anachronistic survival from the past. His contribution was extremely valuable. Curry identified astrology as inherently pluralist and relativist, both characteristics of postmodernism, while its enemies in the western world, whether Christian or scientific, were monist and universalist, both characteristics of modernism. For the last two thousand years, he argued, astrologers have adopted the language of their persecutors, of absolute truth and scientific laws. In these terms astrology is, and has always been, fundamentally postmodernist not in terms of its historical time-frame, but its assumptions, while many of its practitioners have adopted the language which became associated with modernism—'its love affair with all-encompassing grand-narratives' and worship of Progress'; he adds, 'The point about postmodernism, therefore, is not that it has replaced modernism but that the fundamental premises of modernism have been transformed, by a subtle but powerful sea-change, into assumptions. The keynote of post-modernism is not a new consensus but a lack of consensus'.[80]

Some astrologers have turned the sceptics' argument around and agree that astrology finds a natural ally in postmodernism. One is Geoffrey Cornelius, who delivered the following lecture titled 'Astrology: the Post-Modern Shape Shifter', via an on-line conference in November 2010:

---

[79] Stark, 'Atheism, Faith, and the Social Scientific Study of Religion', p. 56.

[80] Patrick Curry, 'Astrology: From Pagan to Postmodern?', *The Astrological Journal* 36, no. 1 (Jan./Feb. 1994): p. 74.

> Despite the valiant efforts of astrologers over the past century, modern astrology has not found a place in contemporary culture. We have still not caught up with the impact of the scientific Enlightenment. Aping science is futile, and attempts to return to our roots, Hellenistic, Arabic, Indian, are sentimental distractions until we face the core dilemma of modern practice: the loss of rationale with the sweeping away of the ancient Cosmos. We examine the argument for a divinatory interpretation of practical astrology as the shift our discipline requires to release its potential and open an intelligent conversation with post-modernity.[81]

Cornelius sees postmodernity as offering a safe haven for astrologers bereft of their pre-Copernican cosmology, not because it encourages the revival of antique astrological techniques, but because it permits a reading of astrology as divination. By removing astrology from modernity, he challenges modern science's right to comment on it. He does not deny that there have been modernising astrologers, but argues that they have failed.

Commentators on other areas of 'alternative' (a difficult word) thought, also see liberation in postmodernism. Stephen Flowers, writing on magic, argues that,

> Furthermore the post-modernist is free of the constraints of modern progressivism: To the modern if it's not new, if its not the latest thing, then it is 'retrograde' or 'reactionary' and hence unacceptable. Post modernists are free to synthesise elements from all phases of human history—in any shape or form that suits their purpose'.[82]

Some modernising astrologers take a similar line to Cornelius. For example, Glenn Perry, who is deeply influenced by the modernizing astrologer Dane Rudhyar (see below), considers that

> What is most interesting about these developments is that, implicit in the new, organismic paradigm of postmodern science are the very principles upon which astrology is

---

[81] Geoffrey Cornelius, 'Astrology: The Post-Modern Shape Shifter', lecture delivered at the International Academy of Astrology Online Conference, 19 November 2010. Recording available: http://www.astrocollege.com/campus/libraries.cgi (accessed 18 April 2010).

[82] Stephen Flowers, *Hermetic Magic: The Postmodern Magical Papyrus of Abaris* (Boston: Weisder Books, 1995), p. 14.

> based... The possibility of a creative synthesis of modern and premodern truths may lead to an integration of psychology and astrology in a new, postmodern, astro-psychology.[83]

Perry's postmodernism, though, is not a rejection of modernism, but a synthesis of its finer qualities with those of the premodern world. Candy Hillenbrand took a similarly nuanced view, looking beyond the modern rather than rejecting it:

> It is time, I believe, for the discipline of astrology to engage in a much-needed philosophical overhaul, to bring itself more in line with more modern, or more correctly, post-modern developments in thinking.[84]

Hillenbrand argued that the world has gone beyond modernism because it was inadequate, not because it was incorrect. Other astrologers have distanced astrology from modernism without espousing postmodernism as an alternative. Robert Hand argued that astrology is pre-modern, since it 'has never been part of the modern world and cannot have a post-modern period'.[85] He does agree that there is a postmodern astrology, but argues that it is characterised by a rediscovery of classical and medieval astrology, the same process which Cornelius rejects as a sentimental distraction.

The reasons why the notion of postmodernity appeals to those who are sympathetic to astrology (as well as those who are critical of it) may be found in Philip Sheldrake's work on

---

[83] Glenn Perry, 'The New Paradigm and Postmodern Astrology', International Forum on New Science, University of Fort Collins, Colorado, 27 Sept. 1991, http://www.aaperry.com/index.asp?pgid=21 (accessed 20 January 2007).

[84] Candy Hillenbrand, 'An Archaic Astrology Cast Adrift in a Post-Modern World',
http://www.aplaceinspace.net/Pages/CandyPostmodern.html
(accessed 20 January 2007); Gerry Goddard, 'Beyond a Post-Modern Astrology: a Response to Candy Hillenbrand',
http://www.astro.com/astrology.net/resp-can.html (accessed 21 April 2010). See also Bill Sheeran, 'Astrology, Patriarchy and Postmodernism', *The Mountain Astrologer* (Apr./May 1999).

[85] Robert Hand, 'Towards a Post-Modern Astrology', Paper Presented at the Astrological Association Conference of the British Astrological Association, York, 2005,
http://www.astro.com/astrology/in_postmodern_e.htm (accessed 20 January 2007).

contemporary spirituality. He considers that postmodernity 'resists attempts to reduce events or people to mere instances of some overarching theory...[and] defends the otherness, particularity and difference of all people'.[86] The notion of 'otherness' being valued rather than rejected, and of astrology recognising the uniqueness of the individual, is appealing to astrologers. The problem for the identification of astrology as postmodern, however, is that astrology does precisely what postmodernism is supposed to reject; it imposes an over-arching theory on a diverse practice. Thus Cornelius, for example, speaks of the recognition of astrology's divinatory nature as 'required'. This opens up what we might describe as the 'post-modern paradox'—that an appearance of diversity of claims from a sociological perspective, is not matched by a recognition of diversity within individual truth-communities. Instead individuals or groups who are identified as postmodern may resist one of the supposed core features of postmodernism.

Patrick Curry follows Bauman in rejecting the notion of the modern and postmodern as necessarily historical periods and preferred to consider them as styles of thought. However, his location of the challenge to modernist thought in recent times comes with its own historical assumptions, such as that modernism in the early twentieth century was characterised by consensus. However, if for example, we consider modernism in early–twentieth century politics (taking modernism as characterised by a worship of Progress), we find anything but consensus: democrats of different shades competed with Nazis and many varieties of Marxism. There was, actually, a complete absence of consensus. The problem is this: do we characterise individuals, groups or ideas as modernist because they lay claim to the absolute truth, or do we consider whether modernism in general, as made up of individuals, groups and ideas, embodies a consensus. The issue is a serious one and, as far as astrology is concerned, suggests that we either should consider its essential nature on the one hand, or its cultural context on the other. Curry argues that astrology is, in its essential nature, postmodern, while astrologers' culturally-conditioned rhetoric has tended to be modern.

---

[86] Philip Sheldrake, *Spaces for the Sacred* (London: SCM Press, 2001), pp. 12–13.

ASTROLOGY AND THE MODERN

Curry had identified a paradox: that astrology is in its very nature postmodern does not conflict with the existence of modernizing astrologers. It is just that the modernists are deluded as to astrology's true nature. The modernising trend in western astrology is evident in the nineteenth century, but was made explicit by the Theosophical astrologer Alan Leo (1875–1917), one of the most influential astrologers of the early twentieth century. Leo was a devout believer in the coming of the Age of Aquarius and argued that astrology had to be reformed in order to serve this purpose. 'I am actuated', he wrote, 'by the primary motive of expressing what I believe to be the true Astrology, for the new Era that is now dawning upon the world'.[87] His stated aim was to 'modernise the ancient system of Astrology'.[88] Leo rejected what he saw as the 'exoteric' (concerned with outer events), predictive astrology of the nineteenth century and developed a modern astrology (he founded a journal called *Modern Astrology* in order to promote his ideas), in favour of an 'esoteric' astrology which emphasised spiritual awareness and, in relation to earlier forms of horoscopic astrology, greater technical simplicity.

The modernist tone was established by H. P. Blavatsky, founder of the Theosophical Society. Blavatsky stated that,

> Astrology is a science *as infallible* as astronomy itself, with the condition, however, that its interpreters must be equally infallible; and it is this condition, however, *sine qua non*, so very difficult of realization, that has always proved a stumbling block to both. Astrology is to exact astronomy what psychology is to exact physiology. In astrology one has to step beyond the visible world of matter, and enter into the domain of transcendent spirit.[89]

In two sentences Blavatsky had set out a manifesto for a modernising astrology: under no circumstances can her assumption of infallibility, and hence implicitly of scientific demonstration, be considered postmodern. Her core

---

[87] Alan Leo, *Esoteric Astrology: A Study in Human Nature* (London: Modern Astrology, 1913), p. v.

[88] Patrick Curry, *A Confusion of Prophets* (London: Collins & Brown, 1992).

[89] H.P. Blavatsky, *Isis Unveiled*, 2 vols (Pasadena: Theosophical University Press, 1976), facsimile of 1877 edition, vol. 1, p. 259.

argument was that astrology, is infallible but that astrologers, being only human, are all too fallible.[90] If only astrologers could improve their understanding of astrology, they would serve the purposes of humanity much more effectively.

Leo's modernising spirituality was developed by the American theosophist, Dane Rudhyar (1895–1985). Echoing Leo's reference to the 'new aera', Rudhyar claimed, with an astonishing faith in his own powers, that it represented the birth of a new epoch'.[91] More cautiously, the *Larousse Encyclopaedia of Astrology* considered that the book 'is generally acknowledged to be a classic'.[92] Rudhyar's own description of the book was that it,

> was an attempt to reformulate traditional astrology in terms of the modern philosophical and psychological outlook… It established new foundations for a consistent system of symbolism, using astrological factors as its symbols. Its goal was the formulation of an 'algebra of life', using organic life-qualities as its primary elements, defining these qualities particularly at the psychological level in terms borrowed from C. G. Jung's analytical psychology.[93]

In 1974, thirty-eight years after its publication, the book was voted second in 'a survey of 100–200 opinions on "The 7 Best Books in Astrology"'.[94] Rudhyar's modernising tendencies were evident his second book, published in 1938, where he issued a call to build a new world couched in the language of Hermetic cosmology

> Today is a new birthday for the ancient gods. New men call for new symbols. Their cry rises, beyond their logical intellects ashamed of mystical longings, for new gods to worship and to use in order to integrate their harrowing mental confusion and to stabilize their uprooted souls. Young gods, fresh and radiant with the sunshine of a new dawn, glorified with the 'golden light' of a new Sun of Power,

---

[90] Annie Besant, 'An Appreciation', in Bessie Leo, *The Life and Work of Alan Leo* (London: Modern Astrology, 1919), p. 8.

[91] Dane Rudhyar, *Occult Preparations for a New Age* (Madras and London: Theosophical Publishing House, 1975), p. 77.

[92] Jean-Louis Brau, Helen Weaver, and Allan Edmunds, *Larousse Encyclopaedia of Astrology* (New York: Plume Books, 1982), p. 244.

[93] Dane Rudhyar, *New Mansions for New Men* (New York: Lucis Publishing Company, 1938), p. xii.

[94] Dean and Mather, *Recent Advances*, p. 3.

ecstatic with virgin potentialities after the banishment of ancient nightmares.[95]

As modernists—as representatives of modernity—Leo and Rudhyar's fellow travellers were Kandinsky, Yeats, Holst, and Breton. They were aesthetic modernisers. An alternative, but allied school of modernisation favoured the development of astrology through what we might call scientific developments, and the accumulation of empirical evidence and the identification of interpretative techniques which work in contrast to those which don't, although often still within a broadly theosophical context. Blavatsky's assumption that astrology is infallible was adopted, but without the edifice of Theosophical spirituality. A key protagonist of this school of thought was the British astrologer, John Addey (1920–1982), one of the founders of the British Astrological Association. Addey believed that

> astrology is evidently about to undergo a rebirth and a period of new growth. It will be no ordinary rebirth and no ordinary period of growth. From being an outcast from the fraternity of sciences, it seems destined to assume an almost central role in scientific thought.[96]

Jeff Mayo (1921–1998), Principal of the Faculty of Astrological Studies, for many years from its foundation in 1948 the main British school of astrology, considered the situation amongst practising astrologers, appealing to science and applauding the rejection of esotericism. He claimed that,

> Astrology as practised today by trained astrological-consultants is, by its correlation to modern psychology and the eradication of many muddle-headed esoteric theories and 'fortune-telling sensationalism', far removed from the astrology of even the turn of this century.[97]

Dennis Elwell, another British astrologer, adopts a third position, being neither a theosophist nor an advocate of science. He does, though, regard astrology as a modernising force:

---

[95] Rudhyar, *New Mansions*, p. xiii.

[96] John Addey, *Astrology Reborn* (London: Faculty of Astrological Studies, 1971), p. 3.

[97] Jeff Mayo, *Teach Yourself Astrology* (1964; repr. London: Hodder and Stoughton, 1981), p. 7.

> There is no area of knowledge, no activity, immune from the revolutionising effect of a genuine astrology… Astrology is the best…hope of religion, because it offers a meeting ground for the scientific and religious views of reality, reconciling many of their differences.[98]

The few astrologers who have engaged with the topic argue that astrology offers a postmodern escape into pluralism, diversity and democracy, a world in which individuals count. But, if modernism is characterised by the self-confident creation of the future in line with a single meta-narrative, Elwell is a modernist. Further, if modernists think 'compulsively about the New' and look for 'new worlds' as Jameson put it, then astrologers such as Alan Leo, Dane Rudhyar, John Addey, and Jeff Mayo, were thorough-going modernists.[99]

CONCLUSION

Unfortunately, the very use of terms such as modern and postmodern encourage scholars to fall into the trap of categorisation: this thing is modern, that is postmodern, as if such distinctions can possibly be made in any other than a rigidly binary universe. When we look at human society with all its rich, messy complexity, such theoretical boxes reduce clarity rather than enhance it. New Age culture may therefore be postmodern in some respects, modern in others. As Hexham and Poewe pointed out, the counter-culture of the 1960s contained elements of both modernism and postmodernism.[100] And so it is with astrology.

Some astrologers may be modernists, others post-modernists. Many may be both. For example, Robert Hand has argued that the development of psychological astrology, the most influential development within modern professional astrology, may be an indicator of a modernist trend within twentieth-century astrology.[101] We might

---

[98] Dennis Elwell, *Cosmic Loom: The New Science of Astrology* (London: Urania Trust, 1987), p. 3.

[99] Jameson, *Postmodernism*, p. ix.

[100] Irving Hexham and Karla Poewe, *New Religions as Global Cultures* (Boulder, CO: Westview Press, 1997), pp. 149–51.

[101] Robert Hand, 'Foreword' in Olivia Barclay, *Horary Astrology Rediscovered* (West Chester PA: Whitford Press, 1990), p. 15.

consider that the argument that astrology is a science that can be proved, or the New Age proposition that its widespread acceptance will change the world for the better, might both be considered modernist without implying that all astrology is modernist. Patrick Curry took a similar line, writing of the esoteric and psychological astrology which was developed at the beginning of the twentieth century that, 'Far from being an irrational aberration, the new occult astrology was perfectly suited to the capitalism and individualism of the age'.[102] But, then he also argues that astrology is postmodern in that, in the astrological consultation, pluralism reigns: 'the astrologer and/or the client', he wrote, 'bring a complex set of values, assumptions, problems and strategies to *every* situation', a situation which can never be repeated and so cannot represent an absolute truth'.[103] The question largely depends on our particular view point. We might stand back from astrology as a whole and be struck by the diversity of competing voices, of multiple narratives, and this may look postmodern. But, if each school of astrology is proclaiming a grand-narrative in which astrology can explain or, at least, comment on, absolutely everything known to humanity, and some of those schools assume that they are engaged in creating a better world, we see unabashed modernism: one of modernity's key features, aside from a belief in the creation of a new world, is the belief in a set of absolute criteria by which judgments can be made and certainty arrived at. And then we can turn to a variety of sociological arguments, promoted by Grace Davie and others, that religious pluralism is not a postmodern reaction to modernity but is actually a feature of modernity. Whatever way we turn the argument, astrology is not part of a postmodern aberration, a symptom of a failure to cope with modernity, a bizarre relic from a superstitious past, as the scientific modernists would put it, but a normal part of the modern world. This tells us nothing about the truth of its claims, but it does enable us to begin to find a position where we can at least assess what its practitioners are doing and how they relate to modern culture. When we consider astrology, then there is indeed a certain postmodern relativism in astrologers' rhetoric, the widespread assertion by astrologers, for example, that the techniques of astrological interpretation are purely matters of

---

[102] Curry, *Confusion*, p. 132.

[103] Roy Willis and Patrick Curry, *Astrology, Science and Culture: Pulling Down the Moon* (Oxford: Berg, 2004), p. 97.

convenience with no intrinsic, objective value: the majority of delegates at two major astrology conferences in the UK and the USA in 1999 and 2002 stated that the reliability of astrological techniques depends on the astrologer using them.[104] Such relativity could undoubtedly be considered postmodern.

Yet time and time again, with a few notable examples, the representatives of particular schools of thought in astrology, the 'traditionalists', supporters of divination, advocates of science or psychology, assert the absolute truth of their positions. Theirs is the grand-narrative of cosmic truth. And how much more true this is of those followers of Leo and Rudhyar for whom the creation of a new world to which everyone, with no exceptions, will be subject, is the overwhelming priority. But, if astrologers are overwhelmingly modernists in their promotion of the modern and their adherence to the meta-narrative of cosmic truth, my research also shows significant subtexts which can clearly be described as postmodern, such as the finding that a significant number regard the techniques of astrological interpretation as a matter of subjective convenience ('each astrologer uses the techniques which work for them'[105]). Even then, though, there is an ancient lineage to support such a proposition; in the influential tenth century work, the *Centiloquium* attributed to Claudius Ptolemy, we read 'He that is desirous to study any Art, hath in his Nativity without doubt some Star of the same Nature very well fortified'.[106] Is astrology, then, postmodernist as mode of thought? Perhaps, but then, why use a word which implies a succession to the modern? The problems of using the word in this sense is that, if we apply it to Ptolemy we have to apply it to his entire cultural milieu: does it really make sense to label Stoics as postmodern? Bauman's statement that postmodern is a

---

[104] Nicholas Campion, 'Prophecy, Cosmology and the New Age Movement: the extent and nature of contemporary belief in astrology' (PhD thesis, University of the West of England, 2004), p. 248.

[105] Campion, 'Prophecy, Cosmology and the New Age Movement', p. 248.

[106] Claudius Ptolemy, 'Centiloquium', in John Partridge, *Mikropanastron, or an Astrological Vade Mecum, briefly Teaching the whole Art of Astrology - viz., Questions, Nativities, with all its parts, and the whole Doctrine of Elections never so comprised nor compiled before, &c.* (London: William Bromwich, 1679), para 3.

state of mind rather than a historical period is half-way to rejecting to the term postmodern as a description of astrology, but does not go far enough.

Astrology exists within a view of modernity in which religion and spirituality are not dying out, as traditional secularisation theory claims, but diversifying. Its survival in the twenty-first century is therefore not an anomaly to be explained, but an aspect of the modern world to be examined on its own terms. Neither, as the failure of the insecurity hypothesis has it, is it an aspect of modernity in crisis: there is just no evidence to support this view. As Bowman and Sutcliffe wrote of New Age culture, the 'alternative' may be now better seen as 'mainstream'.[107] The major part of the astrology of the modern west is not part of the supposed crisis of late-modernity. It is an integral part of modernity itself. The implications are wider than the narrow concerns of modern astrology, though. On the wider level, we should abandon any notion that practitioners or 'believers' in the esoteric, 'alternative spiritualities', or New Age disciplines are somehow excluded from the modern world, standing outside the general flow of history. This is essential if we are to understand the diversity of contemporary spiritual culture.

My starting point for discussion throughout has been the existing body of literature, primarily sociological and historical works. However, as Michael Hill observed acutely, all academic disciplines 'which pursue the goal of a rigorous and systematic investigation of the empirical world sooner or later come up against the "pure" and "applied" dichotomy'.[108] Postmodernism and Modernism may exist in the minds of various writers as 'pure' types, but their application to particular practices is frequently misleading. This is often the case with astrology. Those sociological works which refer to contemporary astrology tend to ignore the actual theory and practice of modern astrologers, its 'applied' nature, and assume *a priori* that astrology should be categorised in 'pure' terms, as postmodern, or a religion, new religious movement, New Age discipline or superstition, and that its claims are false. It is also assumed that astrology can be treated as a single entity, as if all astrologers think the

---

[107] Marion Bowman and Steven Sutcliffe, *Beyond New Age: Exploring Alternative Spirituality* (Edinburgh: Edinburgh University Press, 2000), p. 11.

[108] Hill, *Sociology of Religion*, p. 6.

same and work according to a single code. Yet astrology is, like any other discipline, marked as much by its diversity as by its uniformity. As David Hufford remarked, when arguing that belief cannot be considered in isolation from disbelief, 'we must be prepared to tolerate some theoretical uncertainty and even dissonance while we develop a comfortable theoretical consistency primarily by selectively avoiding pertinent information and by forcing that information into appropriate, preconceived patterns'.[109] In this respect Festinger's notion of cognitive dissonance removes the need to look for consistency of thought or practice amongst astrologers any more than within any other discipline.[110]

Actually, although there may be some phenomena which might clearly be labelled 'post-modern', such as architecture which mixes vernacular styles, or 'modern', such as architecture which rejects the past, once we have moved beyond such tangible examples, the distinctions between the postmodern and modern cease to make sense in most contexts. One person's modern is often another's postmodern. In the arts the distinction has ceased to make sense, and similarly in astrology. Thus, whether astrology is modern or postmodern seems to be largely a matter of individual taste, and an adjunct to whatever argument which is being proposed. Thus for Bauer and Durant astrology is 'late modern' because its advocates are unable to cope with the modern, while for Cornelius it is postmodern because the modern is at odds with its essential nature. Thus astrologer and critic of astrology find common cause in detaching astrology from the contemporary world. As Stuart Sutcliffe said of 'New Age', modern and postmodern are emblems which people adopt to denote their cultural affiliations.[111] As an 'emblem', anyone who has an instinctive idea of what 'the Modern' or 'Postmodern' is can then attach ideas or activities to them. We may then refer to Curry's application to astrology of Bauman's view that modernism and post-modernism describe styles of thought rather than historical

---

[109] David Hufford, 'Traditions of Disbelief', *Talking Folklore* 1, pt. 3 (1987): p. 27.

[110] Leon Festinger, *A Theory of Cognitive Dissonance* (1957; repr. Stanford: Stanford University Press, 1968).

[111] Stuart Sutcliffe, *Children of the New Age: A history of spiritual practices* (London: Routledge, 2003), pp. 9–11.

periods. Individual astrologers or schools of thought in astrology may be described as modern or postmodern. This does not mean that they *are* modern or postmodern. And to suggest that astrology as a whole *is* post modern or *should be* modern imposes a universalising tendency which contradicts the diversity of truth claims which have characterised western astrology since the Hellenistic period.

BIBLIOGRAPHY

Abell, George O. 'Astrology' in *Science and the Paranormal: Probing the Existence of the Supernatural*, edited by George O. Abell and Barry Singer, pp. 70-94. London: Junction Books, 1981.

Addey, John. *Astrology Reborn*. London: Faculty of Astrological Studies, 1971.

Adorno, Theodor. *The Stars Down to Earth*. 1953; reprint, London: Routledge, 1994.

Baldick, Chris. *The Concise Oxford Dictionary of Literary Terms*. New York: Oxford University Press, 1991.

Basil, Robert. 'New Age Thinking', in *The Encyclopaedia of the Paranormal*. Edited by Gordon Stein. Amherst, NY: Prometheus Books, 1996.

Bauer, John, and Martin Durant. 'British Public Perceptions of Astrology: An Approach from the Sociology of Knowledge'. *Culture and Cosmos* 1, no. 1 (1997): pp. 55–72.

Bauman, Zygmunt. *Intimations of Postmodernity*. London: Routledge, 1992.

Bennett, Gillian. *Traditions of Belief: Women, Folklore and the Supernatural Today*. London: Penguin, 1987.

Besant, Annie. 'An Appreciation', in Bessie Leo, *The Life and Work of Alan Leo*. London: Modern Astrology, 1919.

Best, Steven, and Douglas Kellner. *Postmodern Theory: Critical Interrogations*. London: McMillan, 1991.

Blavatsky, H. P. *Isis Unveiled*, Pasadena: Theosophical University Press, 1976, 2 Vols., facsimile of 1877 edition.

Blum, Cinzia. *The Other Modernism: F. T. Marinetti's Futurist Fiction of Power*. Berkeley: University of California Press, 1996.

Bok, Bart J., and Margaret W. Mayall. 'Scientists Look at Astrology'. *The Scientific Monthly* 52 (1941): pp. 233–44.

———, Lawrence E. Jerome, and Paul Kurtz, 'Objections to Astrology: A Statement by 186 Leading Scientists'. *The Humanist* 35, no. 5 (September/October 1975): pp. 44–46.

Bowman, Marion, and Steven Sutcliffe. *Beyond New Age: Exploring Alternative Spirituality*. Edinburgh: Edinburgh University Press, 2000.

Brau, Jean-Louis, Helen Weaver, and Allan Edmunds. *Larousse Encyclopaedia of Astrology*. New York: Plume Books, 1982.

Caird, Dale, and Henry G. Law. 'Non-Conventional Beliefs: Their Structure and Measurement'. *Journal for the Scientific Study of Religion* 21, no. 2 (1982): pp.152–63.

Campion, Nicholas. *A History of Western Astrology*, Vol. 2, The Medieval and Modern Worlds. London: Continuum, 2009.

——. 'Do Astrologers Have to Believe in Astrology?'. *The Sceptic* 15, no. 2 (Summer 2002): pp. 20–22.

———. 'Prophecy, Cosmology and the New Age Movement: the extent and nature of contemporary belief in astrology'. PhD thesis, University of the West of England, 2004.

———. 'Surrealist Cosmology: André Breton and Astrology'. *Culture and Cosmos* 6, no. 2 (Autumn/Winter 2002): pp. 45–56.

Childs, Peter. *Modernism*. London: Routledge, 2005.

Collingwood, R. G. *An Essay on Metaphysics*. Revised edition. Oxford: Clarendon Press, 1998.

Cornelius, Geoffrey. 'Astrology: The Post-Modern Shape Shifter'. Lecture delivered at the International Academy of Astrology Online Conference, 19 November 2010. Recording available: http://www.astrocollege.com/campus/libraries.cgi

Curry, Patrick. *A Confusion of Prophets*. London: Collins & Brown, 1992.

———. 'Astrology: From Pagan to Postmodern?'. *The Astrological Journal* 36, no. 1 (January/February 1994): pp. 69–75.

Dean, Geoffrey. 'Discourse for Key Topic 4: Astrology and Human Judgement'. *Correlation* 17, no. 2 (Northern Winter 1998/9): pp. 24–71.

———, and Arthur Mather. *Recent Advances in Natal Astrology*. Subiaco, Australia: Analogic, 1977.

Dean, Geoffrey, Ivan Kelly and Arthur Mather. 'Astrology' in *The Encyclopaedia of the Paranormal*. Edited by Gordon Stein, pp. 47–99. Amherst, NY: Prometheus Books, 1996.

Docherty, Thomas. *Postmodernism: A Reader*. Hemel Hempstead: Harvester Wheatsheaf, 1993.

Durkheim, Emile. *The Elementary Forms of Religious Life*. Translated by Karen E. Fields. 1912; reprint New York: The Free Press, 1995.

Elwell, Dennis. *Cosmic Loom: The New Science of Astrology*. London: Urania Trust, 1987.

Evans-Pritchard, E. E. *Social Anthropology*. London: Cohen and West, 1967.

Festinger, Leon. *A Theory of Cognitive Dissonance*. 1957; reprint, Stanford: Stanford University Press, 1968.

Flowers, Stephen. *Hermetic Magic: The Postmodern Magical Papyrus of Abaris*. Boston: Weisder Books, 1995.

Glick, Peter and Mark Snyder. 'Self-Fulfilling Prophecy: the Psychology of Belief in Astrology'. *The Humanist* 46, pt. 3 (May-June 1986): pp. 20–25, 50.

Glock, Charles Y. and Rodney Stark. *Religion and Society in Tension*. Chicago: Rand McNally, 1965.

Goddard, Gerry. 'Beyond a Post-Modern Astrology: a Response to Candy Hillenbrand'. http://www.astro.com/astrology.net/resp-can.html

Godwin, Joscelyn. *The Theosophical Enlightenment*. New York: SUNY Press, 1994.

Gollob, Harry F., and James E. Dittes. 'Effects of Manipulated Self-Esteem on Persuasability Depending on Threat and Complexity of Communication'. *Journal of Personality and Social Psychology* 2, no. 2 (1965): pp. 195–201.

Gombrich, E. H. *The Story of Art*, 15th revised edition. London: Phaidon Press, 1995.

Goode, Erich. *Paranormal Beliefs: A Sociological Interpretation*. Illinois: Waveland Press, 2000.

Gray, W. D. *Thinking Critically about New Age Ideas*. California: Wadsworth, 1991.

Greeley, Andrew M. *The Sociology of the Paranormal*. London: Sage Publications, 1975.

Hand, Robert. 'Foreword', pp. 13–18. In Olivia Barclay, *Horary Astrology Rediscovered*. West Chester PA: Whitford Press, 1990.

———. 'Towards a Post-Modern Astrology'. Paper presented at the Astrological Association Conference of the British Astrological Association, York, 2005. http://www.astro.com/astrology/in_postmodern_e.htm (accessed 20 January 2007).

Hawking, Stephen. *The Universe in a Nutshell*. London: Bantam Press, 2001.

Head, Raymond. 'Astrology, Modernism and Holst's "The Planets"'. *Astrology Quarterly* 65, no. 1 (Winter 1994–95): pp. 40–54.

Heartney, Eleanor. *Postmodernism*. London: Tate Publishing, 2001.

Heelas, Paul. *The New Age Movement: The Celebration of the Self and the Sacralization of Modernity*. Cambridge, MA: Blackwell, 1996.

Heine, Elizabeth. 'W. B. Yeats: Poet and Astrologer'. *Culture and Cosmos* 1, no. 2 (Winter/Autumn 1997): pp. 60–75.

Herbrechtsmeier, William. 'Buddhism and the Definition of Religion: One More Time'. *Journal for the Scientific Study of Religion* 32, no. 1 (1993): pp. 1–18.

Hexham, Irving, and Karla Poewe. *New Religions as Global Cultures*. Boulder, CO: Westview Press, 1997.

Hill, Michael. *A Sociology of Religion*. 1973; reprint, London: Heinemann, 1979.

Hillenbrand, Candy. 'An Archaic Astrology Cast Adrift in a Post-Modern World'. http://www.aplaceinspace.net/Pages/CandyPostmodern.html (accessed 20 January 2007).

Hufford, David. 'Traditions of Disbelief'. *Talking Folklore* 1, pt. 3 (1987): pp. 19–29.

Inglehart, Ronald. *Modernization and Postmodernization*. Princeton NJ: Princeton University Press, 1997.

Irwin, Harvey J. *The Psychology of Paranormal Belief: A Researcher's Handbook*. Hatfield: University of Hertfordshire Press, 2009.

Jacob, Margaret C. *Living the Enlightenment: Freemasonry and Politics in Eighteenth-Century Europe*. Oxford: Oxford University Press, 1991.

Jameson, Frederic. Foreword to Jean-Francois Lyotard, *The Postmodern Condition: A Report on Knowledge*. Manchester: Manchester University Press, 1985.

————. *Postmodernism, or, the Cultural Logic of Late Capitalism*. New York: Verso, 1991.

Janis, I. L. 'Personality correlates of susceptibility to persuasion'. *Journal of Personality* 22 (1954): pp. 505–18.

————. 'Anxiety Indices related to susceptibility to persuasion'. *Journal of Abnormal and Social Psychology* 51 (1955): pp. 663–67.

Jardine, Nicholas. 'Imagineering the Astronomical Revolution, Essay Review'. *Journal for the History of Astronomy* 37, part 4, no. 129 (November 2006): pp.471–84.

Jencks, Charles. *What is Post-Modernism?* 1986. Reprint, London: Academy Editions, 1996.

Jencks, Charles. *Post-Modernism: The New Classicism in Art and Architecture*. London: Academy Editions, 1987.

Jencks, Charles. *The Post-modern Reader*. London: Academy Editions, 1992.

Jerome, Lawrence. 'Astrology: Magic or Science?'. *The Humanist* 35, pt. 5 (Sept/Oct 1975): pp. 10, 16.

Jevons, Frank. *Introduction to the History of Religions*. London: Methuen, 1896.

Johns, Derek. 'Why Write Novels?'. *The Author* (Autumn 2008): p. 95.

Kanitscheider, Bernulf. 'A Philosopher looks at Astrology'. *Interdisciplinary Science Reviews* 16, no. 3 (1991): pp. 258–66.

Kelly, I. W. 'Why Astrology Doesn't Work'. *Psychological Reports* Vol. 82 (1998): pp. 527–46.

Klages, Mary. Colorado University, http://www.colorado.edu/English/courses/ENGL2012Klages /pomo.html (accessed 18 April 2010).

Koch-Westonholz, Ulla. *Mesopotamian Astrology*. Copenhagen: Museum Tusculanum Press, 1995.

Leo, Alan. *Esoteric Astrology: A Study in Human Nature*. London: Modern Astrology, 1913.

Linklater, Magnus. 'An academic dispute that is out of this world'. *The Times*, 30 August 2001, p. 12.

Mayo, Jeff. *Teach Yourself Astrology*. 1964; reprint, London: Hodder and Stoughton, 1981.

Miller, Jon D. 'The Public Acceptance of Astrology and other Pseudo-science in the United States'. Paper presented to the 1992 annual meeting of the American Association for the Advancement of Science, 9 February 1992.

Outram, Dorinda. *The Enlightenment*. Cambridge: Cambridge University Press, 1995.

Perry, Glenn. 'The New Paradigm and Postmodern Astrology'. International Forum on New Science, University of Fort Collins, Colorado, 27 Sept. 1991, http://www.aaperry.com/index.asp?pgid=21 (accessed 20 January 2007).

Plug, C. 'An investigation of superstitious belief and behaviour'. *Journal of Behavioural Science* 2, no. 3 (1975): pp. 169–78.

Ptolemy, Claudius. 'Centiloquium'. In John Partridge, *Mikropanastron, or an Astrological Vade Mecum, briefly Teaching the whole Art of Astrology - viz., Questions, Nativities, with all its parts, and the whole Doctrine of Elections never so comprised nor compiled before, &c.* London: William Bromwich, 1679.

Rudhyar, Dane. *New Mansions for New Men.* New York: Lucis Publishing Company, 1938.

Rudhyar, Dane. *Occult Preparations for a New Age.* London: Theosophical Publishing House, 1975.

Sagan, Carl. *Cosmos: the Story of Cosmic Evolution, Science and Civilisation.* London: Warner Books, 1994.

———. *The Demon-Haunted World: Science as a Candle in the Dark.* New York: Random House, 1997.

Sheeran, Bill. 'Astrology, Patriarchy and Postmodernism'. *The Mountain Astrologer* (April/May 1999): pp. 12–17, 105.

Sheldrake, Philip. *Spaces for the Sacred.* London: SCM Press, 2001.

Smart, Ninian, *The Phenomenon of Religion,* London: MacMillan, 1973.

Smithers, Alan. 'Astrology, like literature and music, can invest life with meaning'. *The Independent* Wednesday 4 April 2001, http://www.independent.co.uk/news/education/education-news/alan-smithers-astrology-like-literature-and-music-is-capable-of-investing-life-with-meaning-753186.html

Stark, Rodney. 'Atheism, Faith, and the Social Scientific Study of Religion'. *Journal of Contemporary Religion* 14, no. 1 (1999): pp. 41–62.

Stenmark, Mikael. *Scientism: Science, Ethics and Religion.* Aldershot: Ashgate, 2001.

Sutcliffe, Stuart. *Children of the New Age: A history of spiritual practices.* London: Routledge, 2003.

Tambiah, Stanley Jeyaraja. *Magic, Science, Religion and the Scope of Rationality.* 1984; reprint, Cambridge: Cambridge University Press, 1990.

Thrower, James. *Religion: The Classical Theories.* Edinburgh: Edinburgh University Press, 1999.

Turner, Victor. *The Ritual Process: Structure and Anti-Structure.* London: Aldine Transaction, 2008.

Tylor, Edward Burnett, *Primitive Culture,* Vol. 1. London: John Murray, 1873.

Victoria & Albert Museum, http://www.vam.ac.uk/vastatic/microsites/1331_modernism/the_exhibition.html (accessed 17 March 2010).

Williams, Raymond. *The Politics of Modernism: Against the New Conformists.* London: Verso, 1989.

Willis, Roy, and Patrick Curry, *Astrology, Science and Culture: Pulling Down the Moon.* Oxford: Berg, 2004.

Wolfart, Johannes C. 'Postmodernism'. In *Guide to the Study of Religions*. Edited by Willi Braun and Russell T. McCutcheon. London: Cassell, 2000.
Webster, Charles. *From Paracelsus to Newton: Magic and the Making of Modern Science*. Cambridge: Cambridge University Press, 1982.
Yates, Frances. *The Occult Philosophy in the Elizabethan Age*. 1979; reprint, London: Routledge and Kegan Paul, 1983.
————. *The Rosicrucian Enlightenment*. 1972; reprint, London: Routledge and Kegan Paul, 1986.
Yinger, J. Milton. *The Scientific Study of Religion*. New York: MacMillan, 1970.

Contributors

Bernadette Brady holds an MA in Cultural Astronomy and Astrology from Bath Spa University and is a tutor for the MA in Cultural Astronomy and Astrology at The University of Wales, Lampeter, and tutors for Schumacher College, in partnership with the University of Plymouth, in their MSc programme on Holistic Science. She is currently reading for her doctorate in determinism in western astrology at The University of Wales, Trinity St David, UK. She received the Charles Harvey Award (Astrological Association of Great Britain) in 2006 and the Regulus Award for Theory and Understanding in Astrology (UAC) in 2008.

Nicholas Campion is Director of the Sophia Centre, University of Wales, Trinity St David, Senior Lecturer in the Department of Archaeology, History and Anthropology, and course director of the MA in Cultural Astronomy and Astrology. His books include *A History of Western Astrology* (London: Continuum, 2009) and *Astrology and Cosmology in the World's Religions* (New York: New York University Press, 2011).

Robert Collis is currently an Honorary Research Fellow at the University of Sheffield. He completed his PhD at The University of Turku, Finland, and was previously a student at the University of Sussex. In July 2009 his thesis, entitled *The Petrine Instauration: Religion, Esotericism and Science at the Court of Peter the Great, 1689-1725*, won the inaugural Thesis Prize of the European Society for the Study of Western Esotericism. Robert has written numerous articles on aspects of western esotericism in early modern Russia, as well as co-editing a volume entitled *Freemasonry and Fraternalism in Eighteenth-Century Russia*

Martin Gansten is a historian of religion specialising in astrological and other divinatory traditions in India as well as the west. He has taken particular interest in the South Indian phenomenon of nadi reading, in the development of the method of primary directions (aphesis, at-tasyir) from the early Greek period up to the present day, and in the mutual influences of Perso-Arabic and Indian astrological traditions in the Middle Ages. He is based in Lund University, Sweden.

Nicholas Goodrick-Clarke is Professor of Western Esotericism and Director of the Centre for the Study of Esotericism (EXESESO) in the College of Humanities at the University of Exeter. He is the author of *The Western Esoteric Traditions* (OUP, 2008), studies of Ramon Lull, Paracelsus, John Dee, Emanuel Swedenborg and Helena Blavatsky, as well as a trilogy of monographs on the esoteric-political connection, *The Occult Roots of Nazism, Hitler's Priestess,* and *Black Sun* (NYU Press). He is General Editor of

Western Esoteric Masters Series (North Atlantic) and joint-editor of *Aries: Journal for the Study of Western Esotericism* (Brill).

LIZ GREENE received a PhD in History from the University of Bristol (2010), an MA in Cultural Astronomy and Astrology from Bath Spa University (2007), and an MA and PhD in Psychology from Los Angeles University (1971). She is a qualified analytical psychologist (Association of Jungian Analysts, London, 1983) and a member of the International Association of Analytical Psychology. Her research interests include the Kabbalah, the British occult revival of the late 19th century, and Orphic, Gnostic, early Jewish, and Hermetic astrologies from late antiquity. She is an Honorary Research Fellow at the University of Bristol and a part-time tutor for the MA in Cultural Astronomy and Astrology at the University of Wales, Trinity St David, UK.

DARRELYN GUNZBURG is a part-time tutor for the MA in Cultural Astronomy and Astrology at The University of Wales, Trinity St David, UK. She holds a BA (Hons) from the Open University majoring in the art historical exploration of religious art produced in Italy 1280–1500. Her BA (Hons) dissertation was short-listed for the AAH Bulletin 2006 BA Dissertation Prize, and is being published in St Andrews Journal of Art History and Museum Studies (2010). She's also published books and plays in the fields of playwriting and astrology. She is currently reading for her PhD in art history and astrology at the University of Bristol, UK.

ROBERT HAND has been a student of astrology since 1960 and a full-time professional astrologer since 1972. His books include *Planets in Composite, Planets in Transit, Planets in Youth, Horoscope Symbols* and *Essays on Astrology,* and a number of shorter works on traditional astrology. He has been actively translating traditional astrological texts from Latin in connection with his company ARHAT, and also has an active astrological consulting practice in the Washington DC area. He is also working on his PhD dissertation in medieval history at the Catholic University of America. He is currently the Chairman of the Board of Kepler College.

JAY JOHNSTON is Senior Lecturer in the Department of Studies in Religion, University of Sydney. Her publications include *Angels of Desire: Esoteric Bodies, Aesthetics and Ethics* (Equinox 2008). Areas of research include metaphysics, western esotericism, the role of images in astrology and magic (antiquity to present), philosophy of religion, religion and medicine, angelology.

GARRY PHILLIPSON is a student of astrology, Buddhism and Advaita. He is a tutor on the MA in Cultural Astronomy and Astrology at the University of Wales, Lampeter, where he is working on a PhD looking at theories of truth as they apply to astrology.

* 9 7 8 1 9 0 7 7 6 7 0 1 2 *